PRAISE FOR CATHY GLASS

'Poignant and revealing … real-life stories such as these have helped to move and inspire a generation'   *Sunday Mirror*

'A true tale of hope'   *OK!* Magazine

'Heartbreaking'   *Mirror*

'A life-affirming read … that proves sometimes a little hope is all you need'   *Heat* Magazine

'A hugely touching and emotional true tale'   *Star* Magazine

'Foster carers rarely get the praise they deserve, but Cathy Glass's book should change all that'   *First* Magazine

'Cannot fail to move those who read it'   Adoption-net

'Once again, Cathy Glass has blown me away with a poignant story'   The Writing Garnet, book blogger

'Brilliant book. I'd expect nothing less from Cathy … I cried, of course'   Goodreads review

'… gripping page-turner from start to finish … emotive and heart-wrenching …'   Kate Hall, book blogger

Neglected

ALSO BY CATHY GLASS

THE MILLION COPY BESTSELLING AUTHOR

CATHY GLASS

Neglected

Scared, hungry and alone,
Jamey craves affection

HARPER
element

Certain details in this story, including names, places and dates,
have been changed to protect the family's privacy.

HarperElement
An imprint of HarperCollins*Publishers*
1 London Bridge Street
London SE1 9GF

www.harpercollins.co.uk

HarperCollins*Publishers*
1st Floor, Watermarque Building, Ringsend Road
Dublin 4, Ireland

First published by HarperElement 2022

5 7 9 10 8 6 4

A catalogue record of this book is
available from the British Library

ISBN 978-0-00-850750-3

Printed and bound in the UK using 100%
renewable electricity at CPI Group (UK) Ltd

MIX
Paper from
responsible sources
FSC™ C007454

This book is produced from independently certified FSC™ paper
to ensure responsible forest management.

For more information visit: www.harpercollins.co.uk/green

ACKNOWLEDGEMENTS

A big thank you to my family; my editors, Kelly and Holly; my literary agent, Andrew; my UK publisher HarperCollins, and my overseas publishers who are now too numerous to list by name. Last, but definitely not least, a big thank you to my readers for your unfailing support and kind words. They are much appreciated.

AUTHOR'S NOTE

The definition of neglect is a lack of care resulting in a child's needs not being met. It is a form of abuse and sadly summed up little Jamey's life.

CHAPTER ONE

JAMEY

It was 23 December, just before Christmas, and I was on the sofa in my living room trying to comfort two-year-old Jamey while listening to his social worker and her colleague. Jamey was curled on my lap, his head resting against my chest and his hands covering his face in an attempt to block out what was happening to him. Every so often he stifled a sob. The poor boy was traumatized, and I was doing my best to soothe him as his social worker, Shannon, brought me up to date and her colleague, Nathan – a trainee social worker – took some notes.

Jamey had been removed from his home a short while before, after his mother, Kat, had left him alone in his cot all night while she went to a Christmas party. It wasn't the first time she had neglected her child. The social services had been monitoring her for some months and had also put in place support with the hope that Jamey could stay with her. It hadn't worked; her only child was now in foster care and would be living with me for the foreseeable future. It was sad – even more so because it was just before Christmas.

'Jamey had only just returned home from staying with his aunt – Lacey,' Shannon continued. 'The first night he went back home, his mother goes out partying, leaving him alone from nine o'clock.' Social workers are rarely judgemental, but I could hear the condemnation in her voice. Shannon was an experienced social worker who came across as efficient and forthright. 'Lacey raised the alarm and let us in. Kat was still asleep. Lacey had found Jamey in his cot, sopping wet, thirsty and hungry. She'd changed him and given him something to eat and drink by the time we arrived. Kat is very angry and upset, and is blaming her sister for informing us, but it's not her fault.'

I nodded.

'I'll set up contact for Kat to see Jamey tomorrow.' When a child first comes into care it's usual to arrange contact straight away.

'It's a pity Jamey couldn't have stayed with his aunt,' I suggested. A suitable relative is generally considered the next best option if a child can't live with their parents. It's also the cheapest for the social services.

'She wants Jamey to live with her and is angry with me for bringing him into care. She's going to find a lawyer and apply for guardianship. She's looked after him quite a bit in the past, but it was an informal arrangement.'

'So why hasn't he gone to her now?' I asked.

'Jamey's mother, Kat, doesn't want her sister to have him and says she's got issues of her own. If Lacey puts in an application to foster him, we'll assess her.' A social services assessment is often required even though it's a relative.

'And Jamey's father?' I asked. Shannon had emailed the Essential Information Forms, but I hadn't had a chance to read them as Jamey had been moved at very short notice.

'He never sees him, although we'll try to inform him that Jamey is in care.'

Jamey whimpered and I held him closer.

'Are you all right, love?' I asked, moving his hands slightly away from his face so I could see him. He moved them back again. 'Do you like the Christmas tree?' I asked, tempting him to look. Our house was festively decorated ready for Christmas, although I knew the Christmas spirit would be in very short supply in Jamey's world right now. He'd just been taken from the only family he knew and brought to live with a stranger.

'He's wearing a nappy,' I said to Shannon. 'Is he not toilet trained yet?' Jamey was two and a half years old – an age when a lot of children are using the toilet or a potty, so it was something I needed to know.

'No,' Shannon confirmed. 'His aunt has packed some nappies and clothes, but you will need to buy some more.'

'OK.' The bag they'd arrived with was in the hall.

'There's a security blanket in there too, but it needs a wash,' Shannon's colleague, Nathan, said.

'I wonder if it would help Jamey if he had it now,' I said, thinking aloud.

'I'll get it,' Nathan replied, standing.

He left the living room and reappeared a few moments later carrying not so much a blanket as a grubby piece of cloth that might have once been white but was now grey and chewed around the edges. However, as I gave it to Jamey he pushed it to his face and, eyes screwed shut, began sucking on one corner. The smell and texture would be familiar to him, and no matter how disgusting it might appear to me, it gave him some comfort. I would wash it in time.

As we talked about Jamey I asked Shannon if he was allergic to anything or taking any medication. She said as far as they knew he wasn't. She completed the paperwork that allowed me to foster Jamey and then said she'd have a look around the house before they went. It's usual for the child's social worker to check the foster carer's home when they place a child, and also at most subsequent visits. 'I'll phone you with the time of contact tomorrow,' she added. 'It'll be at the Family Centre. You know where that is?'

'Yes.'

'Would you like to see the house too?' I asked Jamey, as Shannon and Nathan stood.

He kept his eyes closed and the rag in his mouth and shook his head, so I stayed with him in the living room while the social workers looked around the house.

'It's going to be all right, love,' I told Jamey quietly as I cuddled him. His eyes remained tightly shut.

I heard the social workers go upstairs, in and out of the bedrooms and the bathroom, then come down again. They reappeared in the living room.

'There is just you and your daughter living here?' Shannon asked.

'Yes. I've been divorced for many years.'

She nodded. 'Which bedroom will Jamey be in?'

'The one next to mine,' I replied. 'There is a single bed already made up, or do you want him to use a cot?'

'Jamey is used to a cot,' Nathan said.

'Too much so,' Shannon commented. 'He was left in it day and night. He might be better in a bed.'

'I'll try him in the bed and see how it goes,' I said.

'Won't he fall out if he's not used to it?' Nathan asked.

'I'll put cushions along the floor around the bed,' I said. 'It's what I usually do when a child first starts sleeping in a bed.'

They seemed satisfied with this and began gathering together their belongings – coats, laptops and briefcases.

'We're going now,' Shannon told Jamey, coming over to where I was sitting with him on my lap.

He didn't open his eyes or acknowledge her, so she and Nathan said goodbye and saw themselves out. I stayed on the sofa cradling Jamey. He seemed so small and fragile. I was used to having Emma, my granddaughter, on my lap, and although she was a year younger she felt far sturdier and more robust than Jamey. Also, if I'm honest, he smelt as if he needed a bath, but I'd see to that when he felt a bit better.

The Christmas garlands stirred slightly in the warm air rising from the radiator, but the rest of the house was quiet and still. I held Jamey for a few moments longer and then said, 'I wonder what Father Christmas will bring you.' I would need to go into town tomorrow to buy some more presents for him as well as nappies. I'd already bought a few general presents in case a child arrived just before Christmas, but now I could buy more specifically for him.

Jamey didn't respond to my comment about Father Christmas, which was hardly surprising. He was still very anxious so I stayed where I was, my arms around him, and continued talking to him quietly.

'I'm Cathy, I'm a foster carer and I'm going to look after you for a while. I live here with my daughter, Paula. She's an adult and is at work. You'll meet her later today. There's just us and our cat, Sammy. But he's in the garden.' I'd heard him shoot out of the cat flap on the back door in the kitchen as soon as the social workers had arrived. 'I also have a grown-up son, Adrian, who is married to Kirsty. They live in their own flat. You'll meet them on Christmas Day. You'll also meet my other daughter, Lucy, her partner Darren and their baby, Emma.'

I wasn't expecting Jamey to remember any of this or even to be interested, but he would be getting used to the sound of my voice and hopefully learning that I was friendly and wouldn't harm him. When a child first arrives it's impossible to know what life experiences have taught them. Sometimes even the most innocent comment or action can induce fear and panic in an abused child. I stayed where I was with my arms lightly around him, talking softly, for around ten minutes or so. He kept his eyes closed and the rag in his mouth, but his little body began to relax.

I heard the cat flap open and close as Sammy let himself in. Then he meowed as he came to find me. He was braver now the house was quiet and the strangers had gone. He came into the living room, stopped by the door when he saw Jamey, then, with another meow that made Jamey start, came right up to us.

'It's all right, love,' I said. 'This is our cat, Sammy. He has come to say hello to you.'

Finally, Jamey opened his eyes and turned his head slightly so he could see Sammy. Then he pulled himself upright and, taking the rag from his mouth, said, 'Cat.'

I smiled, pleased. It was the first step along a very long road to Jamey relaxing enough to accept me as his foster carer.

CHAPTER TWO

CHRISTMAS LIGHTS

An hour later the only two words Jamey had said were 'cat' and 'car'. The latter when I'd carried him to the toy boxes and shown him an assortment of toy cars. We were sitting on the living-room floor, Jamey on my lap, as I lined up the vehicles, telling him what they were, trying to establish some communication – red car, ambulance, motorbike and so on. Although Jamey wasn't playing with the vehicles or even touching them, he seemed vaguely interested and was watching me in between sucking his cloth comforter. Whether his lack of language was because he was still traumatized from being removed from home or because he didn't know many words I couldn't say. Shannon, his social worker, had said he appeared developmentally delayed, but no formal assessment had been done.

The average two-and-a-half-year-old knows at least two hundred words and some many more. They can put together short sentences and ask simple questions that begin with words like 'where' and 'what'. They have an understanding of how language works. Jamey had been neglected, so it was possible he hadn't been given the stimulus or encouragement to develop his talking, although

I'd have thought his aunt might have encouraged him, given that he seemed to have spent quite a bit of time with her and she was saying she wanted him to live with her. Jamey hadn't asked for his mummy or Lacey, which was strange. I would read the Essential Information Forms later, which I hoped would give me more background knowledge so I was better able to understand Jamey and meet his needs.

Sammy was now curled up on the carpet a little way from us with one eye open, watching Jamey. Every so often Jamey looked at him warily. 'Have you got any pets?' I asked him. He looked blank so I wasn't sure if he didn't understand or didn't have the vocabulary to tell me. Generally, though, he seemed a bit more relaxed, so I was reluctant to move from where we were.

'Would you like a drink or something to eat?' I asked him.

He looked back at me, worried and cautious. Then my mobile suddenly began to ring from the chair where I'd left it, startling Jamey, although its ringtone wasn't loud. I reached out and answered it.

'How is he?' Shannon asked.

'Quiet, but not crying. We're looking at some toys.'

'Good. I've arranged an hour's contact at the Family Centre for tomorrow at eleven o'clock. I was lucky to be given the slot. The centre closes early on Christmas Eve.'

'Is this just with his mother or his aunt as well?' I asked, so I could tell Jamey.

'Just Mum. Also, phone contact on Christmas Day, please – a short call; withhold your number and monitor the call. Can you put it on speaker?'

'Yes.'

'Lacey wants contact and I've told her she can speak to him on Christmas Day too. I've emailed you their numbers and the contact arrangements for the following week.'

'Thank you.'

'I shall be there at the start of contact tomorrow and hopefully I'll have some more clothes from home, but don't hold your breath. Buy what he needs.'

'Yes, of course.' Foster carers receive an allowance towards the cost of looking after the child.

We said goodbye, and while I had my phone in my hand I messaged my family's WhatsApp group to tell them Jamey had arrived and would be with us for Christmas. I knew they would want to buy him a present. When Paula arrived home later I'd give her more details of Jamey, as she would be living with him. I shared information about the child I was fostering with my family on a need-to-know basis.

I put down my phone and continued to take toys from the boxes, hoping to pique Jamey's interest. The smell I'd previously noticed was becoming stronger.

'I think we'd better change your nappy,' I said.

He didn't move or give any indication he'd heard me.

'Jamey, let's go and find you a clean nappy, love,' I said, and gently eased him from my lap into a standing position.

I straightened my legs and stood. I was stiff from sitting in one position with Jamey on my lap. I thought he might be too, as he was standing unsteadily where I'd put him, the cloth pressed to his mouth. It was the first time I'd seen Jamey upright. Nathan had carried him in from

9

the car and then he'd been sitting on my lap. Now I could see just how small he was – short for his age; there was nothing of him. The jogging pants and jersey top he was wearing hung loosely on his skinny frame. He was also very pale. His hair had been cut unevenly as if done at home – without much success.

'OK, love?' I asked him, with a smile, and offered him my hand. 'Let's change that nappy of yours.'

He didn't move so I gently took his hand. 'This way,' I said, and led him out of the living room. He walked, not as a two-year-old, but like a much younger child, unstable on his feet. I wondered if it was because he'd been sitting for so long in one position or if there was another develop-mental reason for it that Shannon hadn't mentioned.

I took him along the hall and to his bag. It was small and grubby and had a broken zip. I searched inside and found two nappies and a few clothes. I had spare clothes in the ottoman in my bedroom that I could use until I was able to buy more. From what Shannon had said, there wouldn't be a lot arriving from home.

'We'll go upstairs to change you,' I said, and guided him to the foot of the stairs.

Jamey was very unsure of the stairs and clutched my hand tightly as we began slowly going up, his other hand gripping the banister as the cloth dangled from his mouth.

'You probably haven't got stairs in your flat,' I said. It could explain why he was so uncertain on them. Most children his age manage stairs easily. I made a mental note to put the stairgates in place.

'In here, love,' I said, guiding him into his bedroom. I'd left the changing mat, baby wipes, disposable gloves and so forth in here in case I fostered another baby. I'd previously washed and disinfected the changing mat and I now placed that on the bed.

'Can you clamber on for me?' I asked him.

He didn't so I lifted him on. As I did he went rigid – stiff with fear.

'What's the matter, love? I'm just going to change your nappy.'

Tears sprung to his eyes and his little face creased as he rubbed his security cloth over his eyes. It was pitiful; the poor child.

'What's wrong?' I asked again, worried.

He shook his head and ground the cloth between his gritted teeth.

'I won't hurt you,' I said. 'But I do need to change your nappy. Can you lie down for me?'

He remained sitting. I couldn't change his nappy in that position, so I gently eased him down. His arms and legs were stiff. Clearly having his nappy changed in the past had been a bad experience. 'We'll soon be done,' I reassured him.

I'd already taken off his shoes downstairs when he'd first arrived, and I now gently removed his jogging bottoms. He was grimacing and as I removed his nappy I saw why. The worst case of nappy rash I'd ever seen. The whole area concealed by his nappy was covered in angry red sores. His bottom was bright red and the creases at the tops of his legs were weeping. It must have been agony for him each time his nappy was changed and cream applied. If cream had ever been used, for I couldn't see any sign of it.

His nappy was sodden, which would aggravate the sores and broken skin. It also contained three small poo pellets, suggesting he was constipated. Not a pleasant sight, but foster carers, like parents, have to deal with unpleasant things when caring for their children.

My immediate concern was how best to clean him without causing him more pain. He was grinding his teeth on the cloth, his eyes screwed shut and his face contorted, and bracing himself, expecting to be hurt.

'I think we'll give you a nice warm bath before we put you in a clean nappy,' I said. I thought this would cause him the least distress. 'Can you walk to the bathroom with me?'

He didn't move so I gently scooped him up in my arms – hoping he wouldn't choose this moment to have another wee – and carried him into the bathroom. I set him down by the bath and he stood watching me as I ran and tested the water. I talked to him gently, reassuring him that what I was doing was going to help him, for I'd no idea what his experience of bath time at home was.

'It's nice and warm. Not too hot and not too cold,' I told him as I tested the temperature of the water. 'I'll put in the ducks. They like a swim.' A bag of bath toys hung from a hook beside the bath and I dropped some of them into the water.

Once the bath was ready, I eased off Jamey's top and lifted him into the soothing warm water. He still had the cloth in his mouth.

'Let's put that down or it will get wet,' I said.

He allowed me to take the rag from his mouth and hang it over the side of the bath.

'Sit down, love,' I said. He was still standing.

He hesitated and then gingerly lowered himself into the water. As he sat there I could see there was nothing of him. The bones in his shoulders, neck and spine jutted out, and I could have counted his ribs. Shannon had said he was slightly built, but it was more than that. He looked malnourished to me. I would have to inform her of what I'd found having removed his clothes, and possibly take him to the doctor.

Jamey sat still for a few moments, not interested in the bath toys, his little face serious and woeful. He wasn't in pain, just lost, and my heart went out to him. At least there weren't any cuts, bruises or cigarette burns on his body, I consoled myself, as I'd found on some of the children I'd fostered.

Kneeling beside the bath, I leant over and began making the plastic ducks bob up and down in the hope of easing Jamey's unhappiness.

'Where's the duck gone?' I said with a smile, holding it under the water. 'Here it is!' I said, releasing the duck so it sprang up.

Jamey watched for a while and then, reaching out, pushed one of the ducks under, not gleefully but mechanically.

'Fantastic! Well done,' I enthused. 'Where's it gone?'

He didn't reply but pushed another duck under, then two together. While he was occupied I began gently sponging his back and neck, then under his arms and across his chest. It was just plain water with no soap so it wouldn't irritate his sore and broken skin. He wasn't dirty as some children were when they first arrived, and he didn't have head lice, so I didn't wash his hair. I'd do that another day when he was more settled.

Having washed his back, chest, arms and legs, I gave him the flannel and asked him to wash around his penis.

He did so and although it wasn't a very thorough wash, sitting in the warm water would cleanse him. He handed back the flannel and reached for his security cloth, having lost interest in the bath toys.

'Let's get you out and dry you off,' I said.

I helped him stand up and then climb out. I wrapped him in the large, fluffy bath towel I had ready. There was so little flesh on him to keep him warm that he immediately began to shiver, his lips trembling, although the house was very warm.

I released the water from the bath and, making sure the bath towel was wrapped snuggly around him, I guided him along the landing towards his bedroom.

'Do you want to go to the toilet before you get dressed?' I asked. I thought I should start getting him used to the idea of using the toilet.

He shook his head, so I guessed someone – either his mother or aunt – had introduced the idea of using a toilet.

'OK. Tell me if you do,' I said. 'Good boy.' I wasn't expecting him to tell me, but I had to start somewhere.

I took Jamey into his bedroom and helped him onto the changing mat. He lay snuggled in the towel while I thoroughly dried him and then gently applied barrier cream all over the sore area that would be covered by his nappy. It was uncomfortable for him but not painful. I fastened the nappy and then dressed him in the clothes he had just taken off. They were clean and later I would find him fresh clothes for tomorrow.

'Good boy,' I said, smiling. 'Let's get you a drink and something to eat. You must be hungry by now.'

I took the bag containing the soiled nappy with us and held his hand as we returned slowly downstairs and went into the kitchen. I dropped the nappy bag outside the back door for putting in the bin later and then thoroughly washed my hands.

'What would you like to drink?' I asked Jamey, who was watching me cautiously.

He didn't reply so I took a carton of apple juice from the fridge. From what I'd seen so far I didn't think Jamey had the fine motor skills needed to use an open cup, so I took out the trainer beaker instead. Also known as a sippy cup, it has a closed lid with a spout and a handle each side, making it easy to drink from. Jamey was still watching me and I threw him a smile, then poured the juice into the cup and added a splash of hot water from the kettle to take off the chill.

'What would you like to eat?' I asked him.

He answered my question with a blank stare, so I began opening cupboard doors and showing him the contents, then the fridge, hoping he would spot something he liked. He would be eating our meals, but for now – on his first day – I just wanted him to eat something. He pointed to a bag of crisps.

'OK, but I'll make you a sandwich to have with it.'

I took him to the table and sat him on the booster seat with the trainer cup in front of him. 'You have some of your drink while I make you a sandwich.'

I could see him from the kitchen where I worked, and he began sucking thirstily on the spout of the beaker. 'Good boy.'

I made him a sandwich with wholemeal bread, cutting off the crusts and then slicing them into triangles so they were more manageable. I arranged some crisps on the plate, together with some sliced cucumber and cherry tomatoes cut in half. It was an attractive and healthy snack.

Given that Jamey was very withdrawn, I wasn't expecting him to show much enthusiasm for food, and I thought I'd probably have to encourage him to eat. However, the moment I put the plate down in front of him he set upon it and began eating the crisps, then the tomatoes, cucumber and sandwiches. He was clearly hungry. I sat with him as he ate and drank and then I refilled his beaker, and he drank half of it.

'Would you like something else?' I asked. 'A yoghurt? Fruit?'

He shook his head.

'OK. We'll have dinner later.' Indeed, we'd be having it in two hours, for it was already four o'clock.

I needed to telephone his social worker and tell her about the condition Jamey was in. It couldn't be left. I took him into the living room to the toy boxes, hoping he might amuse himself while I spoke to Shannon. It was growing dark outside so I switched on the Christmas-tree lights, and they shone magically. Jamey's eyes rounded and he said his third word.

'Lights.'

'Yes, that's right, love. Christmas-tree lights. Well done. Have you got a Christmas tree at home?' Daft question, really, as there hadn't been enough money for food, let alone a Christmas tree.

He shook his head. I could see he was enthralled by the lights, as indeed I was. I feel there is a mystical quality about Christmas-tree lights that you never grow out of. Jamey wasn't interested in the toys but joined me on the sofa as I phoned Shannon. He was still gazing at the lights and as I waited for the call to be answered he rested his head against my shoulder. I put my arm around him and felt the joy and peace of Christmas step that little bit closer.

CHAPTER THREE

PAULA HELPS

'I'll arrange for him to have a medical,' Shannon said as I finished telling her of Jamey's emaciated body, sore bottom and the food he'd ravenously eaten. 'But it will be after Christmas now. How are you treating the sores?'

'I bathed them in warm water, thoroughly dried the area, and then used barrier cream. I'll go to the chemist tomorrow and see if they can recommend something stronger.'

'I'll ask his mother what she uses. I've got to phone her shortly.'

'Could you also ask her if he can have his favourite toy, please? There's nothing in the bag.'

'I'll try again. I did ask her while we were there, but she wasn't happy about letting go of his belongings, to put it mildly. Not that there is much in the flat. What's Jamey doing now?'

'Sitting beside me gazing at the Christmas-tree lights.'

'That's nice. There's no sign of Christmas at his home.'

'That's a pity,' I said, although I wasn't surprised.

I'd fostered other children whose first proper Christmas had been when they'd come into care. Many of them had been much older than Jamey so had missed out for years. I'm sure their parents didn't intentionally deprive them of a good Christmas, but there wouldn't have been much left over for presents if, like Jamey's mother, they were drug- and alcohol-dependent, which many of them were. They're expensive habits and would have first call on their income as they wouldn't be able to face life without them. These substances affect the way the brain works, and I know of many parents who, once clean, were shocked and disgusted at how badly they'd neglected their children – to the point where they'd been taken into care and even adopted, so they'd lost them for good. But while I felt sorry for the parents – no one should suffer the pain of losing their children – the child's welfare must come first.

Shannon wound up by saying she'd see me at contact tomorrow. Jamey was still nestled in the crook of my arm, his little body more relaxed. I put down the phone and looked at him. His eyes were closed.

'Jamey?' I asked, quietly.

He was asleep, bless him, exhausted from the gruelling day. I carefully withdrew my arm from under him and then laid him flat on the sofa to continue to sleep. It would do him good. I took the cloth from his mouth but left it in his hand. I crept quietly from the living room and went upstairs for a throw-over fleece, which I covered him with. Even in sleep his little face was anxious. His brow was furrowed as though he was worrying. I hoped that in time I could take away his pain so that he could play, carefree, as a child should.

Leaving Jamey to sleep, I went into the front room and to my computer, where I took the opportunity to check emails. Shannon's included the Essential Information

Forms and I quickly read them. They gave Jamey's age, date of birth, ethnicity and home address. It appeared he and his mother had been living in a one-bedroom flat; Jamey had slept in a cot in the living room while his mother slept on the sofa, as the bedroom was too damp to use. He didn't see his father and the only extended family was his aunt, Lacey, who was listed under other significant adults. Jamey's mother was twenty-eight and Lacey was thirty. Details of the child's nursery and education were blank. Jamey had no known health issues or allergies, which I knew. The reason for the foster placement was neglect and he was the subject of a court order. Thankfully there was no suggestion he had been sexually abused, and the box on the form for behavioural problems said, *None*. His first language was shown as English, with the comment that Jamey was very quiet and appeared to have limited language skills. *An assessment may be required.*

I was just coming to the end of the forms when the landline rang. I grabbed the handset, hoping it hadn't woken Jamey. It was Joy Philips, my supervising social worker. All foster carers have a supervising social worker whose role is to support, monitor, advise and guide the carer and their family in every aspect of fostering.

'I understand you've got a new arrival,' Joy said. 'Jamey Durrant.'

'Yes, a few hours ago.'

'Sorry I couldn't be there when he was placed. I was in a meeting.'

Some supervising social workers try to be present when a child arrives. This is more important for new carers than those who have done it before and know what to expect and the questions to ask.

'How is he?' Joy asked.

'Asleep on the sofa.' I then told Joy what I'd told Shannon, ending with details of the contact that had been arranged for tomorrow.

'Have you got everything you need to foster him?' Joy asked.

'Mostly. I'll go shopping tomorrow. Thanks for the Christmas card,' I added.

'You're welcome. Have a good Christmas. I'm sure you will. I'm off work for the week and will be back in the New Year. If you need emergency advice you know to contact the duty social worker.'

'Yes.' Most of the staff were taking the week off. Both Joy and Shannon would visit us in the New Year – within a month of Jamey being placed.

Joy and I wished each other a merry Christmas and said goodbye.

I went into the living room to check on Jamey and found him wide awake, lying on the sofa and watching the ceiling decorations as they slightly stirred.

'Hi, love, you're awake. Do you remember where you are?'

He looked at me with large, sorrowful eyes, then pulled himself into a sitting position.

'What would you like to do? Play with some toys?'

He slid from the sofa and stood in front of the Christmas tree. 'Lights,' he said, pointing.

'Yes. Christmas-tree lights. It's Christmas soon.'

He went to the patio windows to look out. It was a pretty miserable day outside, wet and windy. He turned and spotted Sammy curled up by the radiator.

'Cat,' he said, pointing.

'Yes, that's right. Our cat is called Sammy. Would you like to stroke him?'

I went over and began stroking Sammy, showing Jamey what to do – running my hand from his neck, down his back, keeping to the direction of his fur. 'Like this.'

Jamey watched but didn't say anything or want to stroke Sammy. Instead, he returned to the tree, which clearly fascinated him.

'Lights,' he said again.

'Yes, let's count them.' I began counting. 'One, two three.' I got to ten, but Jamey had lost interest and was looking around the room. 'Would you like to play with some toys now?' I asked, going to the toy boxes.

He looked at me carefully, then frowned, straining – a look I recognised from other infants. 'Do you want the toilet?' I asked him.

He didn't reply but filled his nappy, so I took him upstairs to change him. He'd passed a few more pellets. It would take many days before he was no longer consti-pated and was going to the toilet normally, and I'd be monitoring it. The barrier cream was doing its job so changing him wasn't too uncomfortable, and I reapplied the cream.

Downstairs I deposited the nappy bag in the bin outside, washed my hands, and then for the next hour I tried to find something that Jamey might like to play with. But he was overwhelmed and just looked at everything I showed him. Still holding his hand, I took him on a tour of the house so it wasn't so strange. I told him about each room and named some of the items in them – chair, table, computer and so on. Upstairs I said, 'Jamey's bedroom,' as we went in. Then, 'Jamey's bed.'

I showed him the other bedrooms, the bathroom and toilet. 'For doing poos and wees,' I emphasized.

We were about to go downstairs when he tugged my hand, wanting to go into his room again.

'Jamey's bedroom,' I said as we went in. 'Jamey's bed.'

He seemed to be looking for something and I wondered if it was a cot.

'Now you're a big boy you can sleep in the bed,' I said, patting the bed. I drew the curtains while I was in the room as it was dark outside now.

Jamey seemed to want to go into the other rooms again so, still holding hands, we went all over the house for a second time. I switched on lights and closed curtains and blinds as we went. As we were going downstairs I heard a key in the front door. I'd lost track of time. It was Paula returning from work and I hadn't even begun dinner.

'Hello, love,' I said. Arriving in the hall, I gave her a kiss. 'This is Jamey.'

'Hi, Jamey,' she said with a smile, slipping off her shoes. 'How are you?'

Jamey looked at her.

'This is my daughter, Paula,' I told him, then said quietly to her, 'He's not saying much at present, but he likes a hug.'

'Well, that's good,' she said, smiling at him. 'I like hugs too. Would you like a hug now?' She squatted down so she was at his level and opened her arms.

Most children who have a strong attachment to their parents wouldn't hug a stranger, but Jamey went over and cuddled her as he'd been doing to me.

'That's lovely,' she said, clearly touched. 'I'm going to get changed now and then I'll play with you.' Paula liked to change out of her office wear when she arrived home.

I took Jamey with me into the kitchen until Paula appeared, then she kept him occupied in the living room while I made dinner. I could hear the gentle, loving way she was talking to him, coaxing and encouraging him as I had tried to do. He was quiet for most of the time but did say 'lights', 'cat' and 'car' again. I cooked a fish dish for dinner and we all ate together. Jamey was hungry and fed himself, although he used his fingers rather than the child's knife, fork and spoon I'd set out. After dinner Paula took him into the living room again while I cleared up. She reappeared quite quickly.

'I think he's done a poo,' she said, grimacing.

'I'll see to him,' I said with a knowing smile. Paula was a big help with fostering, but changing nappies wasn't her forte. My other daughter Lucy was different. Working in a nursery, she'd had to get used to changing nappies, wiping bottoms and cleaning up accidents just as foster carers have to, but she was no longer living with us.

Once Jamey was clean, I took him downstairs where Paula sat on the sofa and read to him. We had a good selection of early-years picture books, including ones for Christmas. I took the opportunity to sort out the contents of Jamey's bag where I found a pair of pyjamas. At around 7.30 Jamey began rubbing his eyes, clearly tired.

'I'll take him up and get him ready for bed,' Paula offered.

Jamey held onto both our hands, suggesting he wanted us both to go, so that's what we did. Upstairs I took a new child's toothbrush from my spares and Paula helped Jamey brush his teeth and wash his face and hands, while I put a stairgate in place at the top of the stairs. Once they'd finished in the bathroom, we showed him where I slept and then Paula's room before going to his room. Paula helped him into bed and I took spare pillows from the airing cupboard and arranged them either side of the bed so if he fell out in the night it would be a soft landing.

'Would you like your light on or off?' I asked him. 'Or maybe on a little?' It's details like this that help a child settle in a strange room. I turned the dimmer switch up and down to show Jamey. He didn't reply – hardly surprising, as this was all so different to sleeping in a cot in the living room at his home. I left the light on a little.

'I'll leave your door open, so if you need me in the night, call out and I'll come to you,' I told him. 'Night, love.' I kissed his cheek.

'Night, night,' Paula said, and kissed him.

We looked at him, so small in the bed, his little face just visible above the covers. 'Shout if you want me in the night,' I said.

Although Jamey was clearly tired and needed to sleep, I was reluctant to leave him alone. He seemed so vulnerable, and I wasn't sure he would call out if he needed me. The thought of him lying there alone in the dark was heart-wrenching.

'I'll listen out for him if you want to get on with something,' Paula offered. 'I'll be in my bedroom for a while.'

'OK. Thanks, love.'

Paula and I said goodnight again to Jamey and, leaving the light on low and the door open, we came out. Paula went to her room, and I went downstairs to my computer in the front room where I logged onto the council's portal to start my log notes on Jamey. Foster carers in the UK are expected to keep a record of the child or children they are looking after. This includes appointments and the child's health and wellbeing. As well as charting their progress, it can act as an aide-mémoire if necessary. These notes, like most other records, are now stored digitally. There was no sound coming from Jamey's bedroom and ten minutes later, when I'd finished and had shut down the computer, I checked on him. He was fast asleep.

Presently Paula came downstairs and we sat in the living room with mugs of tea.

'I texted Adrian and Lucy and told them Jamey was here and how cute he is,' Paula said.

I smiled. 'Yes, he is a darling, for sure. A lovely little chap.'

'It will be nice having him with us for Christmas,' Paula said. 'I've been thinking a lot about Nana recently. It makes me sad, but having Jamey here to look after will help.'

'Yes, I know what you mean,' I said, and gave her a hug.

My mother had spent last Christmas with us and had died on the morning she was due to return home. I'd found her in bed. We were heartbroken, and as the anniversary of her death approached the memories came flooding back. But Paula was right, having Jamey with us would help, although of course I felt sorry for Jamey's mother, who wouldn't have her son with her at Christmas.

'You're frowning, Mum,' Paula said.

'Oh dear. I didn't mean to. I've got a lot to do tomorrow,' I replied. 'Jamey has contact at eleven o'clock and I need to collect the Christmas order and buy some more presents for his sack, and some nappies.'

'I finish work at twelve tomorrow so I could collect the Christmas order on the way home,' Paula offered. 'I pass the supermarket.'

'Oh, yes, please. That would be a big help,' I said, and kissed her cheek. Then we sat quietly gazing at the tree lights and sipping our tea. 'We'll give Jamey a really good Christmas.'

'Yes, we will.'

CHAPTER FOUR

MEETING JAMEY'S MOTHER

I never sleep well when there is a new child in the house. I'm half listening out in case they wake frightened, not knowing where they are and in need of reassurance. Although Jamey didn't call out, I checked on him twice in the night, but he was fast asleep. The following morning, after I'd showered and dressed, I went in again. He was awake, lying in bed, gazing around the room.

'Good morning, love, you slept well.' He looked fresher. 'It's Christmas Eve today,' I said, opening his curtains. 'We'll get you dressed, then you can have some breakfast, and later you're seeing your mummy.'

Jamey didn't reply or give any indication he had heard me. I was starting to have concerns he might have some hearing loss. He wouldn't be the first child to have gone undiagnosed.

'Jamey, can you hear me?' I asked.

He nodded. Even so, it would be something I'd mention to the paediatrician when Jamey had his medical.

As I helped Jamey wash and dress I could hear Paula moving around in her bedroom, getting ready to go to work. She came to say goodbye.

'Don't forget the Christmas order, and nappies,' I reminded her.

'I won't, don't worry, Mum.'

I knew I was worrying. I was usually very well organized, especially with the Christmas arrangements as it was such an important family occasion, and as usual my children were going to spend it with me. I had planned to collect the food order early and then spend the afternoon preparing for tomorrow before going to church in the evening. Now I was worried I'd run out of time, with contact and looking after Jamey. I wanted everything to be just right. You've got all afternoon and Paula is helping you, I reminded myself.

I talked to Jamey about seeing his mother at the Family Centre and what to expect. 'It's like a big house with lots of living rooms,' I said. 'You'll see Mummy in one of the rooms. It will have chairs and lots of games and toys to play with. I will take you and then collect you at the end and bring you back here.'

Jamey was concentrating on what I was telling him. Children his age can understand more than they can say. As I finished he said, 'Mummy.'

'Yes, that's right, love. You are seeing your mummy later and then I will bring you back here.'

I was planning to leave the house at 10.30 as contact was at 11. In the meantime I set out some toys in the living room for us to play with, but Jamey brought me one of the Christmas books that Paula had read to him, so we looked at that instead. As he was choosing another book my mobile rang. It was Shannon.

'Can you come to the Family Centre fifteen minutes early?' she asked. 'Kat wants to meet you.'

'Yes.' It wasn't unusual for parents to ask to meet the foster carer, although I normally saw them at the start and end of contact as well.

It was then I realised Jamey should really take his mother a Christmas present as he wouldn't see her again before Christmas. The foster carer usually organizes gifts for the child to give to their parents, siblings and any other close family members at Christmas, on birthdays, and Mother's and Father's Day. If I'd had more time, I would have chosen something especially for Kat, but now I'd have to make do from my spares.

'Let's find a Christmas present for you to give Mummy,' I said to Jamey.

I took him upstairs to my bedroom and opened a drawer where I kept some emergency presents. Most foster carers keep a few. I showed him the bath oil and tea light set, the Jasmine-scented reed diffuser, the scarf and the china mug with 'Mum' on it. There was also one with 'Dad' on it, but that wasn't relevant as Jamey didn't see his father. He chose the bath oil set, probably because it was in a brightly coloured box. I took out a sheet of Christmas wrapping paper, sticky tape and scissors, and together we wrapped the gift. Jamey didn't say anything, but I could tell from his expression he was enjoying the task. I then let him choose a Christmas card and, putting a biro in his hand, I helped him write the words inside the card: *Love from Jamey*. And on the envelope: *To Mummy*.

'She'll like that,' I said, and he smiled.

I gave him a hug and felt his little body relax against me. He loved being cuddled. He was such a treasure and very easy to love.

I changed his nappy and applied more barrier cream. Downstairs I took a box of sweet mince pies from the cupboard to give to Kat as a little extra festive present. I put the barrier cream and a spare nappy in a bag to take with us. Normally the carer provides this at contact, and it was important that Jamey didn't stay in a soiled nappy as it would aggravate the sores on his bottom and prevent healing.

We left the house at 10.15 and on the way to the Family Centre I explained again to Jamey where we were going and why – 'to see your mummy'.

'Mummy,' Jamey said. Then, looking out of his side window, he kept pointing and saying, 'Lights.'

'Yes, love, lots of lights. It's Christmas Eve so most shops and houses have their lights on now.' Indeed, some buildings had incredible displays of Santas on sleighs pulled by reindeer with flashing lights, while many houses had a Christmas tree lit in their front-room window. You couldn't help but feel uplifted by all the Christmas lights and Jamey was taking it all in from his seat in the back of my car.

By the time we arrived at the Family Centre I was feeling upbeat and in a festive mood. I parked the car in the small car park to the side of the building, tucked the box of sweet mince pies into the bag and opened Jamey's door, which was child locked. He was holding the gift for his mother with both hands, so I took his arm as we crossed the car park, then walked up the path to the security-locked main door. I pressed the buzzer. The closed-circuit television camera above us was monitored in the office, and a few moments later the door clicked open and we went in.

'Jamey Durrant to see his mother,' I said to the receptionist, who was seated behind a screen to my right. 'His
social worker asked me to come early to meet his mother.'

'I'll tell her you're here,' she said, picking up her desk
phone. 'Can you sign in, please?'

I signed the Visitors' Book and a few moments later
Shannon appeared with another woman. 'This is the
contact supervisor,' she said, introducing her. 'She can
look after Jamey while we talk to Kat in another room.'

I smiled and said hello to her. Contact at the Family
Centre is usually supervised, and the parents are told this
in advance. The supervisor is in the room the whole time
with the child during the contact session and takes notes,
which they send to the child's social worker, who incor-
porates them into their report to the judge for the final
court hearing.

'Mummy?' Jamey asked, looking confused.

'Yes, you'll see her soon,' I reassured him. 'This lady
will look after you for a little while and then you'll see
Mummy.'

He still looked unsure, but when the contact supervisor offered her hand he took it. As they went down the
corridor I heard her ask, 'Is that present for Mummy?'

Jamey replied, 'Yes.'

'This way,' Shannon said to me, and we headed along
the corridor in the opposite direction. 'Thanks for coming
in early. I'm afraid Kat isn't in a very good mood.
Hopefully seeing you will help reassure her. The manager
is with her now.'

'What's the matter?' I asked.

'She's pissed off with me for putting Jamey in care,'
Shannon replied stoically. 'Not that I had any choice.'

I nodded. Shannon was in her early forties and had a direct manner. I thought how frustrating and upsetting her job must be when it was impossible for a child to stay at home. I didn't know how social workers coped, year after year, dealing with so much misery.

We stopped outside a closed door, and I saw Shannon take a deep breath before she opened it. I followed her in.

'This is Cathy, Jamey's foster carer,' Shannon said, pulling out a chair for me to sit on.

'Hello.' I smiled at Kat and the manager.

'About bleeding time,' Kat said. 'Taking my kid and dumping him with a stranger.'

I knew Kat was twenty-eight, but she looked much older and already bore the signs of heavy substance misuse. Painfully thin, she had angry red marks on her otherwise sickly-pale cheeks and forehead. Her hollow eyes had dark circles beneath them and, despite the centre being very warm, she had on layers of baggy woollens, which she clutched protectively across her as if she was cold.

'If you don't need me here any more, I'll go,' the centre's manager said to Shannon. 'I have a meeting soon. Or do you want me to stay?'

'No, you can go,' Shannon replied.

The manager said goodbye and left the room, closing the door behind her.

Kat was agitatedly licking her lips and scratching her arms – more signs of drug dependency. She was glaring at me and I thought now might be a good time to try to defuse some of her anger with a peace offering. I took out the box of sweet mince pies.

'I thought you might like these,' I said, sliding the box across the table. 'Jamey has a Christmas present for you too.'

'I don't want your stuff,' she said in a hostile manner. 'I want my son back!' I felt a bit of a fool.

'You said you wanted to see Cathy so you could tell her about Jamey,' Shannon reminded her.

'He's mine!' Kat said, clearly having little idea of why she'd asked to see me.

'Of course he is,' I said. 'I am his foster carer. Would you like to see some photographs of my home and Jamey's bedroom? It might help put your mind at rest if you can picture where he is.'

'Not fussed,' Kat said, scratching her neck.

'I think that would be nice,' Shannon said to me.

I took out my phone and, tilting the screen so Kat could see, I scrolled through the photos I'd taken for this purpose – of the different rooms, including Jamey's bedroom, and the garden.

'Where's his cot?' Kat demanded as I finished.

'Remember I said he was going to sleep in a bed?' Shannon reminded her. 'He's old enough now.'

'No, he's not,' Kat snapped confrontationally.

'We can see how it goes,' I suggested. 'He slept very well last night.'

'That's because you drugged him.'

I was taken aback. I could understand that Kat was angry at having had her son taken into care, but to accuse me of drugging him was out of order.

'I would never give a child drugs to make them sleep,' I said indignantly.

'That's what they accused me of,' she retaliated, glaring at Shannon. So I guessed that was what had prompted the accusation. 'I don't do drugs any more,' she added.

'No?' Shannon said. 'So if we were to do another hair-strand test now, it would come back negative?'

Kat didn't answer but redirected her anger at me again. 'And you're not allowed to hit him either. I'll report you if you do.'

'I wouldn't hit any child – or adult – ever,' I said. 'I will look after Jamey as if he was my own and give him a lovely Christmas.'

'Of course you will,' she sneered. 'You've got the money to do it. I haven't.'

Kat had a point, although of course a drug habit is very expensive. Even so, I felt sorry for her. She had lost her child into care and her life was in ruins.

'I'm going to see my kid now,' she said suddenly, and stood.

'Are you sure you haven't any more questions for Cathy?' Shannon asked.

'No.'

'You might need this,' I said, picking up the bag. 'It contains a change of nappy and barrier cream.'

'My son didn't have sores when he left me,' she said, snatching the bag. I guessed Shannon had told her what I'd found. 'And neither was he constipated. I feed him proper.' Stuffing the box of mince pies into the bag, she stormed out of the room.

I allowed myself to breathe again.

'Sorry about that,' Shannon said with a sigh. 'I'd better go – I need to be in the room at the start of contact.'

'I'll come back at twelve then to collect Jamey,' I said.

'Yes, please.'

We stood and I walked with Shannon to reception where I signed out of the Visitors' Book and left.

I was very unsettled by Kat. I hate confrontation and don't handle it well. It would play on my mind for some time to come. As a foster carer I do my best for the child and it is hurtful if we are accused of not looking after them or, worse, harming them. It can also lead to the carer being investigated. Thankfully, Shannon wasn't taking Kat's allegations seriously. I hoped that once she was over her initial anger we would be able to work together for Jamey's sake. It's always better for the child if they see their parents getting along with the foster carer.

I was pleased to be out in the fresh air and set off at a brisk walking pace in the direction of the local shops. It wasn't worth me returning home and I knew there was a chemist and café in the parade of shops about a ten-minute walk away.

I went first to the chemist where I asked the pharmacist for some advice about treating severe nappy sores and broken skin. He said to keep the area dry and clean, which I was doing, and he recommended an antiseptic barrier cream that looked similar to the one I was using, but I bought it anyway. He said if the sores didn't clear up or got worse, I should go to the doctor as it could be infected. I thanked him and also bought some more nappies. Then I went next door to the café where I ordered a hot chocolate to take away.

I sipped the drink on the way back to the Family Centre; it was warm and comforting and helped raise my spirits. When I arrived at the centre there were still fifteen minutes before the end of contact so I sat in my car to finish the hot chocolate and took the opportunity to message Adrian and Lucy.

Looking forward to seeing you later for church, love Mum xxx

Adrian and his wife, Kirsty, Lucy and her partner, Darren, and their baby daughter, Emma, would be coming to the Christmas Eve family service with Paula, Jamey and me. It was held at our local church every year. Last year my dear mother had been with us, and I remembered how much she had enjoyed the service, which had become part of our Christmas celebrations. This year she would be with us in our hearts.

Just before midday I went into the Family Centre and to the contact room, aware of how upsetting saying good-bye at the end of contact could be. There were times in the past when I'd had to carry a young child crying and screaming for their parents from the building. It was heart-breaking for everyone, but eventually the parents and the child began to adjust to the contact arrangements and looked forward to the next one.

The door to the room was closed so I knocked and then went in. It was uncannily quiet. The contact super-visor was sitting at the table to my left, making notes. Jamey and his mother were on the sofa; he had a picture book open on his lap and Kat was checking her phone.

As soon as she saw me she stood and said to the contact supervisor, 'I need to get going.' Then to Jamey, 'Bye, be good.' She quickly kissed the top of his head and hurried from the room, brushing past me on her way out. And that was it.

Jamey's gaze followed his mother, although he didn't try to run after her as most children would. Was this the level of care and affection he was used to receiving at home? I wondered. While I wouldn't have wanted him and his mother to have been upset at having to say good-bye, it would have been far more natural than this parting.

'Are you all right, love?' I asked gently, going to him. 'Time to go.'

He obediently put down the book and stood. I picked up the bag containing the spare nappies and cream. They hadn't been used. I would change Jamey once we were home. I noticed the box of mince pies had gone though, so I assumed Kat had taken them with her, until I saw the empty box in the wastepaper basket.

'Kat enjoyed the mince pies,' the contact supervisor said as she packed away.

'Good. All of them?'

'Yes. She hadn't had breakfast. And she's told Jamey she'll buy him a Christmas present when she has the money.'

'OK,' I said and, taking Jamey's hand, led him out of the room.

CHAPTER FIVE

CHRISTMAS

Once home, I changed Jamey's nappy and then made us lunch. He ate well and didn't appear to be unsettled by having seen his mother as most children in care are to begin with. Again, I wondered about the strength of their relationship.

As we ate I kept an eye on the time, aware that we'd have to go out before long. Paula was collecting the Christmas food order on her way home, but I also needed to buy Jamey some more presents. However, just as we finished eating, Paula texted:

I've got the food order. I'm in the toy shop choosing something for Jamey. Do you want me to get him some presents for his sack?

Yes please, love, I texted back. *That will be a big help. Buy what you think he might like. xxx*

I trusted Paula's judgement and I could now spend the afternoon getting ready for Christmas Day.

'Jamey, it's Christmas tomorrow,' I told him excitedly. I scooped him up and gave him a big hug. 'Would you like to help me get everything ready?'

He snuggled his head against my shoulder and cuddled me lovingly. Never before had I fostered a child who'd shown me such affection so soon after arriving. It usually took weeks, if not months, and I wondered if this was a result of the neglect he'd suffered in the past. Neglect doesn't just mean not meeting the child's physical needs, but their emotional ones too. Jamey had all the signs of being deprived of love, attention and affection, and I hoped to make it up to him. Lack of care in the early years can leave devastating and lasting scars on a child, which can follow them into adulthood if not addressed.

With the afternoon now free and with Jamey's help, I set about laying the table in the front room ready for tomorrow. We only used this dining table, which had extending leaves, for special occasions; the rest of the time we ate around the smaller table in our kitchen-diner. Jamey helped me put the festive cloth on the table and arrange the matching paper napkins, then the cutlery. I talked to him as we worked, explaining what we were doing and why. He followed me around in silence, compliant, obedient and probably overwhelmed. I finished the table with a festive centrepiece and then stood back to admire our work.

'Doesn't that look nice!' I exclaimed, lifting Jamey up for a better view. 'All ready for Christmas tomorrow. Now, let's play a game together.'

I couldn't do anything more at present until Paula returned with the shopping, so, holding Jamey's hand, I took him into the living room where the toy boxes were. Whenever he walked beside me I was reminded of how unsteady he was on his feet compared to the average child his age. It was something I would mention to his social worker, and the paediatrician at his medical.

Taking an early-years' wooden jigsaw puzzle from the toy box, I sat with Jamey on the floor. Aimed at twelve-month-olds, the puzzle had six large pieces with a picture of an animal on each, which fitted easily into the sunken spaces on the board. Puzzles like this help a child develop spatial awareness, hand–eye coordination and fine motor skills, as well as being fun.

It soon became clear that Jamey didn't have any idea what to do. I showed him a number of times, lifting out each piece and then putting it back in its correct place while saying the name of the animal in the picture – cat, dog, horse, cow and so on.

'Jamey do it now,' I said, encouraging him.

He picked up the piece with the picture of the cat on it, said 'cat' and then put it into his mouth as a much younger child would.

'Yes, it's a cat, good boy,' I said. 'It goes here.'

I guided his hand to the spot on the board where the piece fitted.

'Well done!' I said, clapping. He looked pleased. 'Now let's put the dog in its place. Where's the picture of the dog, Jamey?'

He picked up the correct piece and made an attempt to put it into one of the spaces, but it wasn't the correct one so it wouldn't fit. I helped him again, then clapped. So we continued, working our way through the six pieces. On the second run-through Jamey not only said the word 'cat', but also repeated the names of the other animals in the pictures as well – 'dog', 'horse' and so on. We did the puzzle a third time and then I reached for a different one.

A few minutes later I heard Paula let herself in the front door. Jamey looked up, startled.

'It's Paula come home early from work,' I reassured him.

I stood, Jamey took my hand and we went into the hall. He looked a bit surprised to see Paula and then smiled.

'Hi, Jamey,' she said. She was laden with shopping.

'Thank you so much,' I said, helping her in with the bags.

'I'll put you-know-what upstairs in your room,' she said, referring to Jamey's presents.

'Yes, please. And tell me how much I owe you.'

Jamey came with me into the kitchen and stood watching me unpack the food and put it away. Paula was upstairs. Then he disappeared from view.

'Jamey?' I called. I closed the fridge door and went to look for him. I knew he couldn't have gone far. He never left my side.

I found him in the hall.

'Are you all right, love?' I asked.

He went to the foot of the stairs and looked up hopefully.

'Are you looking for Paula?'

'Yes.'

'She will be down soon. She's changing her clothes. Come and help me for now.' I still had some fridge and freezer foods to put away. 'This way,' I said, offering him my hand.

He refused to take it and sat on the bottom stair to wait, then made a good attempt to call, 'Paula!'

She came out of her bedroom, having changed out of her work clothes. 'I'm ready now,' she said with a smile, and came down.

She got herself a glass of water and then took Jamey into the living room to play while I finished unpacking the food. I was pleased by what Jamey had just done. It was reassuring. I had little idea how developmentally delayed he was and the Essential Information Forms hadn't helped much, but he'd understood that Paula was upstairs and he'd wanted to see her so he'd exerted his will and waited for her. It may not seem much, but it was an indication that Jamey was processing information more like a child his age should.

While Paula was playing with Jamey I took the opportunity to go upstairs and wrap his presents. Paula had chosen well and there was a lovely selection of early-years' toys, books and games. Once I'd finished, I hid the presents in my wardrobe with Paula's, ready to put in their Santa sacks later. Yes, she still had a sack even at the age of twenty-five! Adrian and Lucy had had one too until they'd left home. Now their presents were under the Christmas tree in the living room.

Downstairs I asked Paula how much I owed her and transferred the money online into her account. At four o'clock I made us a snack and then changed Jamey's nappy ready for church.

Adrian and Kirsty arrived at four-thirty, followed shortly by Lucy, Darren and my granddaughter, Emma. I told Jamey who they were as they arrived, but he hid shyly behind Paula, until Emma took him by the hand and drew him out. They were so cute together, but side by side it became even more obvious how far behind Jamey was in all aspects of his development.

At five o'clock, wrapped up warm, we set off for church. It's at the end of the High Street, about a fifteen-minute walk. It was dark now and lights twinkled brightly from the houses we passed, adding to our festive mood. We chatted gaily as we walked; I was pushing Emma in her stroller. Paula and Adrian took turns to carry Jamey some of the way as he just wasn't up to walking far. I thought that I would need to use my stroller if I took him any distance.

We joined others filing into the church. It was festively decorated and filling up fast. This family service on Christmas Eve is one of the most popular in our church's calendar. We took up an entire row, and as we sat waiting for the service to begin we spotted friends and neighbours and waved to them. Paula and I talked quietly to Jamey about where we were and what to expect. His family weren't church-goers so it was likely this was his first experience of church. He was looking around, taking it all in, but as usual didn't say much. 'Lights,' he said, pointing. 'Book.' I'd brought a book with us to keep him amused if he grew restless. Emma sat on her father's lap to begin with, then made her way along the row to sit between Jamey and Paula, but as the service began she went to her mother.

The service was only half an hour long, relaxed and designed for children, so it didn't matter if a baby cried or a child left their seat. There was no long sermon but joyful carols, and the Reverend told us the story of the birth of Jesus and reminded us that this was the reason we celebrated Christmas. At the end all the children were given a wrapped sweet to symbolize the glorious gift God had given us of his only son, although I'm not sure many of the children realized that as they enjoyed the sweet.

As we walked home my thoughts went to this time last year when Mum had been with us. It had been a cold, clear night and as we'd returned home we'd gazed up at the stars and tried to identify the different constellations – Orion, Gemini, the Plough. There'd been a single star shining brightly, just as there was now, and Mum had said it could be the star of Bethlehem that had led the wise men to Jesus. How long ago those words seemed now, yet how vivid and dear the memory. Although the pain of losing her was easing, in some ways I missed her more than ever. It seemed so long since I'd heard her voice, seen her smile or felt her warm embrace. I had kept her favourite scarf among other treasures and it smelt of her – a mixture of her soap and perfume. I am not ashamed to say that every so often I took it from the drawer and smelt it. We had plenty of photos and video clips of her, yet there was something poignant in the smell of that scarf that brought Mum closer.

Once home, I made us supper and then Adrian, Kirsty, Lucy and family left. They would return tomorrow morning for Christmas Day. It was time for Jamey to go to bed, so Paula and I helped him arrange a sweet mince pie and a drink for Santa on a plate, with carrots for his reindeer, and then set the plate outside the front door explaining to him why. I fetched Jamey's and Paula's Santa sacks and they hung them on the front door while I took some photos. I always take plenty of photographs of the child or children I'm fostering to give to their parents and to include in their Life Story Book, and some for us to keep. Jamey seemed to be relaxed and enjoying himself. 'Sack,' he said, smiling.

'Yes, that's right. It's Christmas tomorrow.'

I took him upstairs to get him ready for bed and just after I'd changed his nappy he did a big poo. His constipation was already easing, and I would talk to his social worker about starting to toilet train him and also having his hair trimmed. It's advisable to discuss issues like this with the social worker and/or the parents, as they can become contentious.

Once Jamey was clean again, I tucked him into bed, kissed him goodnight and went downstairs. Paula and I prepped the veg ready for tomorrow before watching a Christmas film together. Later, when she was asleep, I took the Santa sacks from the front door, filled them with their presents and tiptoed into her and Jamey's bedrooms and left them by their beds.

It was after midnight by the time I was in bed, and then I was up early the following morning to check and baste the turkey. I had set the oven on automatic, and all seemed well. I fed Sammy, and then returned upstairs to shower and dress. As I came out of the bathroom I heard Jamey call out, 'Cathy!' It was the first time he'd used my name.

I went into his room. He was sitting up in bed staring in amazement at his Santa sack, which was overflowing with presents. His little face was a mixture of wonder and delight.

'Father Christmas has been!' I said, smiling. 'Look at all these presents. I wonder what he's brought you.'

Jamey continued to gaze at the sack wide-eyed but made no attempt to open a present.

'Come on, let's see what you've got,' I encouraged him.

I helped him off the bed and he sat beside me on one of the cushions I'd put on the floor in case he fell out of bed.

I heard Paula's bedroom door open. I hadn't disturbed her as I thought she might want a lie-in, but she came into Jamey's room with her sack and another one.

'Father Christmas has left something for you too, Mum,' she said with a smile. 'But I think he was too tired to deliver it last night.'

'Thanks, love,' I said.

'It's from all of us,' she added. 'Lucy and Adrian.'

'That is kind.'

The three of us sat on Jamey's bedroom floor and began opening our presents. He was hesitant to begin with, but, seeing Paula and me gleefully tearing off wrapping paper, he began to follow our example, savouring each gift before moving on to the next, just as Paula and I were doing.

Jamey clearly loved the farmyard set – one of the presents Paula had found for him. When we'd finished opening the presents in our sacks Paula and I told him the names of some of the pieces – tractor, barn, duck pond, farmer, pig and so on. Our Christmas had begun.

Once Jamey and Paula were dressed, we had breakfast, and at eleven o'clock Lucy and family, and Adrian and Kirsty, arrived. I served drinks and savoury snacks with Kirsty's help, and then we exchanged our presents. Lucy and Adrian had gifts for Jamey too, but Emma tried to take them from him. She had been the centre of attention in my family until now and I think there was a little bit of jealousy. I made a point of playing with her until her mood passed.

At dinner time Adrian sliced the turkey as Lucy and I put the vegetables into serving dishes – roast potatoes, glazed parsnips, Brussels, carrots, peas and sweetcorn.

We ate at 2 p.m. seated around the table in the front room with Christmas music playing in the background. Jamey sat nicely eating his food, albeit with his fingers, although I'd laid children's cutlery at his place. Emma, a year younger, was using a child's fork and spoon but was less well behaved, excitement getting the better of her. Darren eventually took her out of the room for a few moments' quiet time.

After we'd eaten we went into the living room to rest for a while before we played games to win prizes off the Christmas tree. There was a prize for everyone, and I would make sure everyone won a game. I thought, before we got started playing the games, that now might be a good time to phone Jamey's mother and aunt, Lacey. Shannon had asked me to call them on Christmas Day but hadn't stated a time. I wondered how fruitful phone contact was going to be given that Jamey had so little language. But Shannon had agreed to it, so as Jamey's foster carer I had to facilitate it. Perhaps he spoke more to his mother and aunt than he did to me, although that wasn't the impression I'd got from contact yesterday.

I explained to Jamey we were going to phone his mummy and Aunty Lacey and then said to everyone else, 'We're just going to phone home.' They understood, as quite often children we fostered had phone contact on Christmas Day.

Taking Jamey's hand, I led him from the living room, expecting to be back in ten to fifteen minutes. Shannon had said it should be a short call, but it was to be over an hour before I returned.

CHAPTER SIX

LACEY

I took Jamey to my bedroom where it was quiet to make the call. Shannon had asked me to use the speaker phone so I could monitor the call and also to withhold my number.

'Mummy?' Jamey asked, puzzled, as we sat side by side on the edge of the bed.

'Yes, love. We are going to phone Mummy and Aunty Lacey, then we can play some more games.'

Their phone numbers had been on the Essential Information Forms and I'd already stored them in my phone. Now I set my phone to private number and speaker. 'Mummy first,' I said to Jamey with a smile.

I pressed her number. It rang for a while, then voice-mail cut in. 'It's Cathy Glass, Jamey's foster carer,' I said. 'I'll try again later.'

I glanced at Jamey, who was expressionless. 'Mummy must be busy,' I told him. 'We'll see if Aunty Lacey is free.'

I pressed her number and she answered within a couple of rings, but the call didn't start well. 'Who is this phoning me on a private number?' she demanded.

'Cathy Glass, Jamey's foster carer. I believe you're expecting a call from him.'

'Oh, I see. I don't usually answer private numbers. This is going to be a complete waste of time as Jamey hardly says a word. I told the social worker I wanted to see him, not have bloody phone contact. He should be living here with me, not in care.'

I glanced at Jamey, who'd heard this, had recognized his aunt's voice and was now looking very anxious.

'Jamey is sitting beside me,' I said. 'The phone is on speaker. It would be nice for him if you could just say a few words. Even if he doesn't answer, he can hear you.'

'Very well, put him on,' Lacey said brusquely. 'Then I'll talk to you.'

Her manner changed as she spoke to Jamey.

'Hi, sweetie, Lacey here. How are you? I've got a Christmas present for you. I thought I'd be seeing you at Christmas, but you'll have to have it after now.'

Jamey was staring at the phone as if it had taken on a life of its own. It was perhaps the only time he'd see a phone used on speaker.

'Say hello to Aunty Lacey,' I prompted him.

'Hello,' he said in a tiny voice.

'Hi. What are you doing, love?' Lacey asked.

He shook his head and buried his face in my jumper.

'He's a bit overcome,' I told Lacey. 'But he's not unhappy.'

'Jamey, I am doing all I can to bring you here,' Lacey said. 'It's not right. You should be with me, not living with a foster carer.'

Jamey could tell from the tone of his aunt's voice that she was annoyed and his little face turned sad.

'I know it's difficult for you and Kat,' I said. 'But I am taking good care of Jamey.'

'Kat had it coming to her,' Lacey said. 'I warned her enough times and now it's happened.'

I took the phone off speaker and put it to my ear. 'It's best Jamey doesn't hear this,' I said. 'If you've finished talking to him, I'll let him join my family so we can talk.'

'Put him on then and I'll say goodbye.'

I engaged the speaker again and encouraged Jamey. 'Say goodbye to Aunty Lacey.'

'Bye,' he said.

'Bye, love. I'll see you soon. You know I love you.'

Jamey nodded.

'I won't be a minute,' I told Lacey.

Holding Jamey's hand, I took him downstairs and into the living room where there was a lot of laughter and fun. 'I'm still on the phone,' I said. 'Could you look after Jamey, please?'

'Come on, let's play with some of your new toys,' Paula said. Jamey went to her.

'Help yourselves to drinks,' I reminded them, and returned upstairs.

'OK, he can't hear me,' I said to Lacey. 'He's with my family in another room. I know it's difficult for you all, but we are looking after him so try not to worry.'

'I'm not worried. I'm furious,' Lacey said. 'They've got no business putting him into care when I could have looked after him. I told that social worker weeks ago I would have him, and then they put him with you and tell me after!'

I knew from Shannon that Lacey had come forward to look after Jamey so presumably would be assessed in the normal way. But I also knew that Kat didn't want Jamey to live with Lacey, claiming she had issues of her own.

'As soon as the offices open after Christmas I'll be finding a lawyer to get him back,' Lacey continued. 'How is Jamey? He was so upset when they took him away.'

'He's quiet, but not upset, and we're making sure he has a nice Christmas.'

'Better than mine then,' she said bitterly. 'Have you met Kat?'

'Briefly yesterday at contact,' I replied.

'I wanted to see him yesterday, but they gave me bloody phone contact instead! If you've met Kat, you'll know what a mess she's in. She looks like a druggie and her brains have rotted from all the stuff she's been taking. Bad enough she's ruined her own life, but I'm not having her ruin Jamey's too. I'm a teaching assistant and I know how far behind he is. I told the social services ages ago, but they kept giving her another chance. I knew it wasn't going to get better and in the meantime Jamey suffered. You know it was me who raised the alarm and let them in?'

'Yes.'

'I should have just taken him back to my place like I've done before, but I thought they needed to see for themselves what was going on.'

'I am sorry,' I said. 'Hopefully it will be sorted out before too long so you can see him.' It was the best I could offer as I didn't know what Shannon's plans were for contact with Lacey. She was angry, which was understandable. She'd assumed if Jamey couldn't live with his mother then he'd live with her.

'I mean, I know our childhoods weren't perfect, but whose is?' she continued, venting her anger and frustration. 'You get over it and move on. Only Kat got in with a bad lot who introduced her to drugs. When she had Jamey I thought things might be different and she'd be able to put him first, but she carried on with her life just the same, like he wasn't there. He was a sickly baby and didn't put on weight properly and began missing developmental milestones. He was very late walking because he spent so much time in that cot! The poor kid is permanently constipated because of the crap she gives him, when she remembers to feed him at all. I look after him when she lets me, but I have to work too, so it's a day here and there. I did what I could and some of the neighbours helped her too so he wouldn't have to go into care. I'm not the only one who went into their flat to find Jamey still in his cot in the middle of the day with Kat passed out on the sofa. She kept him in that cot like a cage. It's right she's lost him, but he should be with me.'

'I understand,' I said. 'You clearly know Jamey very well, so perhaps you could tell me some more about him? His routine, likes and dislikes. It would help me to settle him in.'

'He didn't have a routine when he was with his mother,' Lacey said dourly. 'Only when he came to me. I made sure he was fed, clean and went to bed at a reasonable time, but there was only so much I could do in a day here and there. Kat often forgot to change his nappy and his bottom was red raw. How is it now?'

'Healing slowly. I'm using an antiseptic barrier cream the chemist recommended. If it doesn't heal, I'll take him to the doctor after Christmas.'

'I expect you think badly of me for not doing more,' Lacey said. 'I hoped Kat would get fed up with Jamey in the end so he could live with me permanently.'

'I don't think badly of you. It was a difficult situation. Is there anything else you can tell me about Jamey that will help me look after him? For example, what he likes to eat.'

'Most things. He's just grateful for food. He needs to put on weight.'

'Yes, he does, he's very thin,' I agreed.

'I probably should have done more,' Lacey said, clearly feeling guilty. 'But if I kept Jamey for more than a night, Kat would turn up on my doorstep drunk and accuse me of kidnapping him and threaten to call the police. She's not open to reason. Jamey's got his own bed here and a nice room. Does he have a bed or a cot with you?'

'A bed in his own room,' I said. 'He's slept well so far.'

'Yes, he did with me. He doesn't make a fuss, which breaks my heart. He just lies there looking at you, grateful for any love and attention. Perhaps his anger will come out later.'

'It might. He doesn't have any allergies, does he?' I checked.

'No, his social worker asked me that. And his vaccinations are up to date. I took him for those.'

'Good.'

'I sent some clothes in a bag and his comforter.'

'Yes, I've got them.'

'It's all there was at Kat's. I have more clothes for him here if you need them.'

'Thank you. It's nice if he can have his own things, but I have plenty of spares and I'll buy more once the shops open again.'

'Did the social worker tell you that Kat doesn't want me to have him permanently?' Lacey asked.

'She mentioned it,' I replied diplomatically.

'Did she say why?'

'No.'

'You may as well know. As a teenager I got into trouble with the police. Nothing horrendous. Just petty theft and joy riding in cars. I was cautioned, but it hasn't stopped me getting a job as a TA. Kat is using it as an excuse for not letting me have Jamey. I think she's jealous that I've managed to sort myself out and she hasn't.'

I now had a better understanding of why the social services hadn't placed Jamey with Lacey straight away. If she had a criminal record, they would need to know the details through what is known as a DBS check – Disclosure and Barring Service. A police caution or conviction wouldn't automatically exclude her from having Jamey, but it would be a factor in assessing whether she was suitable to look after him. The assessment could take many months and I wondered if Lacey would have contact with Jamey during that time. It was for the social services to decide.

'I'd better go and join my family,' I said. 'They'll be waiting for me to organize some games.'

'Sounds fun,' she said. 'I know you foster carers do a good job. A child I supported in the classroom last year was in care and I got to know his foster carer quite well.'

'We work closely with the school,' I said.

'I'll let you go then,' she said, calmer now. I had the feeling she would have liked to talk for longer, but it was Christmas and my family were waiting for me downstairs. 'Give Jamey my love.'

'I will. Take care, and hopefully we'll meet before too long.'

'Yes.'

Our conversation had ended a lot better than it had begun. I felt sorry for Lacey. She seemed to have done what she could for Jamey while wanting to keep him out of care. I needed to try Kat again. If she answered I'd fetch Jamey, but I wasn't going to bring him up here unnecessarily if the call went to voicemail.

Taking a deep breath, I pressed Kat's number. A few rings and then a man answered.

'Whoever it is, piss off,' he said, and laughed. I could hear music and voices in the background.

'Is Kat there?' I asked.

'Yes.'

'Can I speak to her, please?'

'I guess, as it's her phone.' He laughed again and then shouted. 'Kat! Phone!'

'Is it my bleeding sister?' I heard her say.

'How should I know?' the man replied. They all sounded very drunk or high.

Kat came to the phone. 'Hello. Who is it?'

'Cathy Glass, Jamey's foster carer.'

'Who?' she shouted, over the background noise.

'Cathy. I'm fostering Jamey. We met yesterday. I've been asked to phone you today so you can speak to him.'

'Really?' she said, slurring her words.

'Would you like to talk to him?'

'Don't mind. Is he staying with you?'

I realized then that Kat was in no fit state to speak to Jamey. If a foster carer is asked to supervise phone contact between a child and their family they are expected to make sure the conversation is appropriate and in the child's best interest. Kat was confused and I suspected she was either drunk or under the influence of drugs. Either way, Jamey shouldn't hear her like this.

'Kat, I think it would be best if I tell Jamey you are OK and then we'll phone you tomorrow.'

'Suits me,' she said, and the phone went dead.

I would note these calls in my fostering log for the social services when I had a chance, but for now I went downstairs to rejoin the party. As I opened the living-room door laughter greeted me. Lucy had organized a children's game and they were all sitting on the floor in a circle clapping their hands to the rhythm of a rhyme. I joined in, and then later quietly told Jamey that his mummy sent her love and we'd speak to her another day. He looked at me thoughtfully for a moment, then gave me a big hug. How confusing all these changes must be for him, I thought. He was coping very well, although, as Lacey had said, his anger and frustration might come out later. I'd found this before with other children I'd fostered.

The rest of Christmas Day continued with games, prizes won from the Christmas tree, more eating and drinking and lots of fun and laugher. Lucy and Darren left with Emma at around ten o'clock, as she was over-tired. After they'd gone I put Jamey to bed. We spent a while trying to find his security cloth, which was under the bed. He hadn't used it all day. I kissed him goodnight and returned downstairs where Adrian, Kirsty, Paula and I played Monopoly until after midnight, when they, too, went home.

Despite missing my dear mother, we'd all had an enjoyable time.

CHAPTER SEVEN

MEMORIES

Boxing Day, 26 December, is traditionally when a lot of families go for a walk, having not been out the day before and having eaten to excess. Of course, I am acutely aware that some families don't enjoy the Christmases we do. My family and I know how lucky we are to have enough money to buy Christmas luxuries. We never take it for granted.

Adrian and Kirsty were spending Boxing Day with her family, and Lucy, Emma and Darren were going to his, so there was just Paula, me and Jamey going for a walk today. Jamey had slept well, and then amused himself with his new toys while I made breakfast. Once we'd eaten and were washed and dressed, I got out the stroller and, snug in our winter coats, we set off.

It was another cold, bright day, just right for a walk. Jamey walked a little and then got tired, so he rode in the stroller the rest of the way. We took a route through our local park and then out into open countryside. The fresh air was invigorating and 'blew the cobwebs away', as my mother used to say. On our way back we stopped off in the park so Jamey could play on the children's apparatus – swings, slide, rockers and so on. I didn't know if his mother or aunt had ever taken him to a park, but he needed a lot of help and encouragement to go on the apparatus.

Once home, I made us hot drinks and then Paula played with Jamey while I put together some lunch – mainly yesterday's leftovers. I waited until the afternoon to telephone Kat to give her a chance to recover from yesterday. Although Shannon's instructions had only asked me to phone on Christmas Day, I thought it was right and fair that, as she hadn't spoken to Jamey yesterday, she should be given the chance today. If she didn't answer, I wouldn't try again as she had contact at the Family Centre tomorrow when it reopened. So mid-afternoon I left Jamey with Paula in the living room and went into the hall to phone Kat.

'Hello. It's Cathy, Jamey's foster carer,' I said as the call connected.

There was silence.

'Kat, are you there? It's Cathy Glass. Jamey's carer. Can you hear me?' There was no background noise as there had been yesterday.

'I hear you,' she finally said.

'Shannon asked me to phone so you could speak to Jamey.'

More silence, then she cleared her throat. She sounded groggy. 'That was supposed to be on Christmas Day,' she said confrontationally.

'Yes. I phoned you yesterday, but there was a lot going on,' I said tactfully. 'So I thought I'd try again today.'

'You didn't phone yesterday,' she retaliated.

'I did. In the afternoon. A man answered your phone and then put you on.'

'So why are you phoning me now?'

'Because you didn't speak to Jamey yesterday.' I was starting to wish I hadn't bothered.

'So where is he?' she asked.

'With me. I can put him on if you feel up to talking to him.' I was having doubts.

'Why shouldn't I be?'

She sounded confused, but I decided to take a chance. 'Just a minute and I'll put him on.'

I took the handset into the living room. Jamey was sitting beside Paula on the sofa with a picture book open on his lap. 'Mummy would like to talk to you,' I told him.

I engaged the speaker and sat next to him as Paula made room for me on the sofa. 'OK, he can hear you,' I told Kat.

'Jamey?' she asked.

He looked at me questioningly. 'It's Mummy,' I said. 'Say hello to her.'

'Mummy?' he asked, in his small, plaintive voice.

'Yes, it's me,' Kat replied.

'Mummy,' he said again, slightly louder.

She didn't reply and then I heard her sob. Jamey and Paula heard her too.

'Kat, are you OK?' I asked. Jamey was looking worried.

All that could be heard was her crying, so I took the phone off speaker and left the room. I assumed that hearing his little voice had been too much for Kat and maybe she'd suddenly realized what she'd lost.

'Kat, it's Cathy,' I said, going into the front room. 'Jamey can't hear us. Are you all right?'

'Of course I'm not fucking all right!' she said, and ended the call.

I didn't phone back. I didn't think it would help and I hoped Kat had friends to support her at this difficult time. It crossed my mind that perhaps I should phone Lacey and tell her Kat was upset. But from what I knew of their relationship, it wasn't good, and also as a foster carer I have to know where the boundaries are. While fostering is often a lot more than just looking after the child or children, and usually involves working with the family, it's knowing when to get involved. I felt to phone Lacey now when I knew so little of her and her sister could be construed as sticking my nose in rather than helping. Another foster carer might have seen it differently; we just have to do what we think is best at the time.

'Mummy?' Jamey asked as I returned to the living room.

'We'll see her tomorrow,' I said with a reassuring smile, and replaced the handset in its cradle.

Jamey accepted this as he appeared to accept most changes and disappointments – resigned and uncomplaining. He returned his attention to the book and Paula carried on reading to him, although I saw her slip an arm around his shoulders and draw him closer. He was so small and vulnerable, you instinctively felt the need to protect and love him, which I'm sure his mother would have done too, had she not skewed her perception with substance misuse. If you are an addict, your whole life revolves around getting your next fix and there's not much left over for anything else, including looking after your children.

Paula, having spent most of the last two days with Jamey and me, now went to her room to listen to music and phone some friends. She was due to return to work the following day. I spent a pleasant afternoon playing with Jamey and used the opportunity to teach him as well, by saying the names of objects, their colour and how many there were; for example, a red car, two ducks, three yellow flowers and so forth. A young child needs to hear a word repeated many times in different contexts before they learn how to use it.

Paula, Jamey and I had supper together and then I began Jamey's bath-and-bedtime routine. The sores on his bottom were slowly healing and as usual I applied plenty of antiseptic barrier cream before putting him in a clean nappy. Once he was settled in bed with his security rag, I kissed him goodnight and went downstairs to the computer in the front room. I typed up my log notes and uploaded them to the fostering portal on the council's website. I also emailed Shannon an update, copying in my supervising social worker, Joy. Having logged off, I made a mug of tea and took it into the living room. Sammy opened an eye to see who it was and then returned to sleep.

It was pleasant to sit quietly after all the excitement of Christmas and the build-up to it. I picked up my phone and began going through the photographs I'd taken of this Christmas, and then last. There were lots of photos of Mum last year. Some with baby Emma in her arms, some of her opening her presents, at the dinner table, pulling a cracker and wearing a Christmas hat. Many we'd taken with a selfie stick so we were all in them. Mum had died in the early hours of 27 December, so one year ago tomorrow. She had been taking medication for a minor heart condition but otherwise had been healthy. None of us had expected her to die that night. She'd come with us on our

Boxing Day walk and afterwards had dozed in a chair for a while. I hadn't been surprised or concerned as we'd had a late night and a long walk. I remember she'd only eaten a little supper, but again I hadn't been concerned as she'd had a good breakfast and lunch. Once she was in bed, I went up to say goodnight. She'd thanked me for a lovely Christmas. 'The best ever,' she'd said.

She was due to go home the following day and I remembered asking her to stay longer. 'As long as you want,' I'd said.

'That's kind of you, dear,' she'd replied with that warm smile I knew so well. 'But I'll go home as planned. We've had a wonderful time and I'll see you all again soon.' Mum took comfort in being in her own home, which she'd shared with my father all her married life before he'd passed away.

I could see she was exhausted so I'd kissed her good night and come out. That was the last time I saw her alive. I went to bed soon after and so had Paula. Adrian was still living with me then, but he was out, and I heard him let himself in in the early hours. The following morning I was up first and made myself a coffee. When I didn't hear Mum get up I didn't think much of it until 9.30 a.m. She never slept in that late. I went into her room where she was still in bed, lying on her back, her head slightly facing away, apparently asleep.

'Mum?' I said. She didn't stir. 'Mum? Are you all right?'

I remember feeling the first stab of fear. 'Mum?' I asked again. But her eyes remained closed.

Her lips were slightly parted as though relaxed in sleep, but I couldn't hear or see her breathing. 'Mum?

Are you asleep?' I tried again. She hadn't moved and my fear stepped up another notch.

I reached out and felt her forehead. She always had such smooth skin. It was warm, but not as warm as it should be. Had she got cold in the night? I wondered, but the heating had been on. 'Mum?'

I picked up her hand and that, too, felt cold and was limp. I put my cheek to her lips and couldn't feel her breath. I felt for her pulse. There wasn't one, and in that instant my world fell apart. My dear mother had passed away in her sleep. With tears running down my cheeks, I fetched Adrian and Paula. Adrian called an ambulance, although we knew it was too late. I phoned Lucy, who came straight over. We sat with Mum as we waited for the paramedics. She looked as serene and beautiful in death as she had in life. But how I wished I'd had the chance to tell her one last time how much I loved her.

I started, jolted back to the present, as my phone buzzed with a text message.

It seemed I wasn't the only one thinking of Mum.

I'm feeling sad, Lucy's text read. *It's the anniversary of Nana's death tomorrow.* There was an emoji of a crying face.

I know, love, I texted back. *I was just looking at photos of us all last Christmas xx*

I miss Nana.

So do I.

Then a message arrived from Adrian. *I've got tomorrow off work and I'm thinking of visiting Nana and Grandpa's grave. Would you like to come?*

I telephoned him and explained I would like to go but

Jamey had contact with his mother at eleven o'clock so I wouldn't be able to leave until after one o'clock.

'That's fine,' he said. 'I'll collect you at one.'

'I'll have Jamey with me,' I reminded him.

'Not a problem. See you both tomorrow then.'

'Thank you, love.'

My parents' grave was in the village cemetery where they'd lived, about an hour's drive away. One of us usually went each month to tend the grave and refresh the flowers. Paula and Lucy had come with me last time.

An old friend phoned for a chat and to ask if we'd had a good Christmas. We were talking for over an hour and then, once we'd finished, I did a few jobs and went to bed. I dreamt of Mum – not surprising given that I'd been looking at her photos and it was the anniversary of her death. But it was a reassuring dream, which left me with a warm feeling that she and Dad were together and at peace.

Paula was up at seven o'clock the next day to get ready for work and left the house at eight-fifteen. Jamey was seeing his mother at the Family Centre and I was expecting details of future contacts once Shannon was back at work. Usually contact arrangements were made when a child first arrived for the weeks to come so everyone could plan ahead. But because Jamey had arrived just before Christmas and as an emergency, Shannon had only arranged the Christmas Eve contact, phone contact and the one today.

Once Jamey was washed and dressed, I made him breakfast and then told him he could play for a while before it was time to leave to go to the Family Centre to see his mother. I didn't explain about going to the cemetery in the afternoon as that would have been too much information for a child his age to take in all in one go. While he still wasn't saying much, he appeared to be understanding, so I hoped it wouldn't be long before he began using words and forming short sentences similar to the average child his age.

We left the house at 10.30 to go to contact and in the car I told Jamey again where we were going and why. He never showed much emotion when I mentioned his mother as another child in care might, sometimes venting their frustration and loss through screaming and crying tantrums. I talked to him as I drove and he pointed to some Christmas lights and also some cars, saying the words as we passed.

I parked outside the Family Centre and signed our names in the Visitors' Book, then we were asked to go to the waiting room because his mother hadn't arrived yet. After fifteen minutes the receptionist came in and said they were trying to contact Kat to check she was on her way, as they hadn't heard from her. We waited another fifteen minutes, during which time I read to Jamey from the books there. Then the centre manager came in and said we should go home. They hadn't succeeded in contacting Kat and it wasn't fair to keep Jamey waiting any longer. This was the Family Centre's policy and Kat would have been made aware of it. We said goodbye and holding Jamey's hand we headed out.

'He's so adorable,' the receptionist said as I opened the door. 'He can come and live with me any day.'

I smiled. That was how Jamey made you feel. He was such a treasure.

He had taken his mother not arriving in his stride and as I helped him into the car he just looked at me questioningly and said, 'Mummy?'

I kissed his forehead. 'Not today, love. Maybe another day.'

Which he accepted as just another disappointment to add to the list of disappointments that had been his life.

Possibly Kat had a good reason for missing contact, and hopefully it was a one-off. Most parents who are fighting to have their children returned to them make contact a priority, arriving early and continually pressing the social worker to increase it. It wasn't until later in the afternoon that I learnt the reason why Kat hadn't attended contact. She hadn't got up in time.

CHAPTER EIGHT

MEDICAL: THE EFFECTS OF NEGLECT

I was sitting in the back of Adrian's car. We had been to the cemetery and were now on our way home. Jamey was in his car seat next to me, eating a snack I'd packed for him. As well as the main meals, I was giving him snacks to help him gain weight. I was trying to catch the crumbs that were falling to avoid making a mess in Adrian's car, which he kept very clean. My mobile rang and it was Shannon.

'Are you free to talk?' she asked.

'Yes.'

'I understand from the Family Centre that Kat didn't attend contact this morning.'

'That's right. We waited half an hour and then the manager told us to go.'

'So I believe. How is Jamey?'

'Taking it in his stride.'

'He shouldn't have to. I've spoken to Kat and she has asked for contact to be changed to the afternoon as she rarely gets up before midday. I assume afternoon contact isn't a problem for you?'

'No.' It's one of the foster carer's roles to take children to and from contact and it is always a priority.

'We'll see how this goes then,' Shannon continued. 'But I'm wondering how Kat looked after Jamey if she never got up before midday. Lacey said she left him in his cot and she's probably right. I'm emailing you the details of future contact, but to give you a heads-up, starting from tomorrow Kat will see Jamey at one o'clock for an hour, two days a week. I'm not making it any later than one.'

'And phone contact?' I asked.

'No, Kat says she doesn't always have her phone with her and it's upsetting and a waste of time as Jamey hardly talks to her. I read your email, thank you.'

'Any contact with his aunt?' I asked.

'Not at present. Lacey phoned this morning, not pleased with me. She's getting legal advice, which she is entitled to do, but I'm not starting face-to-face contact until we are further along with her assessment. You can phone her at the weekend. I've put it in the email.'

'All right. Thank you.'

'I want Jamey to have a medical as soon as possible,' Shannon said. 'I'm hoping they will be able to do it tomorrow morning. I'm waiting to hear. I'll email you the details. I think that's everything for now. I'll need to visit you both, but that will be in the New Year. Did you all have a nice Christmas?'

'Yes, thank you. Did you?'

'Quiet, but a welcome break. I'll be in touch about his medical.'

Half an hour later Shannon phoned again to say that Jamey's medical had been arranged for nine o'clock the following morning.

We'd arrived home by then and Adrian had come in. We were in the living room with hot drinks and a plate of biscuits, sitting on the floor and playing with Jamey.

'Social worker?' Adrian asked as the call ended.

'Yes, about Jamey, not a new referral,' I replied. Adrian worried that I sometimes took on too much.

I returned my attention to the play mat Adrian and Kirsty had bought Jamey for Christmas. It showed a street scene and we were moving toy vehicles and play people along the road that was lined with houses.

'He's very quiet,' Adrian remarked as we played.

'Yes, but he does seem to hear and understand.'

As if to prove the point Jamey pointed to a toy car and said loudly, 'Car.' Then a street lamp and said, 'Light.' After which he began naming some of the toy animals in the field.

'Very good,' Adrian said.

'He'll get there; he just needs time to catch up.'

Adrian stayed for about an hour and then said he'd better go as he had some jobs to do at home. The flat where he lived with Kirsty was a short drive away in the older part of town. It was one of three converted from a large Victorian house and was spacious, with high ceilings, a big kitchen-diner, living room, bathroom and three bedrooms. While it had been structurally sound, they'd done a lot of work inside, modernizing and decorating. Each time I went something had changed.

Jamey came with me to the front door to see Adrian off and then we went into the kitchen. He was never far from my side. He was still holding one of his toy trucks and as I began preparing dinner he amused himself by running the truck around the floor and the walls as high as he could reach in the dining part of our kitchen-diner.

I had a safety gate across the gap between the kitchen and the diner. Every so often, as I glanced over, I caught him watching me and I would smile and tell him he was a good boy and playing nicely, as well as what I was doing. 'I'm cutting carrots with a sharp knife. I have to be careful,' I said. Then, 'This is a big spoon called a ladle.'

'Spoon,' he said, pausing from playing. 'Spoon.' He came over and reached across the gate.

'Can I have the spoon?' I said, handing it to him so he would gradually learn to ask for things.

'Spoon,' he said, and passed it back to me.

'Thank you.'

He grinned, then reached again. 'Spoon?'

'Yes, Jamey wants the spoon.'

I passed it to him and so we continued back and forth for a few minutes. It was a game to him and he chuckled, but he was also learning language. I loved it when he laughed, and I hoped in the future he would laugh a lot more. He looked sad and serious too much of the time.

Once I'd put dinner in the oven, I took Jamey into the living room to look at books and play. We were still there when Paula arrived home. Jamey heard the front door open and jumped as he still did at any unfamiliar sound.

'It's OK,' I reassured him. 'It's Paula come home from work.'

Not wholly convinced, Jamey went to the living-room door and peered out cautiously.

'I think I can see someone hiding behind a door,' Paula called, playfully. 'I wonder who it is.'

Jamey chuckled and, coming out, ran down the hall to greet her.

'That is a nice welcome,' she said, hugging him.

'Have you had a good day?' I asked her, kissing her cheek.

'There weren't many in the office – lots of people have taken the whole week off. I wish I had.' Paula had a trainee position in the offices of a local manufacturing business. Many firms had closed for the week between Christmas and New Year.

Having taken off her coat and shoes, she picked up Jamey. 'I'm going to get changed, then after dinner we'll play with some of your toys.'

'Toys,' Jamey repeated, then said 'Paula' clearly.

'Yes, that's right, love, well done,' I said, pleased.

He then pointed at me and said, 'Mummy.'

Oh dear, I thought. 'I'm Cathy,' I corrected.

Foster carers are expected to discourage the child they are looking after from calling them Mummy or Daddy. It's not considered appropriate, as children coming into care have their own parents. It can also be confusing for the child if the distinction isn't made, and upsetting for the birth parents, who are already struggling to come to terms with someone else looking after their child. It's easier with older children – they understand the difference between a parent and a foster carer – but very young children often automatically use the term Mummy or Daddy for their main caregiver.

'Paula,' I said, pointing at her. 'Cathy,' I said, pointing at me. 'Jamey,' I said, pointing to him.

'Jamey,' he said, pointing to himself.

'Yes, well done.'

Over dinner Paula told me more about her day. As well as there not being many in her office, they'd had a software failure and no one was in from IT to fix it so she hadn't had anything to do for a large part of the afternoon. She asked me about my day. 'How did contact go?'

'His mother didn't arrive,' I said quietly.

'Oh dear. How disappointing.'

I nodded and we left it at that.

Later Lucy telephoned. 'Are you free to talk, Mum?'

'Yes. Jamey's in bed. What's the matter?'

'Nothing. I need to ask you something.'

'Go ahead.'

'You know I'm going back to work part-time in January?'

'Yes.' Lucy had taken extended maternity leave from the private nursery where she and her partner Darren both worked.

'It's only three days a week. I wondered if you could look after Emma for one of the days. She will be with me in the nursery for one day and go to Tina [Darren's mother] another.'

'Yes, of course, love. I can do more if you wish.'

'One's good, thanks. You're sure it won't be too much for you with fostering as well?'

'Positive. Have you been talking to Adrian?' I asked.

'I might have mentioned I was thinking of asking you.'

I smiled to myself. 'It's nice that you're all so concerned about me, but fostering one child and having Emma a day a week will be fine.'

'That's what I thought.'

'When do you start back?'

'In two weeks' time, so I was thinking I'd better start leaving Emma with you for short periods so she can get used to it.'

'Yes. Good idea.' Although I saw my granddaughter regularly, it was usually with one or other of her parents. Emma hadn't spent much time away from Lucy and Darren so I agreed it would make sense to start leaving her with me. Of course I didn't mind – far from it!

'Thanks, Mum,' Lucy said.

'It will be my pleasure. How about the day after tomorrow for her first stay?'

'Great. When I start back I will be working Monday, Tuesday and Wednesday. Emma will be with me and Darren at the nursery on Mondays. Tina would like her on a Tuesday, so can you do Wednesdays?'

'Yes.'

Once we'd finished on the phone, and while it was still fresh in my mind, I emailed Joy and Shannon to advise them I would be looking after my granddaughter on Wednesdays. Foster carers are expected to notify their supervising social worker and the child's social worker of any changes in the household. Having Emma on a regular basis could be construed as a change, although I didn't envisage any problems.

Jamey slept well as usual and the following morning, as I washed and dressed him, I told him we were going to see a doctor at the Health Centre to make sure he was all right. I didn't use words like 'paediatrician' or 'medical', which would have been beyond his comprehension, but talked about the nice doctor who would look in his ears, listen to his chest and measure how tall he was.

We had breakfast and left the house at 8.30 for the appointment at 9. I'd been to the Health Centre before many times and parked in their car park at the rear of the building. Taking Jamey's hand, I led him into reception where I gave our names to the receptionist. The Health Centre had opened fifteen minutes earlier so wasn't too busy. Usually we had to wait, but now we were told, 'You can go straight in. Dr Chabra is in room three.'

I thanked her and, still holding Jamey's hand, took him along the corridor where I knocked on the door of consulting room three.

'Come in!' a friendly female voice called from inside.

The paediatrician was seated behind a table-style desk and studying her computer screen. She stood as we entered.

'Good morning. Have a seat,' she said with a friendly and efficient manner. 'So you're Cathy Glass, Jamey's foster carer,' she checked, returning to her chair and reading from the screen.

'Yes.'

'And you must be Jamey.' She looked at him and smiled. He scrambled onto my lap and buried his face in my coat.

'You're not scared of me, surely?' Dr Chabra asked rather loudly. She meant well but perhaps didn't appreciate all the changes Jamey had been through in the last week. 'His social worker has asked him to have a medical as a matter of urgency,' Dr Chabra said. 'We managed to fit you in. I see from the form she's sent Jamey came into care on the twenty-third of December, suffering from neglect.'

'Yes, that's correct,' I said.

'How is he now?'

'Quiet. He's eating and sleeping well. He was constipated when he first arrived but that has cleared.'

'And his poos are a normal colour?' she asked as she typed.

'Yes.'

'How often does he go?'

'Once a day now. His bottom was sore, but I've been putting antiseptic barrier cream on it and it is improving.'

'Is he still in nappies?'

'Yes. I'm hoping to start toilet training him once I've discussed it with his social worker.'

'Why do you need to discuss it with his social worker?' she asked, glancing up.

'It's advisable.'

She rolled her eyes and returned her attention to the screen. 'Does Jamey feed himself using cutlery?' This would be a standard question as part of his developmental assessment.

'He mainly uses his fingers and sometimes a spoon.'

'At his age you need to introduce infant cutlery.'

'I have,' I replied.

Jamey still had his face buried in my coat but had loosened his grip on me a little.

'Does he hold a crayon and draw lines?' she asked, continuing the developmental assessment.

'Not yet, but I'm teaching him.'

'What about walking?' Dr Chabra asked. 'Can he run and jump?'

'He's a bit unsteady on his feet,' I admitted. 'But he's getting better.' I had to be honest. 'I think he spent a lot of time in his cot before he came into care.'

'Why?' she asked brusquely.

'I don't know all the details.'

'Does he climb stairs?' she asked, typing.

'With help.'

She tutted. 'Can he kick a ball?'

'Not yet.'

'What about stacking beakers?' she asked. 'Jamey, look what I've got.' She opened a lower desk drawer and took out a set of seven brightly coloured stacking beakers. 'Jamey, can you do this?' she asked.

Jamey peered out as Dr Chabra stacked the beakers. 'You have a go now,' she told him.

He buried his head in my coat again.

'Have you seen him do this?' she asked me. I knew it was another development check and that stacking beakers was a skill usually mastered by the age of two, assuming of course that the child has been played with and shown what to do.

'Not yet,' I replied. 'But I have stacking beakers and puzzles at home and I'm gradually introducing them to Jamey. He's only been with me a week.'

She nodded as she typed, entering her findings into the online form.

'Let's have a look at some picture cards,' she said. Returning the beakers to the drawer, she took out six brightly coloured cards, each showing a simple object. 'Point to the house,' she told him.

Jamey didn't.

'Can you show me the dog?' she asked him.

He didn't.

'Can he hear me?' she asked me.

'Yes, I think so. He's just overwhelmed.'

'Let me check,' she said. Standing, she went behind him, out of his sight, and clapped her hands sharply.

Jamey started and turned to look where the sound had come from. She repeated it a second and third time, moving further away, with the same result.

'He seems to be able to hear all right,' she said to me, which is what I'd thought. Then to Jamey, 'Point to the picture of the fish.'

He didn't.

'Let me try,' I said. 'He knows some of these. Jamey, point to the picture of the cat. You know the word cat. A cat like Sammy.'

Gradually Jamey let go of my coat and pointed to the cat.

'Good boy,' I said, and slipped off both our coats as it was warm in the consulting room.

'How many words does he know approximately?' Dr Chabra asked.

'I've heard him use about twenty, but he's learning new ones each day. I continually tell him what new objects are. So does my daughter, who lives with me. He knows lights, tree, car and our names.'

She wasn't impressed. 'The average child his age knows at least two hundred words, and some know a thousand. Does he put any words together to make a short sentence?' I knew it was another indication of his level of development.

'Not yet,' I replied.

She typed and then scrolled down the form. Her expression was professional, neutral. 'Does he play with toys?'

'Yes.'

'Can he follow simple instructions?'

'Yes.'

'OK, let me examine him now.'

Jamey was still on my lap, his head snuggled against me, so I gently eased him into a more upright position. Dr Chabra took an otoscope from the top drawer of her desk and looked first in one of his ears and then the other.

'He's got a bit of wax, but otherwise his ears seem clear,' she said. 'There is no sign of an ear infection.'

'That's good news.'

Returning the otoscope to the drawer, Dr Chabra took a wooden tongue depressor from a sealed packet and then asked Jamey to open his mouth wide so she could look in.

He did as she asked. 'So it seems he *can* follow simple instructions,' she said to me, then looked in his mouth. 'His mouth and throat are clear. But you should start taking him to the dentist to get him used to it.'

'Yes, I will.'

She threw the spatula into the bin and picked up the ophthalmoscope from where it lay on her desk and peered into one of Jamey's eyes. He squirmed away so I held his head steady while she finished the eye examination.

'All seems well there,' she said. 'You don't have any concerns about his eyesight?'

'No,' I replied.

'I'll listen to his chest now,' she said, picking up the stethoscope from her desk. I lifted up Jamey's vest while she listened to his chest and then his back.

'His heart is fine,' she pronounced. 'Now let's weigh and measure him. Can you take off his shoes and bring him over here.'

I did as she asked and, holding Jamey's hand, crossed the room to the scales. I helped him on. 'Have you weighed him?' she asked as she looked at the result.

'Yes.'

'He's very light for a child his age.'

'I know.'

She then measured his height. 'He's in the lower percentile for his height too. Most probably the result of poor nutrition if he has been neglected.'

I threw Jamey a reassuring smile as he was looking very serious. We stayed where we were as Dr Chabra went to her computer and entered her findings. 'I'll send my report to his social worker, but I can tell you now he's got a lot of catching up to do.'

'I know.'

'Bring him to the couch, please, so I can examine him,' she said. 'Can you let go of his hand so I can see him walk.'

I felt bad taking my hand away from Jamey. I then had to encourage him to walk by himself to the couch. He liked holding my hand.

'Climb onto this step-stool,' Dr Chabra told him. 'Then up onto the couch.'

Jamey instinctively reached for my hand to help him.

'No, let's see if he can do it on his own,' Dr Chabra said.

I moved out of reach and Jamey somewhat unsteadily managed to clamber onto the step-stool, then wobbled.

'Onto the couch now,' Dr Chabra encouraged. He couldn't, so she lifted him on. The examination couch was higher than his bed, but I knew at his age he should have been able to climb onto it unaided.

'He's not very strong,' Dr Chabra said to me. 'I suppose that's from being kept in a cot for prolonged periods when he should have been running around. Can you take off his jersey, please? Leave his vest on.'

I did as she asked, and she examined Jamey's arms, chest and back, and then felt his tummy. Jamey was looking at me and again I smiled reassuringly.

'Now his joggers and nappy, please.'

I undressed him and he shivered.

'I'm not surprised he's cold,' Dr Chabra said. 'There's nothing of him.' She looked at his legs and feet. 'I'll give you a printout for exercises and games to help strengthen and develop his muscles.'

She looked at where his nappy had been. 'That's healing,' she said, referring to the sores. 'Where the skin has broken down it will take longer, but it's not infected. Keep the area clean and dry. The sooner he is out of nappies the better. You can get him dressed now.' She returned to her desk.

I put Jamey in a clean nappy and then began to dress him. Dr Chabra glanced over from typing. 'Encourage him to do things for himself,' she told me.

'I do,' I said. 'But it takes him time.'

I helped him dress and we returned to the chair by her desk. Jamey sat on my lap again. The printer was working overtime churning out sheets of paper. Dr Chabra swivelled her chair round to take them.

'Suggested meal plans for his age,' she said, handing me a wodge of printouts. 'Exercises to strengthen muscles, games to help develop his language and motor skills. He's pale and I was wondering if I should send him for a blood test, but it's traumatic for a young child so I think we'll monitor him for the time being. Later he may need speech therapy, but there is a lot you can do at home. A good diet, high in fibre and fresh foods. You can use a multivitamin supplement too. Do you have his Red Book?'

'No.' The Red Book, known by the colour of its cover, is a record of the child's health and development from birth. 'It hasn't been given to me.'

'Do you know if his immunisations are up to date?' she asked. This would have been recorded in the Red Book.

'As far as I know they are,' I replied. 'I understand his aunt took him for the vaccinations.'

'Well, that's something,' she said with a sigh. 'I'll get this off to his social worker with the recommendation that he is reassessed in three months' time – either by your doctor or at this clinic. What are the long-term plans for him?'

'He'll stay in care for the time being. His aunt wants him to live with her and she will be assessed.'

'Let's hope she makes a better job of looking after him than his mother did,' she said dryly. 'The effects of neglect are all too obvious. He's way behind where he should be.'

She handed me the last printout, and I thanked her and left, with Jamey holding my hand. I paused in the corridor outside to put on our coats, and then we continued out of the building. I had known Jamey was a long way behind, but hearing it from the paediatrician was depressing. Hopefully he would eventually catch up, but that wasn't guaranteed. The early years are so important and deprivation can have a lasting effect.

CHAPTER NINE

ANOTHER STRANGER

As I drove home from the Health Centre my thoughts kept returning to Dr Chabra's comments and Jamey's skinny little body. I was getting used to seeing him in the bath and when changing his nappy, but seeing him stretched out on the couch had reinforced just how undernourished he was. It hadn't only affected his weight and height; he was also pale, weak and relatively inactive. I wondered how often he had been fed and I pictured him in his cot, peering out through the slats, with no regular meals or stimulation. The cot had been in the living room as the bedroom was too damp to use. How much of the time was his mother there with him? I wondered. How often had she answered his cries? Babies whose cries aren't answered stop crying as they learn that there is no point because their needs won't be met – hunger, a clean nappy or just being held and comforted. It was heart-breaking to think about.

Jamey dropped off to sleep in the car on the way home and was still asleep as I parked. I carefully lifted him out and carried him into the house. He was like a baby in my arms, not a young child. As I laid him on the sofa he opened his eyes.

'Mummy,' he said.

'No, love, I'm Cathy. You'll see Mummy this afternoon.'

I kissed his cheek, took off our coats and made us a drink. I played with him for a while, then made us a sandwich lunch. We sat at the table in the kitchen-diner, Jamey on a booster seat. I sat opposite him, eating and watching him. There was something very moving about the way he sat there quietly, undemanding and grateful for anything he was given.

'Good boy,' I said.

He looked at me, smiled and then returned to his food.

'Good boy,' I said again a short while later.

'Good boy,' he repeated.

'Well done!' He'd used two words together and I felt like phoning Dr Chabra and telling her! True, he was repeating what I'd said, but it was a start and again confirmed there was nothing wrong with his hearing.

After lunch we left for the Family Centre and on the way I told Jamey the names of things we saw – a man on a bicycle, a woman walking a dog, a boy crossing the road. I wasn't expecting him to repeat back all these phrases, but it would add to his store of familiar words and how they were used.

Arriving at the Family Centre, I parked to the side of the building and helped Jamey out. Then, holding hands, we went up to the front door where I lifted him up so he could press the security buzzer, telling him what we were doing.

I said hello to the receptionist. 'Jamey Durrant to see his mother at one o'clock.' It was now 12.55.

'Can you go to the waiting room?' she said. 'Kat isn't here yet, but she's phoned to say she's on her way.'

'Mummy will be here soon,' I told Jamey as we went to the waiting room.

He sat beside me and I picked up one of the children's picture books to look at. He nestled close and I put my arm around him as I read. He enjoyed snuggling up while listening to a story, just as many children do. The door was slightly open and every so often I heard movement in the corridor outside. Ten minutes passed and then the security buzzer on the main door sounded. I heard Kat's voice in reception, but I couldn't hear what was said. After a moment footsteps hurried past the door, then the receptionist appeared.

'You can go through. Their contact is in Blue Room. Kat is here, but she's going to use the bathroom first as she needs to wash and change her clothes.'

'OK,' I said, slightly puzzled.

'She's arrived in her pyjamas,' the receptionist added.

I didn't comment or laugh and neither did the receptionist. I felt sorry for Kat; she was so disorganized. I told Jamey he would see his mummy soon and, having put away the book, we went along the corridor to Blue Room. Each of the six contact rooms is decorated a different colour and known by that name. The contact supervisor was sitting at the table, ready.

'Kat is here, but she's using the bathroom,' I told her, as I wasn't sure if she was aware.

She nodded.

I took a puzzle from the shelf and sat with Jamey on the sofa as the contact supervisor checked her phone. Another ten minutes passed before Kat arrived. Her hair was damp. She was wearing her coat over jeans and a roll-neck jumper. I assumed her pyjamas were in the plastic carrier bag she was carrying.

'Sorry I'm late,' she said, agitated. 'My alarm didn't go off.' From which I assumed she'd been asleep most of the morning.

'At least you're here now,' I said positively, although I knew her lateness would be noted. 'Here's the bag with the change of nappy should Jamey need it.'

She was scratching her hands, which I saw were very red and chapped. I stood to leave and Jamey stood too, as though he thought he was coming with me. Kat noticed.

'You're staying with me!' she exclaimed, hurt. 'Don't you want to stay?'

'He's just a bit confused,' I said.

'Why?' she asked, confrontationally.

'He's had a lot of changes,' I said, but she wasn't listening.

'I'll collect you later,' I told Jamey, and I headed for the door.

As I did I heard Kat ask the contact supervisor if she could have longer to make up for being late. Usually that wasn't allowed unless there were exceptional circumstances, as the parent(s) know they have to arrive on time. Also, the rooms are often needed for the next session.

'I'll have to ask,' the supervisor replied.

Kat followed me out of the room.

'Where are you going?' I asked.

'To find the manager and tell her I want longer as I was late.'

Jamey came out too, looking very worried and bewildered, followed by the contact supervisor.

'Where's the manager?' Kat asked us, still scratching her hands.

'I don't know, but I can tell the receptionist on my way out that you would like to see her,' I suggested. 'Then you won't miss any more contact.'

'That's a good idea,' the supervisor said, trying to placate Kat.

Kat stared at us, jumpy and undecided.

'Come back inside the room,' the supervisor encouraged. 'Cathy will ask about seeing the manager on her way out.'

Jamey looked from one to the other, baffled, and then Kat returned into the room.

'I'll see you later,' I told him. The supervisor took him back into the room and closed the door. There was only half an hour of contact left.

I stopped at reception and told the staff member that Kat wanted to see the manager to ask if she could have extra time as she was late.

'I'll need to check,' she said. 'But I think that room is needed.'

'I'll come back at the normal time then and wait if necessary.'

Outside I breathed in the fresh, cold air and began a brisk walk towards the local café, wondering if Kat was seriously trying to win back custody of her son. I didn't know the last time she'd used drugs, but she seemed to be struggling to understand what was going on. And arriving very late when contact had already been changed to suit her wasn't going to help her case. Parenting doesn't have to be perfect, but it does have to be reliable and to meet the child's needs.

I bought a take-away tea, which I sipped on my way back to the Family Centre, my hot breath steaming in the cold air. Roll on spring, I thought, but that was months away. The receptionist said Kat had been allowed an extra fifteen minutes, so I went to the waiting room and looked at a magazine. I was expecting to collect Jamey from the contact room. It's normal practice for the carer to take the child to and from the room. However, five minutes later the contact supervisor appeared at the door.

'Kat is going now,' she said.

I went into the corridor, where Kat was saying goodbye to Jamey. 'Bye, be good,' she said, patting him on the head, and hurried off. Jamey watched her go.

'Is everything all right?' I asked the supervisor, taking Jamey's hand. It helps the carer to have some feedback on contact so they can better manage the child's feelings and mood afterwards.

'Kat had to leave to catch her bus,' she said, handing me the bag containing the clean nappies and cream. 'She bought Jamey a Christmas present – a big box of chocolates. They've eaten them all so he probably won't want anything else to eat for a while.'

'I see.'

I said goodbye and we got as far as reception before Jamey vomited a puddle of partially digested chocolate that splattered everywhere.

'I think you've had rather a lot of chocolate,' I said to him as I wiped his mouth. Then, moving him away from the mess, I gave him a sip of water.

'I'll have to get someone to clear that up,' the receptionist said, grimacing.

'Sorry,' I said, although I was grateful it hadn't happened in my car.

'Choccy,' Jamey said, rubbing his stomach, as we left.

'Yes, too much, I think, love.' But it wasn't his fault.

Children often need their sugar consumption to be limited and it wasn't the contact supervisor's responsibility. She was there to observe and record and would only intervene if the child was in danger. It was Kat who should have stopped Jamey from bingeing on the chocolates, although from the sound of it she had gorged on them too.

Jamey was subdued in the car going home and I was on tenterhooks hoping he wouldn't vomit again. He didn't, and by dinnertime he had recovered and ate his meal. Once he was in bed, I looked through the printouts Dr Chabra had given me. Much of the information, especially on nutrition, I already knew from looking after children and foster-carer training, but the printouts on games and exercises to strengthen and develop a child's muscles gave me some new ideas.

The following day Lucy dropped Emma off for two hours and that went well. I put on some music and the three of us danced in the living room, following the moves on one of the printouts. It was a fun activity that could be done indoors and was age appropriate for both Jamey and Emma.

On New Year's Eve all my family came to me, and we saw in the New Year to the sound of Big Ben's chimes on the television and a toast.

Most offices and businesses were back on 2 January and that day Joy and Shannon both phoned for updates and to make appointments to visit. That afternoon Kat was supposed to attend contact but failed to show. We waited for half an hour and then the manager told us to go. Jamey took it in his stride, but when I next phoned Lacey at the weekend (as I'd been asked to do) she latched onto it. She spent some time talking to Jamey, asking him what he'd been doing, and – with encouragement – he'd said 'yes' a few times in response. Then she'd wanted to speak to me.

'Has Kat been going to contact?' was her first question.

'Sometimes,' I said. I didn't want to be drawn into their feud by saying Kat had either arrived late or not at all. Shannon would tell Lacey what she needed to know, which apparently wasn't much at present.

'It's like trying to get blood out of a stone talking to that social worker!' Lacey declared. 'But I've got a lawyer now and she'll have to answer his questions.'

'OK.'

'It's not OK. I should be the one seeing Jamey, not her. I'm the person who's going to be looking after him.' But of course that hadn't been decided yet.

'It's not fair on him,' Lacey continued. 'Keep having to see her!'

'Kat is his mother,' I pointed out. 'Even if it's decided that Jamey can't live with her, he's still likely to see her. Contact arrangements are usually included in the court order.'

'That's different. Once he's living with me permanently I'll take him to see her or she can visit him here at my home. But then he'll have stability. He's all over the place at present. He lived with her, me and anyone else who would have him for a few hours or a night, and now he's with you! He needs consistency in his life and that's me.'

She had a point.

'How is he?' she asked, pausing for breath. 'It's so difficult to judge over the phone because he says so little. FaceTime would be better so I can see him. Do you do FaceTime?' FaceTime is one of a number of online applications that facilitates video calls.

'I could use it, but you will need to ask Shannon first,' I replied.

I heard her sigh. 'I'll get my lawyer onto it.'

'All right, but, Lacey, try not to make an enemy of his social worker. It's better if you can work with her. If Jamey does come to live with you permanently then he will still be monitored by the social services to begin with at least. Did your lawyer explain the process to you?'

'I haven't seen him yet. The first appointment is next week.'

I reassured her that Jamey was being well looked after and I told her of some of the activities we did together. I'm not sure if it helped or not. As we said goodbye I confirmed I would phone next weekend unless I heard any different from Shannon. Lacey was clearly genuinely concerned about Jamey and it did seem a little unfair that she wasn't having contact when she had played a significant part in his life. But the social services would have far more information than I did, so there might be good reason why she wasn't having contact at present.

That evening as I watched the news there was mention of a virus in China that was making people very ill, and some were dying. While I empathized with those affected, I didn't think much of it. There had been outbreaks of illness before in China and other countries and they'd dealt with it.

The first full week of January flew by, and the following Monday, Joy, my supervising social worker, visited. Although I'd been updating her, it was the first time she'd met Jamey. He came with me to answer the front door and then hid behind my legs as Joy came in.

'Hello, Jamey,' she tried, peering around me. But he was having none of it. He moved around my legs so he was out of her line of vision.

'You'll soon get used to me,' she smiled. Joy was in her early fifties, of average height and build, and with a wealth of experience. She was caring, efficient and level-headed.

We went through to the living room with Jamey clinging tightly to my trouser leg. 'I'll make you a drink when he lets go,' I said to Joy.

As soon as I sat down he scrambled onto my lap.

'Hi, Jamey,' Joy tried again, taking out her laptop. 'Did you have a nice Christmas?' She knew from my reports and our telephone conversations that he wasn't saying much.

He buried his face in my jumper in the belief that because he couldn't see Joy she couldn't see him. Joy understood. As far as Jamey was concerned, she was just another stranger in an ever-changing world populated by strangers and uncertainty.

We turned our attention to the business of her visit. As a supervising social worker Joy visited every four weeks (in addition to two unannounced visits each year) when we discussed the child's progress, routine, health, education, cultural needs, contact and any issues that might have arisen. While we talked, Joy observed Jamey to see how he was interacting with me and fitting into my home and family. We also talked about my training needs. New training began at the end of January, and as well as attending sessions as an experienced carer I was expected to facilitate training too.

Jamey hadn't moved from my lap and still had his face pressed against me.

'How does Jamey get along with your grand-daughter?' Joy asked. 'You are going to be looking after her for a day a week.' Part of a supervising social worker's role is to recognize and advise carers on any difficulties that might arise in the carer's family as a result of fostering.

'Yes. I've already been having Emma for short periods to get her used to being left, and that is going well. She is a lot more robust and confident than Jamey – and demanding, if I'm honest.' I smiled. 'I make sure Jamey has his fair share of attention, and it's only going to be for one day a week.'

Joy nodded as she typed. 'Do they play together?'

'Yes, with help.'

Jamey finally looked up.

'Hi, Jamey,' Joy said. 'Are you going to show me some of your new toys?' There were lots of his toys in the living room.

With a small nod, Jamey left my lap and picked up some toy cars and showed them to Joy.

'I can make you that drink now,' I said. 'Tea or coffee?'

'Tea would be lovely, thank you,' Joy replied.

'I won't be long,' I told Jamey. 'I'll be in the kitchen.'

He watched me go but stayed in the living room with Joy. I heard her talking to him as I made the tea and poured him a drink. We continued the meeting by discussing Jamey's care plan and Joy asked me to sign the minutes from our last meeting. She arranged the date for her next visit and then looked around the house as she did every visit. Satisfied that all was well, she packed away her laptop.

'Bye, Jamey,' she said with a smile.

'Bye,' he replied. Which made my day, as I think it did Joy's.

CHAPTER TEN

VERY SAD NEWS

On Tuesday a member of staff at the Family Centre telephoned me to say contact was cancelled that afternoon as Kat was unwell. She didn't say what was wrong with her but assumed she'd be all right for the next contact. On Wednesday I looked after Emma as Lucy had now returned to work. It went well, but when Lucy collected Emma Jamey thought he was going with them.

'This is where you live,' I told him gently. He looked confused.

It would take time before he came to see my house as his home, and then of course he would have another move to permanency. But that wouldn't be until later in the year when a decision on his future had been made at the final court hearing.

Contact was cancelled again on Thursday as Kat was still unwell. I asked that my best wishes were passed to her. On Friday afternoon Shannon visited and the first thing she said was that Kat was in hospital recovering from an overdose, accidental or deliberate she didn't know. She'd been told that morning as it had happened during the night.

'Does Lacey know?' I asked.

'Yes, she's the one who found her and called an ambulance. I'll be speaking to her again later.'

Shannon didn't have any more details. I was shocked and saddened by this turn of events, as was Shannon, and I asked her to give Kat my best wishes. We then had to turn our attention to the business of the meeting. Like Joy, Shannon had an agenda to work to and an online form to complete regarding Jamey and how he was doing in this placement. Her role was slightly different to Joy's as her priority was the child and she had to establish a good relationship with him. This was obviously more difficult with a very young child she would only see once a month.

Jamey sat on my lap to begin with as Shannon and I discussed his needs and progress. After about fifteen minutes he clambered down and went to play with his toys on the floor. Shannon put down her laptop and, sitting beside him, began helping him to do a jigsaw puzzle. He looked at her warily to begin with but stayed where he was and accepted her help. She talked to me as she played with him. She'd read the paediatrician's report and we discussed some of it. I asked her if it was all right for me to give Jamey a vitamin supplement as the paediatrician had suggested and she confirmed it was. She then asked about Jamey's diet and I told her he ate well and the foods I was giving him. She said she wanted me to have him weighed at the clinic every two weeks – more often if he wasn't putting on weight. I made a note.

I told her about the exercises the paediatrician had recommended and showed her the printouts. Leaving Jamey playing, she returned to her laptop and typed up what I'd been saying. Jamey was looking a bit lonely all by himself, so I sat with him on the floor and helped him do another puzzle as we talked. Shannon asked me about his routine and I described an average day. She then asked how childminding Emma would impact on Jamey. I told her much the same as I'd told Joy.

'What are Jamey's self-care skills like?' Shannon asked. 'Most children his age can, with help, dress themselves, brush their teeth and wash and dry their hands.'

'I am encouraging him to try to do things for himself,' I said.

She nodded as she typed, then said solemnly, 'According to the paediatrician he's a long way behind where he should be.'

'Yes, he is,' I agreed.

She looked at me thoughtfully. 'I do wonder whether we should have removed him sooner. Lacey thinks so.'

'I can't say,' I replied. 'I guess there was a chance that Kat might have recovered from her addictions and been able to look after him.'

Shannon didn't reply. How difficult it must be to know when the threshold has been reached to remove a child from home for their own safety.

'Does he have his meals with you?' Shannon asked after a moment.

'Yes, with Paula and me in the evening. Jamey eats with us at the table for all family meals. He was very good at Christmas.'

She glanced at him. 'I can't imagine him giving you much trouble,' she remarked. But she would know, as I did, that Jamey's quiet subservience wasn't healthy and not like the average two-and-a-half-year-old.

'Does he have any tantrums?' she asked.

'No.'

'Does he wake at night crying or screaming?'

'No.'

'What about the sores on his bottom? Have they gone now?'

'Yes, but the skin is still very delicate in parts. I would like to start toilet training him. The paediatrician thought it would help to keep him dry so the skin fully heals.'

'Is he ready for that yet?' she asked.

'I think he might be. He knows when he's about to do a poo.'

'OK, try him,' she said, and typed.

'Will you tell Kat he'll be in pull-ups for contact?' I said. 'I'll bring a change of clothes in case he has an accident.'

'Yes.'

We then discussed Jamey's language skills or rather lack of them. I told Shannon what I was doing to encourage him to talk and showed her the printouts the paediatrician had given me to help.

'He's learning new words every day,' I said enthusiastically. 'He's learnt the names of most of those toy animals he had for Christmas.'

Shannon leant forward and picked up a toy tiger. 'What's the name for this animal?' she asked him.

Jamey just looked at her.

'What's it called? Do you know?' she tried again.

Jamey did know and I was willing him to say the word.

'Tiger,' he said eventually in a small voice.

'Well done!' I exclaimed, and clapped enthusiastically. Shannon smiled politely.

'The paediatrician has suggested speech therapy may be needed,' she said.

'Yes, I know.'

'I was discussing this with a colleague and I think we'll hold off for now and see what his next assessment is like. He's still quite young.'

'I agree. Also, the paediatrician suggested I started taking Jamey to the dentist to get him used to it, so I've booked him an appointment for next Monday.' She made a note.

Shannon finished her visit by asking to look around the house. Jamey came with us and held my hand as we went in and out of the rooms.

'Does he fall out of bed?' she asked in Jamey's bedroom, seeing the cushions I'd arranged around the bed.

'No. He hasn't. I put those there as a precaution, but they haven't been needed. I'll take them away before long. Lacey told me he slept in a bed at her place.'

'Yes, so I understand. I will be visiting her flat as part of her assessment.'

'Lacey has asked if I can video call her so she can see Jamey. I told her to speak to you about it.'

'She did, but I've said we'll review it again when we are further along with her assessment. She can have phone contact for now. It's not definite that Jamey will go to her, although she thinks it is. There's her live-in boyfriend to be assessed too, so it will take time.'

'I wasn't aware she had a live-in partner.'

'No, neither were we until recently.' Shannon didn't say anything further, but from her tone I guessed she and

Lacey had had words. It's important to be honest with the social services, and of course Lacey's partner would need to be assessed for his suitability to parent Jamey. They would also be police checked.

We returned downstairs to the living room, where Shannon gave me the details of Jamey's first review, which would take place at my house the following Friday. 'Can you complete the review forms online?' she said.

'Yes.' I made a note.

All children in care have regular reviews to ensure that everything is being done to help the child, and that the care plan (drawn up by the social services) is up to date.

Shannon said goodbye to Jamey and he came with us to the front door. 'Bye, Jamey,' she said again. 'I'll see you next Friday at your review.'

Jamey stared at her.

'Say bye,' I prompted him.

'Bye,' he said quietly.

'Good boy,' I praised him, and clapped again.

That night on the news there was another mention of the virus in China, which had spread from where it had begun in Wuhan. But other than having sympathy for those involved, I didn't think any more of it, and my pleasantly busy life continued.

On Saturday I telephoned Lacey for Jamey's weekend contact call. I left him in the living room with Paula to begin with as I wanted to speak to her first without Jamey hearing. I guessed she would be angry that she wasn't being allowed video calls yet and also I wanted to know how Kat was.

'Kat was discharged from hospital yesterday evening,' Lacey said. 'The silly cow could have killed herself. They wanted to keep her in so she could see the psychiatrist, but she left.'

'I am sorry,' I said. 'Shannon said it was you who found her. What a shock.'

'It was. Her neighbour phoned me as she hadn't seen Kat for some days and she wasn't answering her door or phone. I have a spare key. When I went in I found her lying in bed. I called an ambulance. Just in time it seems. She'd been in bed for most of the week. Shannon knew Kat had missed contact so alarm bells should have been ringing.'

'I think Kat phoned to say she was ill. That's the message I got.'

'Even so, she could have checked. It's her fault Kat is feeling so low. She often stays in bed if she's having a bad time, but not all week. This wasn't the first time she's overdosed. She might not be so lucky next time.'

'Thank goodness you found her when you did,' I said.

'Kat doesn't think so. She says she has nothing left to live for.'

'That is sad. Can't she get help? Go into rehab?' I asked.

'Only if she wants to. You can't force someone.'

While I was greatly saddened that Kat was in such a dark place, I was even more convinced that Jamey couldn't possibly have stayed with his mother for any longer. Where was he on all those days Kat had spent in bed? I shuddered at the thought.

'I wish I'd just kept Jamey when I'd had the chance, instead of all this,' Lacey said. 'It's going to take forever to sort out. The lawyer said the final court hearing isn't until the end of July.' Which I knew from the care plan. 'It's not just Jamey's life they're messing with, but mine and Andy's too. Poking their noses into our business.'

'Andy is your partner?' I asked.

'Yes. He's got nothing to hide, but like he says, it's an invasion of our privacy to have them looking around our home and asking lots of personal questions.'

'You get used to it as a foster carer,' I said.

'*You* might. But I'm not a foster carer. I'm his family. Jamey is my nephew.'

'I know. But it's still a type of fostering you and Andy will be doing, so you'll have to be assessed just like we are. As far as I know it's standard practice.'

'As soon as I can I'll apply for guardianship,' Lacey said. 'I was talking to the lawyer about it.' Special Guardianship is a court order that can be granted to those looking after a child long term. It gives the family more security as the child can't be removed without a court order. The guardian(s) make decisions and act as parents in day-to-day matters, but the child has to live with them for a year before they can apply.

Lacey continued to have a good moan about Shannon and 'the system' in general, the time everything was taking and that she had been denied video calls for no good reason. I could understand her frustration, but I said, 'Just try to work with Shannon.'

Lacey finished by saying she still had Jamey's Christmas present and she'd drop it off at the Family Centre as she wouldn't be seeing him any time soon. I could hear the sadness in her voice and felt sorry for her, but there was nothing I could do. I returned to the living room so she could talk to Jamey. Engaging the speaker, I said to Jamey, 'Say hi to Aunty Lacey.' Paula left the room to do something else.

'Hi,' Jamey said in a small voice.

'Hello, love,' Lacey said, pleased he'd spoken. 'How are you, little man?'

Jamey looked at me, uncertain. 'Tell her you're OK,' I prompted.

'OK,' Jamey repeated.

'Good. What are you doing, love?' Lacey asked, her voice now thick with emotion.

'Playing,' I suggested to Jamey.

'Playing,' he repeated.

'That's lovely. Do you remember me?'

He nodded.

'He's nodding,' I told her. 'Say yes,' I said to Jamey.

'Yes,' he repeated.

'That's good. Don't ever forget me, will you? You should have your Christmas present soon. I hope you like it. I wanted to give it to you in person so I could watch you open it, but that's not possible.' I heard her voice break. 'I love you,' she said.

'Love you,' Jamey said.

I heard her stifle a sob. 'Bye, love,' she said, and ended the call.

Jamey was looking at me sadly as if he had done something wrong. 'Aunty Lacey is all right,' I reassured him, taking his hand. 'It's not your fault.'

I steered him to the toys and he was soon playing again,

albeit without much enthusiasm. Then he began picking up the toy animals and naming them.

'Pig, cow, horse …'

'Yes, well done! What a clever boy!'

And finally, he smiled.

CHAPTER ELEVEN

REVIEW

Many of the toys Jamey had been given for Christmas had an educational component to them, as most early-years' toys do to encourage learning, as well as being fun. No toys had come from his home, so I was also using the games and puzzles in the toy cupboard, of which I had plenty after twenty-five years of fostering. I was taking every opportunity to play with Jamey and encourage him to talk. I made up little sentences to go with the toy people and asked him questions. 'The lady is going to catch the bus. Where do you think she is going?' 'The famer is milking the cow. What colour are its spots?' 'Those children are playing in the park. The boy is on the swing. Do you like to swing?' and so on. Anything to help develop Jamey's language and understanding. It's what most parents do automatically with their young children and I assumed Lacey had, but the time Jamey had spent with her had been very limited and any good had been reduced or negated by the neglect in between. I was also reading to Jamey and counting objects so he would start to understand numbers. Counting the stairs going up and down was an old favourite, as it is for many parents and carers.

I set aside a Sunday to start potty training Jamey and in the morning I got out the potty, training pants and a picture book that talked about using a potty and wearing 'big-boy pants'.

'No more nappies,' I told Jamey positively.

Praising him, I took off his nappy and helped him step into the trainer pants. I read the book and then explained that he could do a wee and poo in his potty from now on. I wasn't expecting Jamey to suddenly start using the potty; it would take many days, if not weeks, and if he really wasn't ready I would stop and try again in a few months.

I kept the potty with us in whichever room Jamey and I were in and asked him from time to time if he needed to do a wee or a poo. A couple of times he sat on the potty but didn't produce anything and then went in his trainer pants, which was only to be expected to begin with. I knew from potty training my children and others I'd fostered that if I could catch some wee in the potty then the child began to understand. Once they were using the potty it was only a short step to using the toilet.

I had kept the whole of the day free and Paula was out so I devoted my time to playing with Jamey and potty training, but keeping it low-key. He wasn't stressed, but by the evening I hadn't had any success, and had spent the day changing his trainer pants rather than nappies. I put him in his nappy at night as usual.

The following day I put Jamey in trainer pants to go for his dental check-up, so we kept the momentum going. Similar to nappies, trainer pants are designed to absorb moisture so the child doesn't get too wet. I was using the same dental practice my family and I had always used. Although the dentists had changed over the years, they are always very pleasant and good at putting children at ease. I sat in the examination chair with Jamey on my lap as the dentist asked him to open his mouth wide. He was compliant and cooperative in this, as he was in most things.

'You are a good boy,' the dentist said. 'One of my best patients ever!'

Once the examination was over with, the dental nurse gave Jamey a reward sticker showing a smiling molar with the caption 'Superstar', which I stuck on his coat.

'All his primary teeth have come through,' the dentist told me.

'Good. Any problems?'

'Not really. A bit of plaque on the back teeth, so make sure you brush them well and limit his sugar intake – that includes sweet drinks and juice, as well as sweets.'

'I will.'

I thanked her and we left. I thought it could have been a whole lot worse. Many of the children I'd fostered who'd had a high-sugar diet and hadn't visited the dentist regularly had rotten teeth, sometimes leading to extractions, which is very traumatic for the child.

Once home, I resumed potty training. Jamey's pants were wet so I put him in clean ones. I wouldn't have expected anything else at such an early stage. That evening I had the first small success. After dinner when Jamey had had a lot to drink and eat I told him he probably needed to use the potty. He sat on it, and I kept him occupied with a book. As I read I heard him do a wee. I praised him, then ceremoniously took him upstairs to flush it down the toilet. I told Paula what he'd done, and she praised him too.

Jamey had contact on Tuesday and, having not heard anything to the contrary, I assumed Kat was well enough to attend. I packed the potty, spare trainer pants and a change of clothes so Kat could continue with the potty training if she wanted. I thought it might be nice for her to be involved. To my surprise she had arrived early and was already in the contact room talking to the supervisor in a highly excitable voice, about the buses and seeing Jamey. As soon as she saw him she rushed over and, taking his head in her hands, began kissing him all over his face. Jamey looked a bit startled and just stood there.

'I've got us a present. Sweets!' she cried, letting go of his head.

She delved into her jacket pocket and pulled out a large bag of dolly mixtures: small, multi-coloured sweets with soft centres and sugar-coated jellies. I thought it was just as well the dentist couldn't see!

Grabbing Jamey's arm, she took him to the sofa and sat him next to her where she tore open the packet. She began dishing them out. 'Some for you and some for me. Some more for you and some more for me,' and so on. She seemed as high as a kite, or perhaps she was always like that when she wasn't down. It was non-stop – sweets for Jamey and sweets for her. He was cramming them into his mouth faster than he could eat them. I glanced at the contact supervisor.

'Perhaps not too many sweets all in one go,' she said to Kat. 'Jamey was sick last time.'

So I guessed something had been said.

'We like our sweets, don't we?' Kat said, nudging Jamey. She carried on shovelling them into her mouth but didn't give Jamey any more. He was still chewing the last mouthful.

I went over to give her the bag containing the potty.

'What do you want?' she demanded, rudely.

'I've just started potty training Jamey and I wondered if you would like to continue it here?' I explained.

'Not fussed,' she said with a shrug and continued eating the sweets.

'I'll leave the bag here then just in case,' I said. 'It contains everything you need – potty, clean trainer pants, wipes and a change of clothes.' I set it by the sofa. 'Have a nice time. See you later,' I said to them both, and left.

When I returned at the end of the hour's contact Kat was ready to leave and rushed straight out of the door. The bag was by the sofa where I'd put it and I smiled at Jamey as I retrieved it.

'Kat didn't use it,' the contact supervisor told me.

'OK. Not a problem.'

Once home, I helped Jamey into clean trainer pants and we resumed potty training. That evening after dinner I again sat him on the potty, and he obliged by producing a small wee and then did the rest in his trainer pants. But that's normal. My three Ps for potty training are Potty, Patience and Perseverance.

On Wednesday I looked after Emma for the day as well as continuing the potty training for Jamey. Emma was interested in what was going on but at eighteen months was still quite young, and Lucy and Darren hadn't started toilet training her yet. She was tired from an early start and in the afternoon fell asleep in my arms as the three of us sat on the sofa. Jamey was snuggled up beside me and also went to sleep. I closed my eyes for twenty minutes too. Emma stayed with us until five o'clock when Darren finished his shift at the nursery and collected her.

Later, I saw on a news feed on my phone that the Foreign and Commonwealth Office had advised against all but essential travel to the city of Wuhan in China where this new virus was spreading. I had no plans to travel to China, so other than feeling for those affected, I didn't pay it much attention and checked the rest of the news.

Thursday was contact and again I took the bag containing the potty and so forth with me in case Kat had changed her mind and wanted to be involved. She didn't arrive. We sat in the waiting room for nearly half an hour and then the manager told us to go as Kat hadn't been in touch to say she was on her way.

'Do you think someone should tell her social worker?' I suggested. 'Kat was in a bad way the last time she didn't arrive for contact.'

'Yes, I know, I'll tell her.'

As Jamey and I were leaving the building the receptionist stopped us. 'I am sorry. I should have given this to you on Tuesday. I put it in a cupboard for safekeeping and forgot about it. Better late than never.' She handed Jamey a Christmas present.

'That will be from his aunt,' I said, and checked the label: *To Jamey. All my love, Lacey. Xx*

'Sorry,' she said again. 'She brought it in on Monday and I completely forgot.'

'No worries. Thanks for looking after it.'

Jamey opened the present in the car – it was a child's tablet. A lovely present that would give him hours of fun and help him with his learning. Once home, I set it up with a simple game and showed Jamey how to use it. He was riveted, and so was I. It wouldn't replace the traditional games but supplement them. I would thank Lacey when I called her at the weekend.

On Friday morning I took Jamey to the clinic to be weighed and measured as Shannon had asked. The healthcare assistant recorded his details on their system and in a record book, which I took away with me.

That afternoon was Jamey's LAC (looked-after child) review. Shannon, Nathan (whom I'd met when Jamey first arrived), Joy, the IRO (Independent Reviewing Officer) and I gathered in my living room. These reviews are chaired by the IRO, who also minutes the meeting. They are qualified social workers with extra training, but they are separate from the social services. Jamey had come with me to answer the doorbell each time it rang, and now everyone was here he sat on my lap.

LAC reviews vary in size but usually last an hour. This one was relatively small as none of Jamey's family had been invited and there were no other professionals – for example, a teacher – involved yet. The IRO took out his laptop and opened the review by asking us to introduce ourselves, as is usual at all social-services meetings. I was last and I introduced Jamey too.

'So you are the star of the show,' the IRO said kindly to him with a smile. 'Nice to meet you. How are you?'

Jamey buried his face in my jersey.

'He doesn't say much yet,' I said.

'I saw your report for the review, thank you,' the IRO said.

I was asked to speak first and, with Jamey on my lap cuddling me, I talked about how well he was doing; how he'd settled in with my family, ate and slept well and had enjoyed Christmas despite the upset of being removed from home just before. I described his average day and what he liked doing as the IRO took notes on his laptop. I said I'd taken Jamey for a medical and gave the date and what the paediatrician had said, adding that I had begun to get Jamey weighed every two weeks. I read out his weight and height, taken that morning. 'So he's put on a little bit since his medical,' Shannon said, noting his weight.

'Yes.'

'Good.'

I continued with the details of Jamey's dental check-up. As I talked and Jamey cuddled me, I felt I could have been talking about my own child, so close had we become in just a few weeks. It felt so natural parenting him and tending to his needs. I gave him an extra hug as I told the review what he liked to play with, including the tablet Lacey had bought for him. I mentioned I'd begun potty training him and the sores on his bottom had largely healed.

'And contact?' the IRO asked. 'How is that going?'

'It's difficult,' I replied. 'Jamey isn't upset or unsettled by going, but Kat hasn't been there very often.'

'She's missed more than she's attended,' Shannon added.

'Are there any plans to reduce it?' the IRO asked, glancing at Jamey.

'Not at present,' Shannon said. 'Although Kat doesn't want phone contact. Just his aunt has that – once a week.'

'And how is that going?' the IRO asked me.

'Jamey doesn't really talk much but he likes to hear Lacey's voice. She speaks to him for a while and then usually wants to talk to me.'

'His aunt has come forward to look after him,' the IRO confirmed with Shannon. He would have been sent a report prior to the review.

'Yes. We are starting the assessment next week.'

The IRO nodded as he typed.

'Any accidents or injuries?' he asked me. It was a standard question.

'No,' I replied.

'Any allergies or medical conditions?'

'No, although Jamey is small for his age – in the lower percentile.'

'Can he catch up?' the IRO asked.

'Hopefully,' I said. 'He may also need speech therapy in the future.'

'Thank you. And Jamey can stay with you until the final court hearing at the end of July?'

'Yes.'

Shannon went next and began with the date Jamey had come into care and the type of care order. She confirmed that the care plan was for Jamey to stay in foster care until a decision was made at the final court hearing, when he would either go to Lacey or be found a long-term placement.

'Is adoption being considered?' the IRO asked.

'It might be,' she said. 'If it's decided that Jamey won't be able to live with his aunt and her partner, we may apply to the court to have him freed for adoption. We are also trying to trace the father.' I then learnt that the social services had been involved with Kat on and off since Jamey was three months old, when a neighbour had reported hearing a baby crying for long periods. It seemed Kat was living on benefits and subsequent social-worker visits found the flat messy, not properly heated and with no food in the cupboards. Shannon touched on Kat's drug habit and said it was likely she was still using. I learnt that Kat was under the mental health team and there was a suggestion she might be bipolar. This condition used to be known as manic depression and can create extreme mood swings between elation and depression.

The IRO thanked her and then asked Nathan if he wanted to add anything. I guessed that, as a trainee social worker, he'd attended mainly to observe, but he did say, 'I was here when Jamey was first brought into care and I'd like to say how much better he's looking now. He's got colour in his cheeks and his hair is shiny. And the way he's cuddling up to Cathy is really good to see. He always seemed so alone before.'

'Thank you,' I said. 'I am pleased you can see a difference already.'

'I can,' Nathan replied.

'Speaking of his hair,' I said to Shannon. 'Will it be all right if I take him to the barber to get it trimmed? It's rather uneven.'

'I was thinking that but didn't like to say,' Nathan said, with a small laugh.

'Yes, go ahead, but nothing too drastic,' Shannon said, making a note.

Joy was asked if she would like to speak and she said she'd seen an improvement in Jamey too. 'My role is to supervise, support and monitor Cathy in all aspects of fostering,' she continued. 'We are in regular contact by phone and email, and I also visit her every month. She is an experienced foster carer and I am satisfied that Jamey is doing well here and receiving a high quality of care.'

'So no complaints then?' the IRO asked.

'None.'

'Thank you. Does anyone want to add anything else before I set the date for the next review?' he asked, looking around the room.

No one did, but then in the short silence that followed Jamey lifted his head and said clearly, 'Potty.'

It took me a split second to realize he was asking to use his potty. 'Excuse us!' I said. Jumping up from my seat with Jamey still in my arms, I ran from the living room and into the kitchen where I'd left the potty.

Just in time, for as I sat him on his potty he began to wee.

'Good boy! Well done!' I cried, elated. 'What a big boy you are!'

This was a huge step forward as Jamey had finally recognized the feeling that he wanted to wee and had managed to hold it until he was on the potty. Once he'd finished, I covered over the potty and left it to rinse out after everyone had gone. Praising him again, I returned with him to the living room where they were packing away their laptops, notepads and pens.

'I take it there was success,' the IRO said with a smile. They'd heard my cries of joy.

'Yes. Most definitely,' I replied, delighted.

'Well done, Jamey,' Shannon said.

'You are a big boy,' Joy added, while Nathan gave him the thumbs-up sign.

Jamey stood there, the centre of attention, smiling broadly and appreciating the praise. It was a glimpse of the child he could become and a lovely way to end his review.

A few days later it was announced that British Airways had stopped flying to mainland China due to the spread of coronavirus. The first case was diagnosed in the UK. There was a long piece on the news and I could see that concern was mounting. Ordinary people like me, living a long way from the epicentre of the virus, were now starting to worry. But no one could ever have imagined what lay in store for us all.

CHAPTER TWELVE

HOW DIFFERENT HER LIFE
MIGHT HAVE BEEN

That week, Jamey continued to make progress using his potty, so when I next phoned Lacey I told her so, assuming it was something she would like to know.

'I would have done it if he'd been with me,' she said with an edge to her voice. 'But you can't do much with a day here and there.'

'No, absolutely,' I agreed, and wondered if she'd seen it as a criticism of her, which of course it wasn't. 'I've spent all week following him around with the potty and asking him if he wanted to go. It's taken over my life.' I laughed.

'He'll be calling you "Mummy" next,' Lacey replied curtly.

Jamey already had called me 'Mummy' a number of times, but I didn't tell Lacey that, and I always corrected him. I thought this conversation was going nowhere. She'd spoken to Jamey and he was now in another room with Paula so I began to say goodbye.

'Have you seen or heard from his social worker?' Lacey suddenly asked.

'Only at his review,' I replied.

'Review? What review?'

I realized then that Lacey probably hadn't been told of Jamey's review as she hadn't been invited.

'Was the review about Jamey?' she persisted.

'Yes. But reviews are standard and only short. They are just to make sure the child is being properly looked after. Nothing is decided.'

'I don't care. I should have been there!' she said, annoyed. 'And please don't try to cover up for them [the social services]. I'm going to speak to my lawyer first thing on Monday. How dare they have meetings behind my back! Goodbye.' She hung up.

I appreciated that feelings were running high. Relatives of children in care often felt excluded from decision making and that there should be more transparency. They had a point, but it would take a change in policy, practice and legislation to bring it about, so it was no good Lacey going on at me or Shannon, which I hoped her lawyer would explain to her.

On Sunday we were all invited to Adrian and Kirsty's for lunch, which was lovely. They'd decorated the spare bedroom since my last visit, and I admired it. Emma enjoyed all the attention that having the family together brought, and Jamey seemed to like being with her, although he lacked confidence. I thought it would do him good to start socialising with other children on a regular basis, maybe at a playgroup where the parent or carer stayed. I would research to see if there was one meeting locally on either a Monday or Friday – the only two days we were free – and send details to his social worker.

We left Adrian and Kirsty's around six o'clock and the air temperature was already dropping. Overnight it plummeted to below zero. The following morning, when I opened the curtains, I was greeted with a magical winter wonderland of glistening white frost. It sparkled on rooftops, cars, paths, shrubs and trees. It was very pretty, but the roads and pavements were treacherous. As Paula left for work I told her to take extra care when driving. She texted to say she had arrived safely. The weather forecast said the 'cold snap' was set to continue for the week, not surprising as we were now in February, often the heart of our winter in the UK.

I'd booked Jamey's barber's appointment for that afternoon, by which time the sun had come out and the frost had gone. The barber's shop is on our local high street so we walked, but I had the stroller with me in case Jamey got tired and couldn't manage the walk home again. He was wearing a warm zip-up all-in-one padded suit I'd bought him, gloves and a matching hat that had been part of Lucy, Darren and Emma's Christmas present to him. Although it took much longer to walk than if I'd pushed him in the stroller, walking is good exercise and would help strengthen his muscles and generally make him stronger. He was eating well and I was also giving him multivitamin drops as the paediatrician had suggested, but it would take time before he had the stamina of an average child his age.

I made walking fun. 'Big giant steps,' I said, and showed him how to stride.

He smiled and copied me. 'Giant steps,' he said.

'Yes, that's right! Good boy.'

We plodded on, and then he cried, 'Potty!'

Oh dear, I thought.

'Hold it,' I said, and, taking him to the edge of the pavement, I quickly unzipped his suit.

Checking no one was around, I held him over the drain. It was a bit cold for him, but he managed to do a wee.

'Good boy,' I said as I pulled up his pants and zipped up his suit.

It was another small success in his toilet training. Jamey hadn't done a poo in his potty yet and I'd had to clean him after he'd gone in his trainer pants. Not pleasant, but that's part of parenting or being a carer, and I'd dealt with worse. One boy I'd fostered, aged seven, who was very disturbed after being badly abused, had smeared poo all over his bedroom and in his bed. The medical term for faecal smearing is scatolia. It's not unusual for very young children to play with their poo if they get the chance and some children with autism do, but it can also be a result of severe trauma from abuse.

I left the stroller outside the barber's shop as there wasn't much room inside. Dino, the owner, glanced at me as we went in. 'Hello. How are you?' he asked. I knew him from taking other children there.

'Good, thank you, and you?'

'Can't grumble. So you have more children?' He paused from cutting his client's hair.

'Just one. This is Jamey. I think it's his first trip to the barber.' I took off his gloves and hat.

'Hello, Jamey. Who's been cutting your hair?' he asked, raising his eyebrows at Jamey's uneven hair.

'No, not me.' I smiled.

'Don't worry. Take a seat. Enzo will sort him out soon.'

Enzo, a younger man in his twenties, was just finishing with his client, brushing the hair from his shoulders. Jamey and I sat on one of the seats to wait. Jamey was staring wide-eyed at Dino cutting his client's hair.

Dino saw him watching. 'So you want to be a barber like me when you grow up?' he joked with Jamey.

Jamey smiled shyly.

'It's a good job,' I said. 'People always need their hair cutting.'

'You're right there,' Dino agreed.

Enzo's client paid and left, and Enzo took a child's booster seat from the cupboard. He placed it on the barber's chair and I lifted Jamey into the seat. As Enzo draped the black cape around Jamey, he looked very worried.

'It's to keep the hairs off you,' I reassured him. 'They itch if they go down your neck.'

'You look like Batman,' Enzo encouraged.

Jamey reached for my hand and I held it.

'What would you like me to do for the little fellow?'

'A trim, please, to even it up,' I said.

'Sure, but I'll need to take more off here,' he said, pointing to one side. 'To make it even all round.'

'Yes, that's fine, thank you.'

I stayed with Jamey, holding his hand to begin with, but I was getting in Enzo's way, so once Jamey realized having his hair cut wasn't going to hurt and began to relax, I returned to my chair. I could see Jamey's face in the mirror and he could see me. I smiled reassuringly. This was a whole new experience for Jamey, and while he wasn't upset, he was looking solemn. Enzo was lovely and kept reassuring him, as I did, but Jamey was relieved when it was all over. I paid at the till and Enzo offered Jamey the sweet jar.

'Say thank you,' I reminded him.

'Thank you,' he repeated.

'Good boy.'

Jamey managed to walk half the way home and then rode the rest of the way in his stroller. I hadn't been in long when my phone rang.

'Cathy Glass?' a woman asked.

'Speaking.'

'Audrey Bashir, here. I'm the Guardian ad Litem for Jamey. I believe you are fostering him.'

'Yes, that's correct. Hello.'

I'd been expecting to hear from the Guardian. They are appointed by the court in child-care proceedings for the duration of the case. Qualified social workers but independent of the social services, they work within the organization known as CAFCASS (Children and Family Court Advisory and Support Service). They have access to all the files and see all parties involved, including the child, their parents, foster carer and social workers. They report to the judge on what is in the best interests of the child and usually the judge follows their recommendation, which may not be the same as that of the social services. Audrey Bashir made an appointment to visit us on Friday – the only day free that week.

When Paula arrived home from work she admired Jamey's haircut. 'Very smart,' she said, and he smiled.

Although tired after work, Paula always made time for Jamey, either playing with him or reading a story, and hugging him goodnight. Jamey liked his hugs and cuddles and appreciated spending time with Paula. I knew how attached she was becoming to him, as indeed I was.

'Do you think Jamey will go to his aunt?' she asked me.

'At this point I honestly don't know,' I replied.

'But he can't go back to live with his mother, can he?'

'It's highly unlikely. But nothing is decided until the final court hearing when all the reports are in.'

'He could stay here,' Paula suggested.

'He could, love, but I think if he can't live with his family, the social services will want to place him with younger parents, possibly even for adoption.' Which Paula knew. She had grown up with fostering and had had to say goodbye to many children we'd fostered. It's always upsetting, losing a family member, like a mini-bereavement, and for this reason some people who consider fostering don't go ahead. Thankfully for us many of the children we'd fostered were still in touch.

Tuesday was contact again. Kat wasn't there when we arrived but had phoned to say she was on her way, so the receptionist told us to wait in the contact room as she wouldn't be long. The supervisor was there working on her laptop at the table. We said hello and Jamey and I sat on the sofa and I read him a story. Kat arrived about ten minutes late and was highly agitated, saying the bus she usually caught had been cancelled. Then she saw Jamey's hair.

'You've had his hair cut!' she exclaimed. For a moment I thought she was going to complain, then she added, 'It looks nice.'

'Good. I'm glad you like it,' I said, relieved. Putting aside the book I'd been reading to Jamey, I stood ready to go. 'I'll leave the bag containing the potty here.'

'Did you cut his hair?' Kat asked, coming over for a closer look.

'No, I took him to the barber. I'm no good at cutting hair.'

'Me neither,' she said. 'But I couldn't afford to take him to the barber.'

I felt sorry for her. When she wasn't angry there was a much nicer side to her. She was rubbing her hands together, trying to get warm. There was nothing of her and she was wearing a thin denim jacket and jeans.

'Can I make myself a coffee?' she asked the contact supervisor.

'Yes. Do you know where the kitchen is?'

'No.' The contact supervisor couldn't leave the room to show her with Jamey here.

'I know where it is,' I said. 'Shall I make you a coffee?'

'Please,' Kat said gratefully. 'Milk and two sugars, and some biscuits if they've got any. I didn't have time for breakfast.' It was 1.15 p.m.

'Would you like a drink?' I asked the contact supervisor on my way out.

'No, thanks.'

The kitchen was empty. I filled the kettle and then searched the cupboards for the tin of biscuits that was usually there. Parents who were working towards having their children returned had longer contact and sometimes made meals in the kitchen and then ate together as a family. The supervisor stayed with them and included it in their report. I found the tin of biscuits and arranged some on a plate, made Kat her coffee and then returned to the contact room.

I stopped and stared in amazement. Jamey was sitting on his potty.

'Well done!' I said, delighted. 'Good boy.'

'He said "potty",' Kat said, astonished. 'He knew he wanted to go.'

'Excellent. He's doing well.'

I placed the coffee and biscuits on the table and Kat helped Jamey pull up his pants.

'I'll empty it,' I said, going over.

I took the potty into the washroom, tipped the contents down the toilet, then rinsed it well and dried it with paper towels. I returned it to the contact room, leaving it just inside the door so as not to disturb them.

As there was only half an hour of contact left, I sat in the waiting room and looked at some magazines. I felt that the interaction I'd just had with Kat was the best so far and I hoped it would continue.

When I returned to the room at the end of contact Kat was in a rush to leave but did manage to say goodbye.

'Jamey is coming along,' the contact supervisor remarked as I helped him into his snowsuit. 'His mother noticed a difference.'

'Good.'

'She told him you were much better for him than she was.'

'Really? That is sad,' I said.

As we left I thought how different Kat's life might have been if she had been able to get off the drugs and go into rehab. Was it too late for her to get clean and keep Jamey? I didn't know, but the social services would have to be satisfied she was clean and could meet Jamey's needs.

* * *

On Wednesday I looked after Emma for the day and Jamey's success with the potty continued – with the wees at least.

'It would be really nice if you could do a poo on your potty too,' I said after lunch when I had to clean him up again. 'Poo in potty.'

He looked at me and smiled cutely.

On Thursday Kat didn't arrive at contact. Jamey and I sat in the waiting room for fifteen minutes and then the receptionist came in and said we should go as Kat had just phoned to say she couldn't make it today. There was no reason given.

Jamey didn't make a fuss – he never did – but this wasn't fair on him, not at all. Children need their parents to be reliable and consistent in order to feel safe. I knew how chaotic Kat's life must be; addicts' lives generally are. But Jamey wouldn't understand that, and why should he? As far as he was concerned he came to see his mother and she had let him down again. Another child would have become upset and angry, but Jamey just accepted it, which in some ways made it worse. He asked for so little and got even less. Was it really impossible for Kat to get to contact to see him for two hours a week? Outside, I gave him a big hug and then helped him into the car.

That evening on the news I learnt that a third case of coronavirus had been confirmed in the UK and there were a few more in other countries. But they were isolated incidents, and those in the UK could all be linked to one person who'd picked it up abroad. So that was reassuring, wasn't it? Pandemics were the stuff of disaster movies and couldn't really happen in the twenty-first century, could they?

CHAPTER THIRTEEN

THE GUARDIAN

The Guardian ad Litem, Audrey Bashir, arrived promptly at 11.30 a.m. on Friday morning. Jamey came with me to answer the doorbell.

'Hello, Jamey,' she said. 'I don't suppose you remember me.'

He hid behind my legs.

'I saw him last year,' she told me, coming in. 'When he was with his mother.'

Audrey was a tall, slender woman in her fifties, wearing black trousers and a pale-blue jumper under her winter coat. She slipped off her coat and hung it on the hall stand. I showed her into the living room and offered her a drink.

'Just hot water, please.'

'Sure? Nothing else?'

'No, thank you. I'm on a detox diet.'

Jamey wasn't ready to let go of my leg yet and came with me, but I left him on the other side of the safety gate as I went into the kitchen to boil the kettle and pour the hot water. We returned to the living room where Audrey was looking at the photographs on the walls.

'Which are yours?' she asked, referring to the children's pictures.

I pointed out photographs of Adrian, Lucy and Paula. The rest were of my parents, family gatherings and the children we'd looked after.

'You've been fostering a long time,' she said, sitting in the armchair close to where I'd placed her drink. 'So you understand my role?'

'Yes.'

She took a pen and reporter-style notepad from her bag. 'I like to take notes the old-fashioned way,' she said with a smile. 'Then, when I type them up, it gives me added time for reflection.'

I nodded. Guardians, like social workers, often had their own style.

'So how has Jamey been with you?' she asked. 'Talk to me about him, please. He obviously feels very comfortable with you.'

Jamey was snuggled beside me on the sofa. Audrey went to take a sip of her drink and stopped. 'It's a bit hot yet.'

'Would you like some cold water in it?' I asked.

'No. It's fine. I'll let it cool.'

I started talking about Jamey as Audrey listened, nodded and occasionally took notes. I began when he'd first arrived, very upset, but I said he'd settled in quickly and was eating and sleeping well and had enjoyed Christmas. I talked about our routine, including the time he spent with Emma on Wednesdays. After a while Jamey grew braver – or perhaps he was just bored – and, slipping from the sofa, went to his toy box. The Guardian watched him.

'Are those toys all his?' she asked after a moment.

'Yes, there are others in his bedroom and dotted around the house.'

'Did any come from home?'

'No, but Lacey bought him that lovely tablet.' I pointed to where it lay.

'I understand Lacey is very eager to see me,' Audrey remarked dryly. 'I believe she has telephone contact only at present. How is that going?'

I told her and, aware that Jamey's future lay in the Guardian's hands, I then ventured to ask: 'I understand adoption may be considered if Jamey can't live with Lacey.'

'It is one option to be considered,' was all she said. Some Guardians are more forthcoming than others, although it was still early in the proceedings, so she was probably still gathering information and hadn't come to a conclusion or recommendation yet.

Audrey asked about Jamey's health and development, and I touched on his medical, although she'd seen the paediatrician's report. I spoke honestly and impartially. Eventually her mug of hot water was cool enough for her to drink and she drank it down in one go. I offered her a refill, but she declined, then she sat on the floor with Jamey and tried to engage with him, but he wasn't inter-ested. She returned to her chair and we continued to talk about Jamey's needs and progress. She was with us for nearly two hours, then, putting away her notepad, she said, 'I'll see him again in a few months. I'll be in touch.'

I stood ready to see her to the door when she paused and asked, 'What is your opinion on where Jamey should live in the future? All foster carers have one.'

I was slightly taken aback by her directness. 'From what I know I don't think he can go home unless Kat dramatically changes her lifestyle,' I said.

'Do you think that is likely to happen?'

'I really can't say.'

She said goodbye to Jamey and he stayed in the living room while I saw her out. As I closed the door I wondered how Lacey was going to get on with her. Audrey was very direct, with an unusual, quirky style, but I thought she was also very astute and wouldn't take kindly to being told what to do.

On Saturday, when I phoned Lacey for contact she seemed more upbeat and didn't mention ending our previous call rudely with a curt goodbye. Neither did I.

'Hi, Lacey,' Jamey said spontaneously, which pleased her.

She asked him how he was and what he'd been doing, and I prompted him to tell her, including that he liked playing on the tablet she'd given him. She told him what she'd been doing and then wound up with lots of kisses blown down the phone. Jamey went to play while Lacey spoke to me.

'Andy and I have to see someone from the court next week,' she said. 'Do you know anything about it?'

'The Guardian?'

'Yes, that's her. What's it all about? Jamey doesn't need a guardian. He has me.'

Doubtless Lacey would have been told of the Guardian's role, but I could appreciate how confusing it might be so I did my best to explain to her who the Guardian was and what she did.

'So she's supposed to be impartial and tell the judge what is best for Jamey? That's what our lawyer said.'

'Yes, that's right.'

'I can't wait. We'll start with me having proper contact. I want to see Jamey and he needs to see me.'

It wasn't really the Guardian's role to intervene in the present contact arrangements, but I didn't correct her. I felt sure Audrey would set her straight.

'Have you seen this Guardian woman yet?' Lacey asked.

'Yes, once.'

'And?'

'I just answered her questions. She didn't give me any feedback.'

'I hope you put in a good word for me. That poor boy is going to forget what I look like soon.'

'Would you like him to have a photograph of you?' I suggested. 'I usually frame some photos of the child's family and put them in their bedroom.'

'I'd rather he saw me in person, but I suppose that's better than nothing for now. Has he got a photo of his mother?'

'No, not yet. But he sees her.'

'I'll get one printed and drop it in at the Family Centre,' Lacey said.

'Great.'

After dinner that evening Jamey did his first poo in the potty. Needless to say, I was delighted. Paula less so, but she knew it was another milestone and praised him. Once he was using the potty confidently, I could start him using the toilet. I already had a child's toilet seat for when it was needed. The great advantage of the potty was that it was within reach, so I didn't have to worry about him making it to the toilet in time – a problem for young children.

The weather continued cold and frosty. Kat attended contact on Tuesday but not Thursday. No reason was given; she just didn't arrive. Lacey had dropped by at the centre on Wednesday and left an envelope at reception. Inside were two photographs – one of her and the other of Kat – which was kind of her. However, Kat's photo had been taken some years ago when she'd looked much younger, healthier and more fresh-faced, before drugs had ravaged her body and prematurely aged her. I showed them to Jamey and he pointed to Lacey and said her name straight away. Then he looked at the one of Kat and said uncertainly, 'Mummy?'

'Yes, that's right, love. It's a picture of Mummy when she was younger.'

I assumed that either Kat or Lacey had preferred to send this photo, which showed her in a better light, rather than a more recent one. The next day I bought photo frames and stood both pictures on a shelf in Jamey's bedroom.

When I telephoned Lacey at the weekend I thanked her for the pictures and told her Jamey had recognized her immediately. I'd assumed she'd be pleased as she'd been worried he would forget her. But she snapped at me.

'Of course he did! Like I told the Guardian, Jamey knows me as well as his mother. So it's not right I still can't see him. That Guardian was useless! All she did was take notes and ask stupid questions about stuff I'd already told his social worker. I showed her Jamey's bedroom here where his toys and clothes are. I told her he'll have outgrown them by the time he gets here. If he ever does!'

So I guessed the meeting hadn't gone well.

'I got annoyed with her,' Lacey continued. 'Then I burst into tears. I felt such a fool. But talking about Jamey made me upset so I had a real go at her. I bet she holds it against me.'

'I'm sure she won't,' I said. 'She'll appreciate how upsetting all this is for you.'

'She's coming back to see us both another time,' Lacey said. 'Andy as well. We've got the social worker coming next week too. It's non-stop and they ask the same stupid questions about our childhoods and how it might influence our parenting. I just want Jamey here again. He's missing me. I can tell from his face.'

I considered this. 'Have you seen Jamey recently then?' I asked after a moment, with a stab of unease.

'On Tuesday, coming out of the Family Centre.'

'You were there?'

'Yes, I've been a couple of times. I don't work Tuesday afternoons. Why? Aren't I allowed to go there?'

'I don't know. Does Shannon know you go?'

'No. And it's not like I go in and cause a fuss, although I'm tempted to. I just sit in my car and watch him leave with you.'

'Lacey, I don't think you should make a habit of it.'

'Why not? No one knows. Unless you tell them.'

This was difficult. 'I'll have to tell his social worker. I'm sorry, but at present you're only supposed to have telephone contact.'

'You old misery! I wish I hadn't told you.'

So did I. But as a foster carer I had a duty to tell the social worker of anything relevant to the child.

Lacey didn't give me the chance to explain; she hung up. I didn't call back. She needed time to calm down.

That evening I included what she'd said in my log notes and left it at that. I'd fulfilled my obligation and what action was taken, if any, was for Shannon to decide, assuming she read my log notes. Had it been anything more serious I would have drawn her attention to it, but I thought Lacey sitting outside the Family Centre on her day off to catch a glimpse of Jamey required compassion rather than concern.

In my email to Shannon I asked her if I could send Lacey some current photographs of Jamey and said that I had a set for Kat too. She replied telling me to send the pictures to her and she'd pass them on to Lacey and Kat. It struck me that she was being quite cautious in allowing Lacey any form of contact with Jamey. I assumed this was because if it was decided that Jamey couldn't live with Lacey then she'd have encouraged a bond between them that couldn't be maintained. If Jamey was adopted, he would probably only have 'letterbox' contact with his mother (when the parents are allowed to send the child a letter with a card at Christmas and on their birthday) and none with Lacey. Sad though that was, Jamey was young enough to have a fresh start.

As February continued concerns about the coronavirus grew. Cases were increasing across the world and passengers on a luxury cruise ship were being confined to their cabins after an outbreak on board. Unable to leave and with provisions running low, they were appealing to the government to do something and fly them home.

Meanwhile, in my less exotic but safer front room I printed some photos of Jamey for Kat and Lacey, which Jamey and I posted in the box at the end of the road. I was also taking photographs for Jamey's Life Story Book. Foster carers are expected to start or continue a Life Story Book for the child or children they are fostering. It is a record of the child's time with the carer and includes photographs, sometimes video clips on a USB stick, and memorabilia; for example, a child's first drawing or, for older children, merit certificates from school. It's an aide-mémoire which the child takes with them when they leave to supplement their own memories of their time in care and help them make sense of their past. It was especially important for a young child like Jamey who may only have limited memories of his time in care.

I took Jamey to the Health Centre to be weighed and measured and he'd put on another three ounces, which was good. The healthcare assistant entered it in the record book and on their system. I would also add it to my log notes.

On Friday morning we went to a playgroup held in a church hall not far away. Shannon had agreed it would do Jamey good. It was for two hours and run by a registered childminder, Carol, and her daughter, Lauri. There were about a dozen adults there with their children, and a small charge was made to cover the cost of drinks, a snack and the hire of the hall. Carol and Lauri were very welcoming and clearly loved working with children. They organized activities, including circle games and songs. There was also time for free, unstructured play.

Jamey was reluctant to begin with and wanted to sit on my lap, but then after a while he joined in and seemed to enjoy himself. It gave him the opportunity to mix with other pre-school children so I would try to go every Friday.

I had been due to attend training on Thursday that week but it had clashed with contact and contact always takes priority. In fact, a lot of the training arranged for the year was being held on Tuesdays and Thursdays, which was now difficult for me. I phoned Joy and explained the issue and we agreed I would make up the training when I could, although it had to be done by the end of the year. It was especially frustrating as Kat seldom attended contact on Thursdays, but I was still having to take Jamey on the off-chance she would arrive.

Both Joy and Shannon made their next scheduled visits in the last week of February when we discussed Jamey's progress, general health and wellbeing, and contact. Neither of them had anything new to tell me, but Jamey was more responsive and less shy. I think he was gradually getting used to having people come into the house. As well as the professionals connected with his case, my family and friends also visited.

As we saw Shannon out Jamey said, 'Bye,' without being prompted.

'Bye, Jamey,' Shannon said with an encouraging smile. 'See you soon.'

Little did either of us know we wouldn't be seeing each other in person for a very long time.

CHAPTER FOURTEEN

COVID-19

Ordinary people like me were now talking and worrying about what had become known as Covid-19. We were checking the news for any updates or new information on the spread of the virus. Scientists were being interviewed and a spokesperson from the World Health Organization (WHO) began appearing regularly on our television screens issuing statements. Interviewers asked if this was a pandemic and were told it wasn't, that while many countries were affected by coronavirus, it hadn't reached the level of a pandemic. Few believed it would.

Life continued much as normal. Wales confirmed its first case, but it was in someone who had recently returned from holiday abroad where there had been an outbreak. Likewise, three further cases in England were in people who had recently returned from abroad, which most of us found reassuring. These were still isolated cases that could be attributed to sources abroad. That was until the start of March when new cases began to be reported in the UK in people who hadn't travelled abroad.

Have you seen the news, Mum? Adrian texted.

I had and, worried, I phoned him.

Then the situation suddenly began to move very quickly as the government in the UK published a plan for dealing with coronavirus, which was now being likened to the flu pandemic of 1918 when one-third of the world's population became infected and 50 million people died. The plan included scenarios ranging from a mild outbreak to a severe one. It was very worrying. People overseas were now dying from the virus and then the first death from Covid-19 was confirmed in the UK. Heart-wrenching video footage began to be shown of patients struggling to breathe and on ventilators. Our Chief Medical Officer grimly announced that we had moved into the second stage of dealing with the virus from containment to delay, suggesting a pandemic was inevitable. The following week the WHO officially declared it a pandemic.

I think there was a sense of disbelief that this was actually happening. It was like being caught in a disaster movie. Surely the human race was too advanced to be at the mercy of a virus? Something you couldn't even see. But viruses, I learnt, were very clever. They'd been evolving for over a billion years and while they needed a host (for example, us) to survive, they'd become adept at entering our bodies, where they could thrive. The virus, I read, inserted its genetic material into the host cell and took over its function. They make us sick by killing or disrupting our cell function. Our bodies often respond with fever because heat inactivates many viruses, giving our immune system a chance to fight back and produce antibodies. I vaguely remembered studying all this at school, but suddenly it became terrifyingly relevant.

Even so, for the time being our lives were continuing much as usual: going to work, shopping, seeing friends and family, and I was busy looking after Jamey. He was now using his potty confidently and would either fetch it or say 'potty' when he needed to go. This was wonderful, and although he still wore trainer pants he wasn't having many accidents at all. He was also remembering the new words and skills I was teaching him; for example, how to dress himself, use cutlery and colour in pictures. However, it wasn't until Lucy commented when she collected Emma one Wednesday afternoon that I fully appreciated just how far Jamey had come.

'When you think back to Christmas and compare him to how he is now, he's so much more confident and asks for things. He's becoming his own little person.'

She was right, and while Jamey still had a lot of catching up to do compared to the average child his age, he had improved tremendously. He was due to have another medical at the end of March and I was looking forward to hearing what the paediatrician had to say when she checked him over. He also had his second review coming up the same week and I was planning on asking if Thursday contact could be suspended as Kat was making no attempt to attend. It wasn't fair on Jamey and was a waste of time when we could be doing other things.

We were halfway through March and the days were growing longer. The evenings and nights were still very cold, but some days there was a spring-like feel to the air. Birds were singing and starting to nest-build and early-flowering bulbs were blooming. Jamey and I were spending more time outdoors when we played in the garden or a park. On Wednesday I took him and Emma to our local park; to get there Emma rode in the stroller and Jamey walked beside me. He rose to the occasion and suddenly seemed much older beside a younger child.

'Push Emma,' he said.

'You can help me push, yes, love,' I replied.

We continued pushing the stroller together until Emma saw what was happening and cried, 'No, Jamey!'

She liked her own way and to have all my attention. Now they were spending every Wednesday together they were more like brother and sister, playing nicely and then squabbling. If there was a squabble – usually over a toy Jamey had and Emma wanted – I made sure I dealt with it fairly, otherwise Jamey would have given in to Emma each time.

While we were in the park and I was going from one piece of play equipment to another, helping Jamey and Emma on and off them, pushing a swing, turning the roundabout and generally making sure they were safe, a woman my age remarked I had my hands full. We got talking and she told me she looked after her grandson two days a week. Inevitably the conversation turned to the pandemic and how worrying it was. She said people were starting to panic buy and asked if I'd stocked up. I hadn't, and I quietly thought she might be exaggerating. However, after we'd said goodbye and I was on the way home, Lucy telephoned.

'Mum,' she said, anxiety in her voice. 'It seems the shops are selling out of basic items and Emma is low on nappies. Can you look after her for a bit longer this after-noon while I go to the supermarket?'

'Yes, of course, love.'

'Do you need anything?'

I had a quick think, but I was concentrating on Emma and Jamey as they'd both wanted to walk home so I didn't give it a lot of thought.

'I'll be doing a normal weekly shop tomorrow so don't worry,' I said. 'I'll get what I need then.'

'Sure?'

'Yes. I'll give Emma some dinner, so don't worry.'

'Thanks, Mum.'

Either Lucy or Darren collected Emma – whoever finished their shift first – usually arriving by 5 p.m.

We continued home where, exhausted from walking and playing in the park, Jamey and Emma both fell asleep on the sofa, which gave me a chance to start preparing dinner for later. They slept for nearly an hour. Paula arrived home at 6 p.m. but there was still no sign of Lucy. Then Darren texted to say he would be collecting Emma. He'd just left work and was on his way. He arrived at 6.30.

'Lucy's only just managed to buy some nappies,' he said. 'She's been searching the shops for over an hour. It's mayhem out there. People are panic buying.'

Paula agreed. 'A woman at work went out at lunch-time to buy hand gel, but she couldn't get any anywhere.'

'They'll have restocked the shelves by tomorrow,' I said. 'I'll go a bit earlier than usual.'

The following morning after breakfast I explained to Jamey we were going shopping, and we arrived at the supermarket at 9.30 to find most of the shelves empty. There was no toilet paper, cat food, tea bags, pasta or soap, which were all on my list. I asked an assistant when they would restock their shelves and he said he wasn't sure, that their stock room was empty and they were waiting for deliveries. The government were advising us to wash our hands regularly so I could understand why all the soap had gone, but why cat food and pasta? Panic buying had created a shortage.

I bought the few items they did have that were on my list and then I spent the rest of the morning going from one supermarket to another, trying to buy the other items. Eventually I discovered toilet paper and cat food in a small corner shop that others hadn't thought of yet, but I'd wasted most of the morning. There was just enough time to go home and give Jamey lunch before we had to leave again for the Family Centre. As we entered the receptionist said, 'Oh, you needn't have bothered. Kat phoned to say she isn't coming as she is worried about catching Covid.'

'I see,' I said, trying to hide my frustration. 'It would have been really helpful if someone could have phoned to save me a wasted trip.'

'Sorry, I thought someone had.'

'No worries,' I said, and left.

Poor Jamey had spent the day so far getting in and out of the car, so instead of going straight home I took him to a small animal sanctuary in a park close by. It housed some birds and small animals that had been rescued and were now recovering. I'd brought my children here when they were little, and other children I'd fostered. It survived on donations and voluntary help and, while small, it was something new for Jamey. He peered interestedly at the birds recovering from injury in the aviary and said, 'Birds.' Three ducks waddled around a small pond and quacked as we passed. A barn owl had his own enclosure; he was a permanent resident as he couldn't fly.

'Look at his big eyes,' I said to Jamey. 'Owls can turn their heads two hundred and seventy degrees.'

As we looked, the owl swivelled its head round and then closed one eye as if winking. Jamey was fascinated, and so was I.

That night I put away the cushions that had been around Jamey's bed, as he'd never fallen out. I also put away his security rag. He hadn't used it since he'd first arrived and it had lain discarded in a corner of his room. At night he now snuggled up to one of the soft toys we'd given him. As well as Christmas presents, my family and I often bought him a small gift. I didn't throw away his rag, though, as it was part of his life story, as were the clothes he'd arrived in. In years to come he might be interested to see them, so I put them all away to pass on to his forever family.

Once Jamey was tucked up in bed, I said goodnight.

'Night,' he said, with the cutest smile, peeping out from over the duvet.

'Sleep well, love,' I said.

As I leant forward to kiss his forehead, he wrapped his arms around me and gave me a big hug. 'Cathy, Mummy,' he said.

I knew what he meant.

'I'm like a mummy to you,' I said, and held him close.

That evening on the news we were told not to panic buy as there was plenty for everyone! Not in my experience, I felt like shouting at the television screen, and Paula nodded in agreement. We had started to make a point of watching the evening news together for the latest on the pandemic, and sometimes we struggled to take in the enormity of what was unfolding. The government was now advising anyone with a new, continuous cough or a fever to self-isolate for seven days, and that the elderly and those with underlying health conditions should take particular care. Some countries were imposing travel bans and insisting people wore a face mask in public places. Our Prime Minister announced that millions of pounds would be available for research into a coronavirus vaccine and rapid diagnostic testing. He said he was also going to start holding a daily televised press conference to update the nation on the fight against the pandemic. The news ended with a piece about the drastic fall in the value of shares as stock markets around the world reacted to the chaos and uncertainty of the pandemic. Not that I had any shares, but the news was all doom and gloom.

On a lighter note, jokes about the scarcity of toilet paper were now circulating on social media. I laughed out loud as I forwarded some of them to my family and friends. Thank goodness we still had our sense of humour, I thought.

In the next update from the government we were 'advised' to avoid non-essential travel and contact with others, to work from home if possible and avoid visiting social venues such as pubs, clubs or theatres. Large gatherings – for example, football matches and music festivals – should not take place. Theatres and cinemas closed, but there was some confusion about what we should or should not be doing, for this was advice, not law.

When I phoned Lacey at the weekend she said she was still going into the school where she worked as a teaching assistant, but there were rumours that the government would soon be closing schools, which was happening in other countries affected by the pandemic.

On Tuesday, having not heard anything to the contrary, I took Jamey to the Family Centre for contact. As soon as the receptionist saw me she picked up her phone and said, 'I haven't heard from his mother. I'll call her now and see if she's coming. I'm not sure what's happening.'

I waited with Jamey in reception while she made the call.

'Are you on your way?' she asked Kat. I couldn't hear her reply, but then the receptionist said, 'I'll tell her. Thank you.' Replacing the handset, she said to me, 'Kat's not coming. She's worried she'll catch coronavirus. She says she'll come when the virus has gone away.'

Fair enough, I thought, although it crossed my mind that Kat probably stood a greater chance of dying prematurely from drug- and alcohol-related issues than the virus.

'Does that mean she's definitely not coming on Thursday and next week?' I asked.

'I don't know,' the receptionist replied. 'She didn't say. You'll have to ask his social worker.'

Which is what I did. Once home, I emailed Shannon, telling her what Kat had said and asking if I should bring Jamey to the Family Centre for contact. She didn't reply. But it wasn't long before my question was answered as the Prime Minister soon announced strict new rules aimed at reducing the spread of the disease. We were all told to stay at home, except for shopping for essential items (such as food and medicine). We were allowed one form of outdoor exercise each day (such as walking, running or cycling), either alone or with others who lived in the same household, but we had to socially distance ourselves from others. We could leave the house if we needed medical attention, to provide care to a vulnerable person or to travel to and from work if the work could not be done at home. Schools were to close except for key workers and children considered vulnerable. Whole households would now have to quarantine for fourteen days if someone had a symptom of Covid-19, and those who were at high risk should isolate themselves for twelve weeks. Non-essential shops, libraries, places of worship, playgrounds and gyms were to shut, and the police were to be given powers to enforce the rules, including the use of fines. Similar measures were being introduced in other countries. Although the term lockdown wasn't actually used, it very quickly became known as that.

'Do you think I'll have to go to work?' Paula asked me, concerned.

'I've no idea, love. I suppose it will depend on whether you can work from home. I'm guessing your boss will tell you.'

I texted Lucy: *Is your nursery closing? x*
I don't know. We're waiting to hear x

I texted Adrian, asking him if he still had to go into the office. He worked for a firm of accountants. He replied, *Not sure yet. I could work from home with the right software.*

More news of what had become known as our fight against coronavirus dominated our television screen.

There were interviews with scientists, doctors, statisticians and commentators, all giving their views on the spread of the virus and how it should be contained. More harrowing video footage from countries that were further into the pandemic than we were showed hospital wards at capacity and mass burials. Yet out of this came a sense of camaraderie and solidarity. People were unifying and helping others. I thought of my dear mother and her strength and stoicism and could almost hear her say, 'Don't worry, dear. We will come through this together.'

CHAPTER FIFTEEN

CLOSER TOGETHER

Paula received an email from the management at her work, subject line: *Covid-19*. It said that, following the latest government restrictions to prevent the spread of coronavirus, the offices would be closed for most workers until further notice; they should work from home where possible and department managers would be in touch to confirm arrangements. Paula was in her dressing gown when she read the email and had been about to get ready for work. I was in Jamey's bedroom helping him dress.

'But, Mum, I can't work from home,' Paula said, worried. 'I don't have access to the files on my laptop.'

'I'm sure they've thought of that, but you could email your departmental manager and let them know.'

'Do you think I should? Won't they think I'm being rude?'

'No, love. It's up to you, but that's what I'd do, or reply to the email you've received. It lets them know you've read the email and are concerned. What's happening now is unprecedented. It will take time for businesses to adjust.'

She returned to her bedroom, not wholly convinced. I finished helping Jamey dress – allowing him to do most of it himself – then took him downstairs for break-fast.

I was just wondering how Lucy, Darren, Adrian and Kirsty were faring with the announcement of lockdown when Lucy texted. *Nursery closed today. Might have to go in tomorrow. Depends how many children we have. I'll let you know about Emma.*

OK, love, take care xx, I replied. Lucy and Darren were key workers.

As Jamey ate his breakfast, I telephoned Adrian. It was the time he would normally be leaving for work, but he was staying at home awaiting further instructions from his boss. He thought it was likely he would be working from home, but the school where Kirsty worked was closed. He said they may reopen a small part of it for the children of key workers and those children considered vulnerable.

The same uncertainty appeared to run through the social services. Shortly after 9 a.m. I telephoned Shannon and Joy to ask about contact arrangements but was met with their out-of-hours answerphones, so I left messages. We were due to have contact that afternoon so when I hadn't heard anything by 11.30 I tried them both again, with the same result. Kat had said she wasn't going, but I needed confirmation from Shannon. I telephoned the Family Centre and the manager answered. She said they were closed until further notice and that she was only there to phone those who had contact over the next few days and to turn away anyone who arrived. She said she'd already spoken to Kat and I was next on her list. She added that I needed to ask my child's social worker about future contact arrangements.

Half an hour later Joy returned my call and confirmed all face-to-face contact was being suspended until further notice and Jamey should speak to his mother on the phone instead, which she hadn't wanted to do.

'So you want me to try on a Tuesday and Thursday?' I checked.

'Yes. We are looking into using video-conferencing calls like Zoom, Microsoft Teams, WhatsApp or Skype. You're all right using that technology?'

'I expect so. I use WhatsApp and Skype, but I've never heard of the others.'

'No, neither had I,' Joy admitted. 'It's going to be a bit of a learning curve. Nothing's been decided yet, so just phone his mother for now. There will be an email going out to all carers before long.'

'And should I phone Lacey, his aunt, as usual at the weekend?'

'Yes, I assume so.'

I explained the new arrangements as best I could to Jamey, then made the three of us lunch. At one o'clock, when Jamey would normally have seen his mother, I phoned her as Joy had said. It went through to voicemail, so I left a message. 'Hi, Kat, Cathy here, Jamey's foster carer. I think you've heard that the Family Centre is closed so it's just phone contact for now. I'll try again in ten minutes.'

I tried every ten minutes for the next hour, but Kat didn't answer. I tried once more at 2.15 and then left another message. 'Hi, Kat, it's Cathy, I hope you are OK. I'll try again on Thursday.' I wasn't unduly worried that she wasn't answering as the manager of the Family Centre had said she'd spoken to her earlier.

Paula had taken my advice and emailed her departmental manager but hadn't received a reply, and she'd spent the morning wandering around looking worried and not sure what she should be doing.

'If you haven't got access to the files you need then you can't do anything,' I said. 'You've done all you can and it's a nice spring day so let's go out for a walk.'

'Are we allowed to?' she asked, concerned.

I had to stop and think. 'Yes, we are one household so we can go for a walk each day as long as we keep away from others. Let's take Jamey to the park.'

I didn't bother taking the stroller as Paula was with me to help if Jamey got tired and needed to be carried. We set off on a slow walk up the road towards our local park. Despite the weather being fine, the streets were deserted, which was rather unsettling, eerie, post-apocalyptic. Paula thought so too. When we arrived at the park the gates were shut and padlocked.

'What?' I exclaimed. 'I can understand the children's play area being shut off.' The government had said playgrounds would be closed. 'But why the whole park?'

Paula checked the padlock, but it was definitely locked. As we turned to retrace our footsteps a woman walking her dog came towards us.

'Is that gate closed too?' she sighed.

'Yes.'

'I've just tried the other two. The whole park is locked up. Seems a bit excessive to me.'

I agreed.

'I thought we were being encouraged to go out for a walk and have some fresh air each day,' she said, keeping her distance.

We chatted for a few minutes while maintaining social distancing, which felt strange, then we said goodbye and set off for home. Jamey could play in our garden, but what about all those families, especially in flats, who didn't have their own garden and relied on communal outdoor spaces and public parks? How would they manage? They couldn't be expected to stay indoors for weeks on end. I guessed their only option was to walk the streets.

Paula, Jamey and I spent most of the afternoon in the garden where Sammy joined us. Paula played with Jamey while I tidied up the garden from winter. Paula had her phone in her jacket pocket and checked it regularly in case her work contacted her again, but they didn't. It was a very unsettling time for many, and later Lucy texted to say she didn't need me to look after Emma the next day. The nursery was open but only a few children were attending so they didn't need all the staff. Lucy was working and Darren was going to stay at home to look after Emma. Childcare was exempt from the restrictions on households mixing.

I texted back, telling Lucy to let me know if they needed any help and to stay safe. I was concerned that she was going to work where she could potentially contract the virus. At that point I didn't know when I would see any of them again. We couldn't just visit each other as we usually did.

Despite all the uncertainty, Jamey was largely unaffected by the changes, although that wasn't true of other children in care. The following day I heard from two foster-carer friends who were struggling. One was looking after a brother and sister, aged seven and nine, who were used to seeing their mother three times a week and were understandably distraught at not seeing her at all. Another carer was looking after a girl of fourteen who, having been told that contact had been cancelled for the time being, stormed out of the foster carer's home and went to see her family anyway.

It was a similar story when I logged into the online support group for foster carers I was a member of. To maintain confidentiality, our identities and those of any children we looked after were anonymized. It was a useful platform for keeping in touch with other carers, pooling our knowledge and generally supporting each other. I soon learnt that many carers were experiencing difficulties and that local authorities were responding at different rates. Some carers had already begun using video calls to replace contact, while others hadn't received any instructions at all. I guessed it would take time before a cohesive policy was formed and we were all advised what to do.

Later that day I spoke to Adrian to see how he and Kirsty were getting on. He said he was now working from home and Kirsty was preparing lessons for the children in her class so they could continue their learning from home online, as was happening in other schools.

Paula finally received an email from her departmental manager saying he was setting up a Zoom telephone conference the following morning for 9 a.m., which threw her into a bit of a spin.

'I don't know what to do,' she said. 'I've never used Zoom before.' She showed me the email, which contained a number of links, phone numbers, login codes and instructions. It did look a bit daunting.

'We can have a look at it later when Jamey is in bed,' I suggested. 'I need to know how to use it too.'

Paula nodded but didn't look reassured. She returned to her bedroom and then reappeared half an hour later, having worked out what to do. She showed me. It wasn't difficult if you just followed the instructions. I think it's the prospect of new technology that can throw us into panic mode.

That evening on the news we were given the latest grim figures of those who had died from Covid-19 and those who'd tested positive. Sadly, included in the death toll were two NHS doctors and a British diplomat abroad. Prince Charles had tested positive so clearly no one was exempt. The Prime Minister warned us that stricter measures would be imposed if we didn't all follow government guidelines. Parliament closed for a month. We also learnt that nurses who had left the profession or retired were being asked to return to help as hospitals filled up. There was nothing optimistic in the news that night, and the whole concept of being in a pandemic felt surreal.

The following morning Paula was up and dressed at the time she would have normally gone to work in preparation for the conference call her manager had arranged, although it was by phone and not video, so she wouldn't be seen. At 8.45 she disappeared into her bedroom with her laptop, ready to log in, while I kept Jamey downstairs playing quietly.

'Where Paula?' he asked.

'In her room. She will be down soon.'

He had begun to ask 'where' questions – 'Where Sammy?' 'Where drink?' 'Where bus?' and so on. I was pleased, as this was another step in the development of his language skills.

Paula was in her room for the next hour. I heard her voice a few times and also that of a man in the conference call who was rather loud. It was just before 10 a.m. before she finally appeared, looking relieved.

'How did it go?' I asked her.

'Yes, good. It took me a few minutes to log in, but I wasn't the only one. Some of the others had difficulties and joined the meeting late.'

'Well done. What have they said about work?'

'They're going to send me some files to work on, but they will see how it goes. They've already had some orders cancelled and they're expecting more cancellations during lockdown. They mentioned a government scheme to furlough workers. I've just been reading about it. It seems that, rather than make employees redundant, the employer can keep them on and they receive eighty per cent of their salary even though they are not working. Then, once lockdown is lifted, they go back to work.'

'Hopefully it won't come to that,' I said, ever the optimist.

Paula had a trainee administrative position in a manufacturing firm, and I thought it was a great pity that her first permanent post after leaving college was now under threat.

That afternoon at 1 p.m. I telephoned Kat.

'Who's that?' she asked blearily.

'Cathy, Jamey's carer.'

'Why are you phoning?'

'It's Thursday. I've been asked to phone you on Tuesdays and Thursdays when you used to have contact.'

'OK. How is he?' she asked, no less groggily.

'He's doing well. I'm keeping him busy. I tried to phone you on Tuesday. Did you get my messages?'

'I guess so.'

'Would you like to speak to Jamey now, or is this not a good time?'

'I'll talk to him if he's there.'

'I'll put him on.'

I engaged the speaker and then said to Jamey, 'It's Mummy, say hello.'

'Hello,' he said in a small, tentative voice.

'Hi, pet. Are you being good?'

'Yes,' he replied, without being prompted.

'What have you been doing?'

I mouthed 'playing' and Jamey said, 'Playing.'

'So I'll see you on Tuesday then. I'm still in bed and I need to get up now.'

I took the phone off speaker and said, 'Kat, the Family Centre is closed during lockdown, so I think I'll be phoning you again next Tuesday.'

'Really?' She sounded confused, as if she might have just woken up.

'I'll put Jamey back on,' I said, and engaged the speaker again.

Then I heard a male voice ask who she was talking to.

'My son,' she replied. Then to Jamey she said, 'I have to go. I'll see you next Tuesday.'

'We'll phone,' I managed to remind her before the line went dead.

'Where Mummy?' Jamey asked, looking puzzled.

'She had to go, love.'

He accepted this in his own quiet way and was soon playing. Phone contact with Kat hadn't worked in the past and it seemed it wasn't any different now.

I received a text from the playgroup Jamey had been attending on a Friday saying that due to government restrictions it was closed until further notice, which I'd assumed. Shannon emailed to say that Jamey's review was being postponed, and I received a phone call from the Health Centre cancelling his second medical.

'Can we rebook it?' I asked.

'No, because we don't know when we will be able to reopen.'

It seemed our worlds were closing in. It was the first time I could remember a review ever being postponed. They took priority over everything. When Paula and I tuned in for the Prime Minister's daily briefing he announced another grim milestone: the number of deaths in the UK from coronavirus in a single day had passed 100, and thousands had tested positive, so the virus was spreading 'exponentially'. It was a word we were going to hear repeatedly in the weeks to come. That, and the 'R' number, which measured the rate at which the virus was being passed on.

The only upbeat part of the news was video footage from around the world showing those in lockdown coming out of their homes once a week to clap and praise their healthcare workers and generally raise morale. We were now being asked to do a similar thing at 8 p.m. that evening and each Thursday in what was being called 'clap for carers', although it included all key workers.

I wasn't sure people would do it. But at 8 p.m. I opened my front door and tentatively peered out to see some of my neighbours doing the same. Paula was at my bedroom window, which overlooked the street. I went further out and stood on the pavement as others were doing up and down the road as far as I could see. Someone began clapping and we all joined in; whistles blew and pan lids clashed – anything to communicate our praise and thanks. Then someone began to play a recording of the song 'You'll Never Walk Alone' and my eyes filled. It was so moving, all of us together in a crisis.

We kept the clapping going until the music stopped, but even then we didn't immediately return indoors. Maintaining social distancing, we began talking to each other, even those we didn't really know well. Men began striking up conversations with other men, and children played in the deserted road. An elderly lady, Jean, whom I knew by sight, appeared at her garden gate further up the road and I called over to her.

'Do you have everything you need?'

'Yes, thank you, dear. My son has done my shopping for me.'

I gave her the thumbs-up sign. 'Let me know if you need anything.'

'Thank you. I will,' she called back. 'Everyone is so kind.' Then another neighbour began talking to her.

It was half an hour before the street cleared and I think we all returned indoors feeling uplifted. I know I did. What had just taken place – that camaraderie – wasn't often experienced in modern society, and of course the nurses, doctors and key workers appreciated our display of thanks. The news was full of it, with video footage of some areas. Lucy, Adrian and some of my friends texted to say they'd been outside clapping and what a lovely atmosphere there'd been. It seemed the pandemic that had forced us apart had, in fact, brought us all closer together.

CHAPTER SIXTEEN

MEETING THE CHALLENGE

The next day the Prime Minister and other Members of Parliament tested positive for Covid-19 and had to self-isolate. It was another timely reminder that none of us was safe. Some of them had symptoms, but others didn't. It seemed to be a worrying trait of the virus that you could have it and infect others without realizing it or being ill yourself. Also on the news was the story that a senior government advisor had been caught breaking the lockdown restrictions, and he was being castigated by the media – rightly so. If we all had to follow the restrictions, so should he.

Paula was sent some work to do and sat at the table in the front room with her laptop while I kept Jamey amused in another room. We made some cookies – he loved working with the dough, although clearing up afterwards lasted longer than the activity itself! Paula joined us for lunch and said she only had about another hour's work to do and was wondering what she should do then. I suggested she let her manager know once she'd finished.

After lunch I took Jamey into the garden. It was mild for the time of year so we just needed our warm trousers, jumpers and jackets. I took the early-years toys from the shed and, once he was playing, I started weeding the flowerbeds. I could hear other children playing in gardens around me. It was strange on a weekday when they would normally have been in school. I was kneeling to weed and every so often Jamey would run over, throw his arms around my neck and give me a big hug, then run off again. It was a bit of a game, so I chased after him and he chuckled. He seemed interested in what I was doing so I found the child's gardening tool set in the shed, and he knelt beside me and began digging the earth. He liked getting messy in the soil and learnt some new words – for example, 'plant', 'snail', 'worm', 'spider' and 'yucky'. Paula finished her work and joined us, playing football with Jamey while keeping an eye on her phone in case her manager called or emailed, but he didn't.

On Saturday when I telephoned Lacey I began by asking her how she was, not just out of politeness, but a genuine enquiry as to whether she was well. It was a question being asked by many now, and most emails and texts began with the words: *I hope you are well*. She said she was and had been into the infant school where she worked part time as a TA, supporting some vulnerable children and those of key workers. She said there were only fifteen children in the whole school, but they were expecting more the following week. They had moved the tables apart and had hand sanitizer in the room, but it was difficult to stop young children getting close to each other, especially when they played. They were providing each child with a meal and checking with the parents that they were coping. The TA's role, like the teacher, has an element of social care anyway, but it was more pronounced now we were in lockdown and families were isolated.

'How are you all doing?' Lacey asked.

'Good, considering,' I replied. 'Jamey is content to play at home.'

'I understand that video calls are being used to replace contact,' she said. 'I asked for a video call right at the start and was told they weren't used for contact. I'm pushing for it now. I've left messages at the social services and also with my lawyer. But everything is taking ages. Is Kat having a video call?'

'No. Only a phone call. We haven't started using video calls yet.'

'Typical! They need to get a move on.'

I sympathized but didn't say too much, for even if we did start using video calls there was no guarantee Lacey would have one, as they seemed to be replacing face-to-face contact, which she didn't have yet. I had no idea what stage her and her partner's assessment had reached, but I guessed it had been put on hold or was taking longer than normal, as was the case in other matters due to lock-down.

'I'll put Jamey on to speak to you,' I said, and engaged the speaker. 'Say hello to Aunty Lacey,' I told him.

'Hello, Aunty Lacey,' he said very clearly.

'Hi, love. Nice to hear you. What have you been doing?'

'Snailing,' he replied.

'Sailing?' she asked, puzzled, although I guessed what he'd meant.

'I think he's trying to tell you he found some snails in the garden,' I said.

'Yes, snails,' Jamey said excitedly, and she laughed.

I prompted Jamey where necessary and they had a reasonable conversation for a child his age. Jamey was getting used to the phone and, of course, he knew more words now so was better able to express himself.

That afternoon Paula, Jamey and I went for a walk. We needed a change from the house and garden. We saw other households also going for their daily walk. Sometimes we just said hello and continued past, while other times we stopped to talk for a few minutes, always maintaining social distancing. It was weird standing so far apart, and also having to step into the road or a driveway to pass each other if the pavement was narrow. I usually hug a friend or good acquaintance on meeting, but now the government had told us to stay two metres apart, so like most people we were abiding by that. We didn't have to wear face masks at that time; that would come later. The park gates were still closed and now a large printed notice was tied to them:

CLOSED DUE TO COVID.

So we walked up and down the roads and then home again.

I telephoned Adrian and spoke to him and Kirsty. They'd been out for a walk too. Lucy made a WhatsApp video call to my mobile, which was great as I got to see them all, including Emma, although she was a bit confused and tried to grab the screen when Paula and I waved and talked to her.

The following afternoon we went out for a walk again in what was becoming part of our new daily routine. As we passed Jean's house – the elderly lady I'd spoken to when we'd been clapping for our carers – she opened her front door to let out her cat.

'Hi, Jean,' I called, pausing on the pavement. 'How are you?'

'I'm all right, thanks, can't grumble, there's worse off than me. How are you?'

'Good.'

We talked for a bit about Covid and the devastation it was causing around the world, with Jean at her front door and us well away from her on the pavement. As we were preparing to leave I asked, 'Have you got everything you need?'

'Yes, apart from tea bags.' She sighed and rolled her eyes. 'I am a fool. I forgot to put them on the shopping list for my son. I'm right out, but it can wait until next week.'

'I could get you some from Dells Stores,' I offered. 'We're walking in that direction.' Dells Stores was a small corner shop in the High Street that most people knew about and was open seven days a week, 6 a.m. to midnight.

'Would you, dear? Thank you. That is kind. I'm not a coffee drinker and I miss my cups of tea. Normally I do my own shopping, but my son doesn't want me to go out. I suppose I have to be careful at my age.'

'Absolutely. I'll get you some tea bags. Is there anything else?'

'No, thank you, dear.'

I said I'd drop them off on the way back and we continued up the road to Dells Stores in the High Street, only to find they were completely out of tea bags and other basic items. I asked the store manager when they were expecting more in and he said he didn't know as panic buying was still creating shortages and some warehouses were empty. He said that some large stores were starting to ration items like tea bags, hand soap, toilet paper and canned goods as people were stockpiling. He thought he might have to do the same. The last time I'd heard of rationing was in connection with the Second World War when there was a real shortage of many items. But this shortage was due to people buying more than they needed and storing it, which meant that people like Jean went without. I was still doing my normal weekly shop and with just the three of us we weren't getting through that much. Even so, there would come a point when we ran out of essential items.

But of course I wouldn't let Jean go without her cups of tea. When we finished our walk we returned home where I took two sealed packets of tea bags from the box and, leaving Jamey with Paula, I returned to Jean's house. I put the foil-wrapped packets on her doorstep, then rang her doorbell and stood well back. She came to the door with her purse in her hand and then, seeing the packets at her feet, looked at me questioningly. I explained what had happened and she thanked me.

'There should be plenty there to see you through,' I said. 'But let me know if you run out again.'

'Oh, bless you, dear,' she said, picking them up.

She was so grateful and wanted to pay for them, which of course I didn't accept. But I did leave her my landline and mobile numbers in case she needed anything in the future. I knew that her son and immediate neighbours were looking out for her, but you can't have too many supporting you in a time of crisis.

The news that evening included the rising death toll and the number of those testing positive both in the UK and around the world. We were told that 'things would get worse before they got better' and that the current restrictions could be in place for six months!

On Monday, as the Health Centre was closed for routine appointments, I weighed Jamey at home and entered his weight in the record book they had given me. I was still taking plenty of photographs of Jamey, some now showing life in lockdown. I was also updating Joy and Shannon regularly by email and they replied thanking me and said they would be in touch, but that I should phone if I needed any help in an emergency. Paula received some more work and around lunchtime I opened an email from the director of children's social care for the county. It had been sent to all foster carers in the region and began by thanking us for all we were doing in these extraordinarily demanding circumstances. It said that supervising social workers (SSWs) were working hard to contact all carers and gather information to find out what help they needed. It went on to say that to minimize the spread of the virus there would be no more home visits for the time being, and supervisory sessions would be by phone or virtual conferencing. An emergency number was included for anyone unable to get in touch with their SSW. Training, support groups and other meetings where foster carers gathered would be postponed, while reviews would take place online.

There was then a paragraph about school-aged children, which said that in line with government guidelines foster carers could be considered as key workers, so children in care should still be able to attend school. Then followed a similar paragraph to the one that had been appearing at the end of Joy's and Shannon's emails: *If any member of the household contracts coronavirus they should stay home for fourteen days, seek medical assistance if necessary, and advise their supervising social worker and the child's social worker.* There were links to various NHS websites that offered further help and advice, including one on our emotional health and how to talk to our children about coronavirus.

I'd just finished reading the lengthy email and had filed it in my fostering folder when Joy phoned.

'Sorry I haven't been in touch sooner but we've had to prioritize our most vulnerable children. How are you all?'

'All right – plodding along, like most people,' I replied.

'Is anyone in your family having to shield, considered vulnerable, ill or displaying signs of coronavirus?' Joy said. 'I have to ask.'

'No, we are all well,' I confirmed.

'Have you been in contact with anyone who has tested positive or is awaiting a test result or displaying symptoms?' she asked.

'No.'

'And you're aware of and following the lockdown restrictions?'

'Yes, and Paula is working from home.' I assumed Joy was noting this or ticking boxes on a spreadsheet as she paused between each question and sounded rather formal.

'No one in the house is over seventy, pregnant or has a serious medical condition?' she checked.

'No.'

'I need to ask you what would happen in the event of you being unable to care for Jamey due to you becoming ill yourself.'

I thought of saying that I couldn't afford to be ill as I was too busy, but I knew this wasn't a time for flippancy.

'I suppose it would depend on how ill I was,' I said, balking at the idea. 'Paula is one of my nominated carers and she lives here, so she would look after Jamey if I couldn't or if I had to self-isolate in one room. But if I was in hospital, I don't know what would happen. Lucy is my other nominated carer, but she is in a different household.' The implications of me being ill in the present circumstances became all too apparent.

'So we'll say Paula then,' Joy said.

'Yes.'

'And you know that if anyone in the household displays symptoms, they need to self-isolate?' Joy checked.

'Yes.'

'Did you receive the email from our director?'

'Just now.'

'Do you have any questions?'

'Not really. Jamey isn't in school or nursery, and the playgroup I've been taking him to has stopped. I'm weighing him at home as the Health Centre is closed. His next medical has been cancelled and I've let Shannon know.'

'Thank you. How is he?'

'He's doing all right. Playing in the house and some-times the garden. We go out for a walk each day. He's still eating and sleeping well.'

'And telephone contact?' Joy asked. 'I saw your update.'

'It's about the same. Lacey talks to him, but the calls to his mother are problematic.'

'Shannon will be in touch to rearrange Jamey's review. It will be online, as will my next visit. I'll let you know the details once I have them. If you need any help or advice, either phone me or the emergency number on the director's letter.'

'I will, thank you. Have any of the carers been affected?' I asked. At that point I didn't know anyone personally who had contracted the virus.

'One family is having to self-isolate pending testing,' Joy replied.

'Oh dear. I hope they're OK.' I didn't ask who, as it was confidential, but it was another indication of just how close the virus was coming.

Joy wound up by saying Shannon would be in touch to confirm future contact arrangements and, telling me to 'stay safe,' said goodbye. Her manner had been more sombre and serious than usual, less chatty, and I felt even more keenly the menace of this unseen enemy that was crossing the world and threatening our lives.

Half an hour later Shannon phoned. It seemed it had taken a while for the social services to mobilize and address what needed to be done, but now they were meeting the challenge of coronavirus. Shannon began much the same as Joy had, by asking how we were and if anyone in the family was ill, displaying signs of the virus, self-isolating or waiting for a test result. I gave her the same replies I'd given Joy, but not knowing me as well as Joy did she asked for more information about Paula and her movements. I said she was working from home and obeying the lockdown rules as I was, and the only time we left the house was to go for our daily walk and shopping. Although in future I thought I would go to the supermarket alone to reduce the risk of one of us catching the virus.

Shannon then asked specifically about Jamey and his routine, health and general wellbeing, as she would have done at a visit. She asked to speak to Jamey and I tried, but other than 'hello', and then 'yes' when she asked him how he was, he didn't say anything. She understood. She said the Family Centre would still be supporting contact, but it would be virtual and they would email me with details of the app and login codes. Contact would take place on the same days and at the same time as before.

'I see from your updates that telephone contact hasn't been a success so hopefully this will be better,' Shannon said. 'I've explained to Kat what's happening, and from this Saturday Lacey's phone call will be a video call, and again the Family Centre will send you the login details.'

'I imagine Lacey is pleased,' I said.

'Only a little,' Shannon replied. 'Her assessment has slowed due to coronavirus, but she needs to understand this is beyond my control and affects us all. I'm organizing Jamey's review. It will be virtual. I'll send you the details and where to get technical support if you need it.'

'Thank you, and how are you?' I asked.

'Not good, if I'm honest,' Shannon replied. 'My mother is in a care home – no visitors are allowed, and now I've just heard they have a case of coronavirus. Not my mother, but a friend of hers.'

'I am so sorry,' I said.

'Thank you.' She sighed.

It was easy to forget that social workers had their own problems as well as those of their clients.

That evening on the news we learnt that the government was arranging to fly home thousands of tourists stranded abroad due to airport closures, cancelled flights and coronavirus restrictions. The daily death toll was still rising, as was the number of those testing positive, and now there was a shortage of PPE (personal protective equipment), used by clinicians and care workers to protect themselves from infection. After the news came a short piece about a research study that had just been completed in the UK, which had found that since lockdown more people were suffering from anxiety and depression. I couldn't stand any more bad news and switched off the television and phoned a friend.

CHAPTER SEVENTEEN

STAY AT HOME

O n Tuesday morning details of Jamey's contact with his mother arrived by email from the Family Centre. I read the instructions, reread them and then, leaving Jamey with Paula, went to the computer in the front room to download and install the app needed. I would use this computer rather than my phone as the screen was much bigger, which should make the experience better for them. I didn't know what device Kat would be using, as the app could be used on a desktop computer, laptop, tablet and phone. Fifteen minutes later I had it set up and felt quite pleased with myself. Over the years foster carers have been expected to keep up with the changing technology. Most documents and reports are now filed and accessed online through the local authority's portal. But, like Paula, using a video-conference call app was new to me. I wondered how Kat would manage.

Just before 1 p.m. I explained to Jamey about the video call – that he would be able to see his mother on screen as well as talk to her. I took him into the front room where I pulled up another chair in front of the computer. Once the call connected I would move to one side but remain in the room, as Shannon expected me to monitor this call just as I had been doing the telephone contact. I logged in and then waited for Kat to do the same. The minutes ticked by and she didn't appear – just a message stating we were waiting for someone else to join the meeting. I waited some more, checked it wasn't my fault and that I had connected properly, then, picking up the handset for the landline, I called Kat's mobile. She answered.

'Kat, it's Cathy. I'm logged in for the video call that the Family Centre has set up. Are you ready?'

'No. I haven't done all that stuff,' she said groggily. 'It's too complicated.'

'I see. Have you told Shannon or the Family Centre?'

'No.'

'I could – perhaps they can offer some help. Do you want to talk to Jamey on the phone now instead?'

'Yes.'

I engaged the speaker on the handset and told Jamey to say hello, which he did. Kat made an effort to talk to him, although she sounded rougher than usual and kept clearing her throat with little dry coughs. Jamey replied 'yes', 'no' and 'playing' in answer to her questions but kept looking at the computer screen, expecting to see his mother. After about five minutes, when the conversation had dried up, he slid from his chair and went to play.

'He's gone,' I told Kat. 'I think it would be better for you both if you could see each other. Do you have any apps on your phone for making video calls, like WhatsApp?'

'Yes, I've got that.'

'I'll let Shannon know. Perhaps we can use that.' Although if we did, it would mean that Kat had my mobile number and at present she hadn't been given my contact details. Would it cause a problem? I didn't know. Generally, if a child is placed in care voluntarily then the parent is given the carer's contact details, but if they are the subject of a court order, as Jamey was, then usually they aren't.

'How are you?' I asked Kat before we said goodbye.

'I don't feel so good,' she admitted, with another cough.

'What's the matter?' I asked, concerned.

'I've got a sore throat and I'm hot. I think I've got a temperature.'

'Perhaps you should phone your doctor for advice. They might suggest a Covid test.'

'I was thinking that. There's so many in this house. I could have caught anything.'

'I thought you lived in a flat?' I asked.

'No, I moved. After they took Jamey I lost my child benefit and couldn't afford the flat, so I came here. It's cheap, but there's loads of us. Shannon said it's no place for a child, but then I'm not likely to get Jamey back so it doesn't really matter.'

I felt for Kat. She seemed to have lost everything, but what she'd just said demonstrated the importance of lockdown to reduce the spread of the virus. Had Kat attended contact at the Family Centre she could have brought infection from other residents in the house with her, spread it to passengers on the bus, then to staff at the Family Centre and to Jamey, who would have brought it home to us.

'I think you should phone your doctor,' I said again, and she agreed.

I checked on Jamey; he was playing in the living room, so I phoned Shannon. The call went through to her voicemail and I left a message saying that the video call to Kat hadn't taken place as she wasn't able to install the app so she'd spoken to Jamey on the phone instead. I said she had WhatsApp and asked if I could use that on Thursday for contact. I also said she wasn't feeling well and had a temperature and a cough. It was important Shannon knew.

Paula had finished the work she'd been sent for the day, so we went out for a walk. While we were out my phone sounded with a text message. It was from a friend who lived about three miles away. I'd spoken to her on the phone last week and she'd been fine then, but now I was shocked as I read her message. Her whole family was in quarantine after her son had tested positive for Covid-19, although he only had mild symptoms. Paula knew the family and was concerned too. I texted back wishing her son a speedy recovery and asking if they needed any shopping. If so, to text me the list and I'd leave it on their doorstep as I couldn't go in. She replied thanking me and saying her sister was dropping off some shopping and wished us well. She finished: *No idea how he got it so take care xx*. It was the first person I knew personally to have a family member with Covid and it was very worrying.

That evening another friend, Siobhan, who was a foster carer, phoned for a chat – or rather to offload. I found that many of us were using the phone more now, whereas normally we would have met. Siobhan had three teenagers, all boys: two of them her own, and one a looked-after child called Ted. He was fifteen and had come to them six months ago having been through many foster placements before. He'd had a very abusive childhood and was angry, volatile and took drugs. Siobhan had put in a lot of work with him and with the help of therapy twice a week, and a good social worker and outreach worker, he had begun to settle down. But now, in lockdown, the counselling and outreach work had stopped, his school was closed and he was spending too much time online – not doing his schoolwork but in touch with the lads who had got him into trouble before. Siobhan said he kept leaving the house to meet the lads and she thought he was using drugs again.

'Apart from his own health, he's putting all my family at risk,' she said, understandably anxious. 'I'm not sure how much more I can take. It's stressful enough having everyone home worrying about catching the virus, and our shop closed, without Ted playing up.' She and her husband managed an off-licence.

'Have you told Joy all this?' I asked. We had the same supervising social worker.

'Yes, but what can she do? She's spoken to Ted's social worker and there's a chance that counselling might resume online next week, but Ted's already saying he's not interested. He says he wants his independence and to live in a hostel, but that's not going to happen. He's only fifteen. It's such a pity – we were doing OK before all this, and now I don't know what's going to happen. I am worn out and my own boys are starting to play up too.'

We were on the phone for nearly an hour, although Siobhan did most of the talking. I am not sure if I was any help, but sometimes just listening is enough. As we finished I realized that, compared to what some families were going through, I was having it relatively easy. We were all well, Jamey was thriving and making good progress, and my family all still had jobs.

The following day, 1 April, was traditionally April Fool's Day when people play practical jokes on each other. However, this year there was little frivolity, hoaxing or prank-playing as the world continued to battle against the spread of coronavirus. The death toll was rising, as was the shortage of PPE, putting frontline workers at risk. Now there was also a shortage of Covid testing kits as countries scrambled to buy what was available. Face coverings in public were already mandatory in some countries and there was talk of similar happening in the UK, so I went online and bought a box of twenty disposable masks for the ridiculously inflated price of £20. There were already feedback comments saying the seller should be ashamed of themselves for making money out of the crisis. It was immoral, but like others I paid the price. If we did have to start wearing masks, I needed to be prepared. I could afford it, but what about all those who couldn't?

Shannon emailed with details of Jamey's online review with links and codes to log in. It was to be held the following Wednesday and chaired by the same IRO, only virtually. She also said that I could use WhatsApp to phone Kat for contact and that the Family Centre had been informed.

That afternoon, once Paula had finished her work, I left Jamey with her while I went supermarket shopping. Things had changed since my last visit and I now had to join a socially distanced queue outside, standing on markers two metres apart. The store was limiting the number of shoppers inside and a member of staff positioned at the door was only allowing someone in as another left. Thankfully it wasn't raining as the queue took a while to feed in before it was my turn.

A large notice just inside the store's entrance asked us to follow the one-way system and to keep two metres apart from other shoppers. It felt like an assault course as I steered the trolley up and down the aisles, sometimes pausing or manoeuvring around another shopper who was too close. Despite the government having asked us to shop responsibly and only buy what we needed, many of the shelves were still low on stock or empty. I managed to buy some toilet paper, but there was no flour or eggs, which was a pity as we sometimes liked to bake and make pancakes. Tinned and dried foods were low too, but I managed to get the two tins of baked beans I needed. However, there was an abundance of chocolate Easter eggs. The shelves were full – I assumed because many events had been cancelled. Easter was only ten days away and, while it wouldn't be the family gathering it usually was because of lockdown, Paula and I would make an Easter-egg hunt for Jamey. I bought a selection of small chocolate eggs to hide and three baskets. It was just a pity that my granddaughter wouldn't be able to join us. She'd been too young last year but would have enjoyed it this year. I also bought eggs for her, Lucy, Darren, Adrian and Kirsty for when I next saw them.

While most shoppers seemed to be following the rules – socially distancing and only buying what they needed – when I arrived at the checkout it was different. Someone was complaining about the wait and then a customer ahead of me in the queue began remonstrating with a member of staff because he wasn't allowed to buy a dozen cans of tuna fish. They had been confiscated and put in a trolley that contained items from other customers who'd been trying to buy more than was allowed. He wasn't happy.

'But they're for my cat!' he exclaimed indignantly, as if that made it all right.

'Lucky cat!' one woman called out sarcastically. 'I wish I could afford tuna!'

He glared at her, cursed the cashier and, instead of checking out, kicked his trolley and stormed off, leaving behind his unpaid shopping for a member of staff to put away. It was uncomfortable to witness. Feelings were running high and you could feel the tension in the air. Everyone was stressed and I was pleased to be out of there and on my way home.

As I pulled onto the drive, Paula opened the front door, Jamey at her side. I assumed she'd come to help me unload the car. She had, but she also wanted to tell me something.

'Mum,' she said, looking serious. 'My manager phoned while you were out.'

'I hope you were able to concentrate with Jamey there.'

'Yes, he was quiet. But I am being furloughed from next Monday.' I stopped what I was doing to look at her. 'There just isn't enough work for me,' she added.

'I see. You wondered if it might come to this. Well, at least you're getting paid.'

'Eighty per cent of my salary, then once lockdown is over I should be able to return to my job, but it will depend on how quickly business picks up.'

I could tell she was worried, and I reassured her as best I could as we took the shopping into the house. Like thousands of others, her job was now uncertain because of the lockdown caused by the pandemic. I told her she wouldn't need to pay me her rent while she was on less money. She, like Adrian and Lucy had (when they'd lived at home), made a small contribution towards the household costs out of her monthly salary, as most of her friends did.

Paula texted Lucy and Adrian and told them she was being furloughed. Adrian replied by text that he was still working normal office hours at home and Kirsty was teaching her class online. Their jobs seemed safe, but it was different with businesses like the one Paula worked for, which relied on trade and selling their goods.

Lucy then phoned Paula and said that Darren was being furloughed too. When they'd finished talking I spoke to her and she explained that with so few children attending the nursery, they only needed a few members of staff. Half of them were being furloughed, including Darren, but as Lucy was part-time they said she could still go in. Lucy and Darren had all the bills to pay on the flat they rented as well as the costs of raising a child, and I told Lucy if they needed any money to let me know and I'd help. I hoped my family already knew that I would always help them, but it didn't hurt to remind them. There were reports on the news of financial hardship created by the pandemic, especially in low-income families who were already struggling and were now being hit hardest by reduced hours or closed businesses. Commentators said that social and economic inequality was becoming more pronounced now, not just in the UK but around the world.

On Thursday we went for a walk in the morning and then after lunch I made the video call to Kat's phone. She didn't answer the first time but did on my second attempt. I could see and hear her well and she could see and hear me. She appeared to be standing outside. I could see a brick wall and a fence, and although the weather was mild she seemed to be shivering.

'How are you feeling?' I asked her, mindful she hadn't been well on Tuesday.

'OK, it was just a cold.'

'Did you contact your doctor?'

'No. I'll only get another lecture.' I assumed she meant in connection with her lifestyle. But it wasn't my business to tell Kat she should really get checked out, so I said I'd put Jamey on. I returned to the living room, where he'd been looking at a picture book with Paula.

'Mummy is on the phone,' I said, and held it so he could see the screen. Paula slipped from the room.

'Mummy,' he said intrigued, pointing at her.

'Yes, it's me,' Kat said. 'Can you see me?'

He nodded.

'I can see you too, you just nodded.'

He looked completely bemused.

'What are you doing?' Kat asked, her teeth chattering.

'Looking at a book,' I prompted Jamey.

'A book,' Jamey said, and picked up the picture book Paula had been reading to him.

'I can see it,' Kat said. 'It's got a picture of a bear on the front.'

Jamey smiled and, pointing to the picture, said, 'Bear.'

'I know, I can see it,' Kat said. She was still shivering.

'Where Mummy?' Jamey asked, meaning where was she.

'I'm at the back of the house where I live. I moved.' She shivered again.

'Are you cold?' I asked. She nodded. 'Can't you go inside to talk?'

'No, there's too many in there.'

She continued to talk for another few minutes and then said, 'I've got to go now. I'm freezing. Be a good boy. Bye, love.'

'Bye, Mummy,' Jamey said, and gave a little wave.

She waved back and then ended the call. I thought the video call had gone reasonably well – better than the phone calls.

'Mummy gone?' Jamey asked.

'Yes, love, for now. You'll speak to her again next week.'

'Bye, Mummy,' he said quietly, and then picked up the book for me to read.

That night on the news we learnt that a number of temporary hospitals were being erected around the country in preparation for a big influx of coronavirus patients. Upsetting footage was shown of interviews with distraught relatives who'd lost a loved one and exhausted nurses struggling to cope. This was clearly a warning to us all to abide by the rules and minimize the chances of catching coronavirus. The weather for the coming weekend was forecast to be sunny, but we were told to stay at home and not go to the coast, parks or country beauty spots. We must not travel, and again I was reminded how lucky we were to have a garden.

At 8 p.m. Paula and I went outside to join in the weekly applause for our NHS staff and other key workers. As before, someone played 'You'll Never Walk Alone' and there was a warm, unifying atmosphere of mutual support. When the clapping stopped we waved to each other and talked to those within earshot, always keeping our distance. I saw Jean at her gate talking to a neighbour. She hadn't phoned me, so I assumed she had everything she needed.

CHAPTER EIGHTEEN

MORE BAD NEWS

O n Saturday I woke with a mixture of apprehension and anticipation at the prospect of making the video call to Lacey. It would be the first time she and Jamey had seen each other, albeit virtually, since he'd come into care just before Christmas. I wasn't sure how he'd react. He'd heard her on the phone, but this was a whole new experience – one Lacey had been pushing for all this time. I hoped she wasn't disappointed or that Jamey was upset.

I wanted to make sure the call connected first, as I was doing with Kat, so just before the contact was due to start I left Jamey with Paula in the living room and went to the computer in the front room. I knew from other foster carers that many were having problems with the conferencing apps – as were social workers – and some were proving more reliable and easier to manage than others.

I followed the login instructions I'd been sent by email and was momentarily startled to see a full-size screen image of my face. Struth! Was that really me? Is that what others would see? It was far more detailed on the large screen of the monitor than the smaller image on my phone during WhatsApp calls. I looked slightly worried, which didn't help the frown lines, and I could see grey roots along my parting, which couldn't be addressed until we were out of lockdown. Then a woman appeared in a small box in the bottom right-hand corner of the screen together with a voice. 'Cathy, is that you? It's Lacey.'

'Yes, hi. Just a second – I need to make you bigger.'

'I'm big enough already,' she joked.

I moved the cursor over various icons at the top of the page until I found the one I needed so that Lacey's image filled the screen and mine was reduced to the small box.

'Sorry about that,' I said. 'This is new to me. I can see and hear you. Can you see and hear me?'

'Yes, fine. I'm using my laptop.'

'It's nice to meet you at last,' I said, smiling.

'And you,' Lacey replied.

I could see a passing resemblance to Kat, but that was all. Lacey was a healthy weight, with full cheeks and a glowing complexion, unlike Kat who was gaunt and sickly-looking. Lacey was older than her sister, but could have been much younger, so profound was the difference.

'I'll get Jamey now,' I said. 'I wanted to make sure I got through to you first.'

'Yes, please, and then we can talk at the end.'

'You know I'll be in the room as I was with the phone calls?'

'Yes, Shannon said, although it seems a bit ridiculous considering he used to stay with me.'

'It's procedure,' I said, and left to fetch Jamey.

Now Lacey had been granted virtual contact she was less angry and the good-humoured side of her nature was becoming apparent. Her eyes were bright and smiley, and she was very different from the person I'd spoken to on the phone when Jamey had first come into care.

'Aunty Lacey is going to talk to you on the computer in the front room,' I told Jamey. It was difficult trying to explain video contact to a young child. I hoped he would just adapt and get used to it.

I took him into the front room and helped him onto the chair in front of the monitor. At first he seemed to think it was just a picture of Lacey on screen, but then she moved and he jumped and gave a little cry of alarm.

'Hi, Jamey!' Lacey said, waving.

He stared at her, his eyes rounding in disbelief.

'Say hello,' I prompted. 'It's like the call to Mummy, only bigger.'

'Hi, Jamey,' Lacey said again, waving some more.

'Lacey,' he said, struggling to believe she was there.

'Yes, it's me. I love you, darling. How are you? I'm so pleased I can see you at last. I've missed you so much.'

His little face said it all. 'Miss you,' he said, and I was sure he wasn't just repeating what she'd said. He had missed her, dreadfully, but lacking the language to express himself he had internalized his feelings. Now he began to cry.

'Oh, love,' I said, putting my arm around him. 'It's all right. There is nothing to be upset about.' It was heart-wrenching. 'Aunty Lacey is in her home. You used to go there sometimes. Do you remember?'

Jamey nodded tearfully and I dried his eyes.

'Don't be upset,' Lacey said, close to tears herself. 'Look what I've got.' She held up a teddy bear. 'It's Bertie Bear, from the book I used to read to you.'

Jamey stared at the screen, clearly trying to make sense of his memories. At his age he should have some recollection of the times last year when he was with her.

'Bertie,' he said quietly but loud enough for Lacey to hear.

'Yes, that's right. I keep him in your bed waiting for you to return. Your other toys are in your room too. I expect you have plenty there, so I'll keep them here for you.'

'Lacey,' he said again, watching her, mesmerized.

'Yes, and Andy is here. We're so looking forward to seeing you again and when you can come to live here.'

Jamey looked confused.

'Lacey, I think it's best not to raise his hopes at this stage,' I said gently.

'Point taken,' she replied easily. 'What have you been doing?' she now asked Jamey.

'Playing,' he replied.

'On the tablet I gave you?'

'Yes.'

'What else have you been doing?'

'Where Bertie?' he asked, for the bear was no longer in view.

'He's here,' Lacey said, picking him up. 'Do you remember the song I used to sing to you?' And she began to sing 'The Teddy Bears' Picnic', which was an old favourite of ours too:

'If you go down in the woods today
You're sure of a big surprise
If you go down in the woods today
You'd better go in disguise!

For every bear that ever there was
Will gather there for certain
Because today's the day the
Teddy Bears have their picnic ...'

As Lacey sang she made the bear dance. Jamey was enthralled, and finally his expression lost some of its seriousness and he smiled.

'More,' he said, as she finished.

'OK.' She was pleased and sang it again.

I encouraged Jamey to join in and he said the odd word. When she finished she sat the bear beside her and asked Jamey if he'd spoken to his mother. I think she was just trying to make conversation. He nodded.

'I've spoken to Mummy,' Lacey told him. 'She's all right.' So I assumed they'd reconciled their differences. Lacey then asked Jamey what else he'd been doing and he said, 'Book.'

'You've been looking at some books?'

He nodded. 'Paula.'

'With Paula?'

'Yes.'

'That's my daughter,' I said.

'Yes, Shannon told me. Do you like books, Jamey?' Lacey asked.

'Yes.'

'I read books to the children at the school where I work.'

And so the conversation continued, much more easily now they were able to see each other. After about twenty minutes Jamey grew restless, which was hardly surprising for a child his age. Lacey noticed it too.

'Do you want to go now?' she asked him.

He nodded. He was trying to get off the chair. 'We'll call again next Saturday,' I told Lacey.

'If not before,' she replied. 'I'm pushing for more contact. I'll say goodbye to Jamey first and then we can talk.'

'OK.'

'Bye, Jamey. I love you. Big kiss.' She blew him kisses and Jamey blew one back. 'Bye, love.'

'I'll just settle him in another room,' I said.

We went into the hall. Paula was upstairs now and I called up to ask her if she could look after Jamey while I spoke to his aunt. She appeared on the landing and Jamey went up to her while I returned to the computer.

'I think that went very well,' Lacey said as I sat down.

'Yes,' I agreed.

'So you'll tell Shannon it went well?'

'Yes.'

'Good. I need all the help I can get. This is doing my head in.' Now Jamey couldn't hear, she was free to have a rant. 'Why does everything take so long? I leave messages and send emails and no one replies. Not just the social worker, but the bloody lawyer too. I know people are working from home, but how long does it take to pick up the phone or reply to an email? I'm thinking of changing legal firms …'

Lacey continued to have a good moan, then asked if I'd heard anything about their assessment.

'No,' I replied honestly. 'But as a foster carer I wouldn't expect to. Is the date for the final court hearing the same?'

'As far as I know. Why? Could it change?'

'Not usually, but there's a lot of uncertainty at present. I think most family court cases are being conducted virtually. You will need to ask Shannon.'

'I have. I've left messages, and the lawyer is supposed to be finding out what's going on.'

I appreciated Lacey's frustration, but there really wasn't much I could say. Once she'd finished, I confirmed that I'd phone her at the same time next Saturday unless I heard otherwise and we said an amicable goodbye.

The rest of our day continued as planned. We went for a walk, taking care to keep our distance from those we passed, then, as the weather was fine, we spent the rest of the afternoon in the garden. Jamey said Lacey's name a few times and when he did I would say something like, 'Yes, you saw her on the computer, and you will see her again next Saturday. She's at home now.'

Later, when we were indoors, he went to the computer in the front room and, pointing to it, said, 'Lacey.'

'She's gone now, love. We'll see her again next weekend.'

'Bye, Lacey,' he said quietly, and came away.

That evening, after I'd read Jamey some stories in the living room, I said it was time for bed and to say 'night, night' to Paula.

'Night, night,' he said, going to her for a goodnight kiss as usual.

'Night, night,' she said, kissing and hugging him.

Jamey knew his bedtime routine now and we began down the hall with the intention of going upstairs, but instead he went into the front room. Going to the computer screen, he said, 'Night, night, Lacey,' and gave it a kiss. It was so touching.

'That's nice,' I said. 'Did Aunty Lacey used to kiss you goodnight?'

'Yes,' he replied, and came with me upstairs. Once he was ready, I tucked him into bed, kissed his forehead, then added one from Lacey and Mummy. He smiled, pleased.

Downstairs, I settled on the sofa in front of the television with Paula for the latest news on Covid. Some people had ignored the stay-at-home order and had gone to country beauty spots. But worse was that a five-year-old had died from the virus – the youngest victim so far. It was heart-breaking, as were the figures from the rising death toll. Paula and I watched the rest of the news in morbid silence and then I suggested we watch a film. She readily agreed. We wanted to keep abreast of what was happening, but it was depressing.

Sunday was another dry, mild day so we went for our usual walk and returned home to play in the house and garden. To be honest there wasn't much else we could do in lockdown, and I was grateful that Jamey was content to play. Had we not been in lockdown I would have taken him to parks, activity centres, the zoo and other places of interest. But now all of our lives had been curtailed, and fortunately he was young enough not to fully appreciate what he was missing. I would make it up to him once lockdown was lifted.

The seriousness of the situation created by the pandemic was emphasized later that day when the Queen took the unusual step of broadcasting an address to the nation and Commonwealth. We were told before it began that it had been filmed by one cameraman wearing protective equipment, otherwise it could have broken current guidelines and jeopardized the safety of those involved. It was watched by 24 million viewers and the Queen's words were a sombre rallying cry. She thanked all NHS staff and frontline workers, and those of us who were helping by staying at home. She said she hoped that in years to come we would all be able to take pride in how we'd responded to the challenge of the pandemic. She said that around the world we were seeing heart-warming stories of people coming together to help others; for example, by delivering food parcels and medicines and checking on neighbours. She said that although self-isolating was hard for everyone, it presented the opportunity to slow down, pause and reflect. She finished by saying we should take comfort that better days would return when we would be with our families again.

Later we learnt that the Prime Minister, Boris Johnson, who'd been self-isolating at home after testing positive for coronavirus, had been admitted to hospital for 'tests'. We were assured his life wasn't in danger and this was a precautionary measure. That evening I telephoned Lucy and Adrian to make sure they were well and coping, and also filled in the online forms for Jamey's review on Wednesday. Although I was now using video calls, a conference call where a number of us would be present was a whole new experience for me. I prepared a few notes for what I needed to say at the review, as I would have done if we'd met in person.

On Monday, the first day of Paula being furloughed, she wandered around not sure what she should be doing.

Even though she'd only had a few hours of work a day in the previous week, it was something to focus on and she'd felt productive. Now she didn't have any work and couldn't socialize with friends or visit Lucy and Adrian. Darren had also been furloughed, but he was looking after Emma while Lucy was at work, so he was fully occupied. Like many others were doing, Paula decided to have a clear-out – a job she'd been putting off for years – and began sorting out the contents of the drawers and cupboards in her bedroom, sometimes with Jamey's help.

Joy and Shannon both telephoned for updates on how Jamey was doing in preparation for his review on Wednesday. I took the opportunity to ask Shannon how her mother was. She said that although she hadn't contracted the virus in the care home, others had. She still hadn't been allowed in to see her, but they'd spoken on the phone when her mother had become very emotional and begged to be taken home. I felt for Shannon and I knew from the news that thousands of others with relatives in care homes were similarly affected, as homes had stopped all visits for fear their vulnerable residents would catch the infection.

Later that day the country was told that the Prime Minister had been transferred to intensive care as his symptoms had worsened. He had been given oxygen but wasn't on a ventilator. The Foreign Secretary was going to deputize where necessary and the Queen was being kept informed. I then received a text from my friend Siobhan who was fostering Ted, saying that her father was ill in bed at home with what they'd thought was flu, but he'd tested positive for Covid. I phoned her straight away. She was very worried and said her father had no idea where he'd caught it from. Her family hadn't seen him for some weeks, so it wasn't from them. Her mother was nursing him at home and Siobhan was phoning her every few hours to see how he was. She added that she hoped Ted would learn from this as he was still breaking lockdown to go out, thereby putting lives at risk.

CHAPTER NINETEEN

TALKING HEADS

Tuesday was Paula's birthday and I made it as much of an occasion as I could in lockdown and said we would do something special with the rest of the family once restrictions had been lifted. Of course she understood. Jamey and I watched her open her presents and cards, which had arrived by post and I'd hidden away. Later I cooked one of her favourite meals – sausage and pasta bake with garlic bread and green salad, followed by fresh fruit trifle and cream, then birthday cake. Adrian and Lucy phoned to wish her a happy birthday and said, as I had, we would meet up when we could.

Also, that day there was finally a glimmer of hope in respect of the Covid figures. The number of new cases in the UK was not accelerating as fast as predicted, although it was too early to say if the outbreak had peaked. Nevertheless, we grabbed this small piece of optimism. Surely this meant the end was now in sight, and people would stop dying and our lives could return to normal? Paula shared my optimism. She was looking forward to a time when she would be able to resume work and see her friends again.

When I phoned Kat that afternoon for Jamey's video contact she didn't answer. I tried a few times between 1 p.m. and 1.30, although Jamey didn't know. Kat would see my missed calls when she next checked her phone, and I entered what had happened in my log. I didn't know if Kat had been invited to the review the following day. It would be usual at this stage in childcare proceedings.

At 4 p.m. my mobile rang and it was Kat. Not a video call, but a phone call.

'I've just woken up,' she said. 'I had a bad night.'

'I'm sorry to hear that. Do you want to speak to Jamey now?' I asked. He and I were in the living room and he was sitting a little way from me playing with some toy people.

'Yes, that's why I'm calling,' Kat replied bluntly.

'Just a minute.'

I engaged the speaker and took my mobile to Jamey. 'Mummy wants to talk to you,' I said, sitting beside him.

'Mummy,' he said quietly, and touched the screen, expecting to see her image as he had the last time.

'It's a phone call,' I explained. 'You can talk to her, but you can't see her.'

'Mummy?' he said, and touched the screen again.

'Jamey, are you there?' Kat asked impatiently.

'He is, Kat, but I think it would be better if he could see you. Can I call you back on video?'

'No, you can't, I'm not up yet.'

I turned to Jamey. 'Say hello to Mummy.'

'Hello,' he said in the same small voice.

'You sound like a mouse,' she laughed. 'Squeak, squeak. Are you a mouse? We have a mouse in the house. A mouse in the house,' she giggled. 'More than one. Lots of mice, trying to hide.' Then she continued to gabble in an agitated manner about all sorts of unrelated matters. A dirty saucepan by her bed, a half-eaten pot of noodles she was thinking of having for breakfast. She could see her toe poking through her sock. They weren't her socks. She thought she had bed bugs. It was a one-sided conversation, a monologue, where she rambled on without any reference or relevance to Jamey. 'Mummy is still in bed. Naughty Mummy. She should be up by now. I wonder if that stinky social worker will tell her off. I think she might. Never mind. It is what it is …'

I left her to talk for a while, hoping it would improve, while Jamey stared at the phone, befuddled. Then he began to look worried. I was there to monitor the call and ensure the conversation was a good experience for Jamey. It wasn't, so finally I interrupted.

'Kat, Cathy here. Have you got something you could tell Jamey that would interest him or maybe ask him what he's been doing?'

'I'm talking to him, aren't I?' she snapped. 'Can't he keep up?' Then to someone else in the room, 'And you can shut the fuck up too.'

Enough was enough. 'Kat, we'll say goodbye now and phone you at one o'clock on Thursday,' I said.

'We'll say goodbye now,' Kat mimicked me. 'Suit yourselves,' she said, and ended the call.

Jamey just sat there looking sad and confused, and I regretted answering her call. Foster carers sometimes have to make snap decisions like this, and it hadn't been the correct one. I wondered if Kat was under the influence of a substance as she'd seemed high and irrational. It was possible. I put away my phone and distracted Jamey with the toy people. He was soon playing again, although I'd have to include what had happened in my log.

On Wednesday morning, ten minutes before Jamey's review was due to start, I left him with Paula in the living room while I went into the front room for the conference call. It was likely the IRO would want to see Jamey as part of the review, at which point I would bring him in, but he couldn't be expected to sit at the computer for any length of time. By eleven o'clock – the time the review was due to start – I had managed to log into the meeting and so had the IRO, who was hosting and chairing it. I could see him in gallery view, the same IRO as last time. He was in his living room in front of a bookcase. Suddenly he looked up at me. 'Welcome,' he said. 'You're Jamey's foster carer.'

'Yes, that's right. Cathy Glass.'

He lowered his gaze to type, then made eye-contact again and said, 'I think Jamey's social worker has logged in too. Are you there, Shannon?' he asked.

There was silence, then Shannon appeared in the gallery. 'Yes. Sorry, I was just taking a call on my mobile. I've switched it off now. Nathan, my trainee, should be here too.' Judging from the background, she seemed to be in her office.

'I'm here,' Nathan said, his live image joining us in the gallery.

'Thank you. According to my list of attendees,' the IRO said, 'we are waiting for the Guardian ad Litem, Audrey Bashir, the foster carer's supervising social worker and Mrs Durrant, Jamey's mother.'

'Mrs Durrant can't make it,' Shannon said.

'Even though it's an online meeting?' the IRO queried.

'That's correct,' Shannon confirmed.

The IRO typed – I assumed minuting her absence as he would have done in a physical review.

While we waited for the others I tried not to fixate on my on-screen image, although I adjusted my fringe. What is it about these devices that highlights our flaws? Shannon's office ceiling lights were casting a downward shadow on her face, creating eye-bags she didn't normally have. And the IRO's laptop was positioned too low so he had to crane his neck forward when he spoke or typed, which gave him the appearance of a large eagle with very bushy eyebrows.

As we waited for Joy and the Guardian to join us I could hear Jamey's voice coming from the living room as he played with Paula. Nathan picked up a sandwich that had been off-screen and took a bite.

'Lunch?' the IRO asked him good-humouredly.

'Yes, sorry. I've had a busy day.'

'Carry on by all means while we're waiting for the others,' he said.

I felt I was starting to get the hang of a conference call. The active speaker was highlighted in the gallery as soon as they began to speak so it was obvious who had started to talk, and only one person spoke at a time. I began to relax and watched the others as Nathan chewed and the IRO typed.

The Guardian joined us.

'Hello, everyone,' Audrey Bashir said, then she introduced herself. She hadn't been at the previous review.

As we said hello our images flashed on screen like contestants on a television gameshow. I noticed Audrey had some rather nice curtains in her living room, although I didn't comment. It occurred to me that video-conferencing calls were quite intrusive, and we needed to be careful about what was on display in the room behind us. Washing airing on a radiator, for example, wouldn't create a very good impression. There were bookshelves on the wall behind me and I thought they could do with tidying later.

The IRO noted that Audrey was present and we waited for Joy. Shannon put the time to good use and began reading a paper document. Nathan finished his sandwich and washed it down with a can of fizzy drink.

'That's bad for your teeth,' I couldn't help but say.

'That's what my mother says,' he replied. I guessed I was probably the same age as his mother.

Finally, Joy appeared looking a bit flustered. Shannon put away her document as Joy began talking. I could see her lips moving but couldn't hear her voice. I thought it was something wrong my end and began checking settings until the IRO said, 'Am I the only person who can't hear Joy Philips?'

'I can't,' Shannon said.

'Me neither,' the Guardian agreed.

'Joy, can you hear me?' the IRO asked.

She appeared to say yes and continued moving her lips dumbly.

'We can't hear *you*,' the IRO said.

Joy looked at her keyboard and talked some more, I guessed trying to work out what was wrong.

'Check you haven't got it on mute,' Nathan suggested.

Joy concentrated on the right of her screen, presumably checking dialogue boxes, then suddenly said, 'Is that better?'

'Yes, I can hear you,' the IRO said. 'Can everyone else?'

We all said we could and our images flashed in the gallery in quick succession.

'Sorry about that,' Joy said. 'I'm not on my usual computer.'

'Don't worry,' the IRO said. 'We're all having to get used to this new technology. My eleven-year-old son showed me what to do.'

The IRO then officially opened the meeting by welcoming us to Jamey's second review. 'I appreciate that some of us are working from home, so if there are any interruptions or background noise please don't worry. I shall be chairing and minuting this review as I would normally do. So let's start by seeing Jamey, then we'll hear from Cathy how he is doing.'

'He's with my adult daughter in another room,' I said. 'I'll fetch him. I won't be a minute.'

'Thank you.'

I stood and went quickly down the hall and into the living room. 'Jamey, love, I need you to come to the computer in the front room for your review.'

'Lacey there?' he asked, remembering the last time he'd sat at that computer, and stood.

'No, not Lacey, your social worker and some others.'

He didn't seem impressed and was about to sit down again and carry on playing.

'Come on, love, you can play once you've spoken to them. You won't be long.'

'Go on,' Paula encouraged. 'I'll wait here for you.'

I gave Jamey my hand and he came with me into the front room where I sat him on my lap in front of the monitor. He stared in amazement at the gallery of images as they smiled and said hello.

'Welcome, Jamey,' the IRO said. 'Do you remember me from your last review?'

I thought it was highly unlikely, and Jamey was still staring in awe at the screen. Then he said to me, 'Television?' loud enough for everyone to hear.

'Yes, like a television,' I said. 'But it's really the same as when we saw Aunty Lacey on Saturday, only there are more people now.'

Jamey returned his attention to the gallery images. 'There's Shannon,' I told him, pointing. 'And Nathan, who was with you when you first came here.' Nathan waved. 'There is Joy and Audrey, who have been here too. And that's the IRO you have also met.'

'How are you, Jamey?' the IRO asked.

Intrigued, Jamey touched his image on the screen.

'You are looking very smart,' the IRO said. 'I think you've had a haircut since I last saw you.'

Jamey rubbed his hair and the others smiled.

'What have you been doing this morning?' the IRO asked him.

Jamey didn't respond; he was too enthralled by the talking heads.

'Playing with toys,' I suggested.

'Toys,' Jamey said.

'Very good. Any toys in particular?' the IRO asked. 'What do you like doing?'

Jamey tapped his image on the screen.

'You were playing with the dinosaurs just now,' I said.

'Dine-e-saws,' Jamey said, as he usually pronounced the word.

'Not real ones, I hope,' the IRO joked.

Jamey poked his image again.

'Can you see me?' the IRO asked him.

Jamey nodded.

'I can see you too. Can you tell me how you are? Are you well?'

'Yes,' Jamey said.

I don't think the IRO expected Jamey to answer all his questions fully, but he was trying to learn enough to gauge how he was.

'Do you have everything you need?' he asked.

Jamey wasn't yet three years old so he wouldn't know that, and he buried his head shyly in my shoulder.

'Shall I describe Jamey's routine?' I suggested.

'Yes, please,' the IRO said.

I would have done this as part of my report, but we were doing things slightly differently today.

'Jamey sleeps well,' I began. 'He always has. He wakes around seven o'clock when I help him wash and dress. His self-care skills have come on tremendously. Then we go downstairs for breakfast. He eats at the table and likes cereal with fruit for breakfast. Sometimes porridge with a sliced banana, and sometimes a yoghurt. He feeds himself using children's cutlery.'

'So that is an improvement,' the IRO said, pausing from note taking.

'Yes, he's doing very well. He's also potty trained now,' I added.

'Excellent,' the IRO said as he typed. 'Please continue.'

'Our routine at present is limited by lockdown so Jamey usually plays in the morning and then we go out for a walk. My daughter Paula, who lives with me, has been furloughed so she comes too, and also plays with him.'

'That's a big help then,' the IRO said. 'I know some carers I've spoken to are finding lockdown very challenging.'

Shannon and Joy agreed.

'Yes, we're having it relatively easy here,' I said. 'There's Paula and me with just Jamey to look after.'

'No challenging behaviour then?' the IRO asked, with a smile.

'No, not yet. I would normally take him out more to activity centres and similar, but everything is closed, even our local park. So after our walk we return home and either go in the garden or play in the house.'

'The parks are reopening,' Shannon said. 'The government has said they should remain open and only close in exceptional circumstances so people have somewhere to go.'

'Yes, I saw that,' Joy said.

'Great. Hopefully ours will reopen too,' I said.

'Lacey?' Jamey suddenly asked, looking up.

'No, love, not today,' I replied.

'Does he like talking to his aunt?' the IRO asked.

'Yes, we made the first video call last Saturday on this computer, which is why he expects to see her on this screen now.'

The IRO made a note and then looked at me to continue.

'Jamey spends the rest of the day playing or doing activities Paula and I organize, like dough modelling, painting, baking and the exercise routines the paediatrician recommended. Physically he's much stronger now:

he can climb stairs, run and jump. He also likes looking at books and playing on the tablet Lacey bought him. We usually have dinner between five-thirty and six and then it's story time, and he has a bath around seven o'clock, then goes to bed. He's wearing pull-ups still at night but is dry during the day, which is normal for a child his age.'

'Thank you,' the IRO said.

As we waited for him to finish typing, Jamey's attention was suddenly drawn to the door as Sammy strolled in and he slid from my lap. Sammy ran off down the hall and Jamey followed.

'Has Jamey gone?' the IRO asked. 'I can't see him.'

'Yes, he's gone after our cat. Shall I bring him back?' I heard Jamey go into the living room where Paula was.

'No, I've seen him. That's sufficient. Perhaps you could continue by telling us how contact is going.'

The review usually wanted to know this. I glanced at my notes and told them how Jamey had been after contact at the Family Centre and now that we were phoning his mother and Lacey. I assumed the IRO had also been made aware of the contact supervisor's reports.

'Thank you,' he said. 'I see Jamey was due for a follow-up medical. Did that happen?'

'No, it was cancelled due to lockdown. I haven't been given another date. The Health Centre is closed so I haven't been able to have Jamey weighed either. I am doing it at home. He's still putting on weight. Do you want the figures?'

'Yes, please,' the IRO said.

I reached for the record book and read out Jamey's weight gains as the IRO made a note.

'Speech therapy was mentioned as well.'

'We agreed to monitor it for now,' Shannon said. 'Although that service is closed too at present.'

The IRO typed and then asked me about Jamey's overall development. I emphasized how well he was doing while acknowledging he was still behind his peer group and the average child his age.

'Is he likely to fully catch up?' the IRO asked.

I wasn't really qualified to answer that – it was for the paediatrician to say – so I said, 'I think he stands a good chance, it will just take him a bit longer.'

'I'll arrange another medical with an assessment once the service is running again,' Shannon said.

The IRO then asked me, 'Any accidents or illnesses?' Which was another standard question.

'No,' I replied.

'Is there anything else you want to add.'

'Only that Jamey is a lovely child and a pleasure to look after.'

Shannon was asked to speak next and began by confirming Jamey's legal status and then said that the date of the final court hearing was unchanged at present. The care plan was the same – that Jamey would either go to Lacey or be found a long-term foster placement. I then learnt that Kat was no longer objecting to Jamey living with Lacey, feeling it was better than him being in long-term foster care. However, Lacey's and Andy's assessments were still ongoing. Shannon hadn't been able to visit them again due to lockdown and all the checks and references were taking longer than usual, so it was possible the final court hearing might need to be postponed.

The Guardian agreed, and then gave her report. She said there was a backlog of childcare cases waiting to be heard as the Family Court was only sitting for emergency hearings, but they were now starting to hear cases virtually. She said she'd seen Jamey twice prior to lockdown: once with his mother at home before coming into care, then with me. Again, she gave no indication of what her recommendation would be, if indeed she'd formed an opinion yet.

The IRO thanked her and then asked Joy if she wanted to add anything. She said that as my supervising social worker she was in regular contact with me by phone and email and would visit again once the restrictions were lifted. She said she had no concerns about Jamey's care and was pleased to see him making good progress. Nathan agreed that Jamey appeared happy and well cared for.

The IRO thanked us all, set the date for the next review, which he said he hoped would be held in person, and we said goodbye. I closed the app, returned to Jamey and Paula, and our lives in lockdown continued.

CHAPTER TWENTY

BONNIE

G ood Friday is an Easter bank holiday when many go to church, but that wasn't an option this year as all services were cancelled due to coronavirus restrictions. There was a short service online, which I watched, and then we went for our daily walk. We took the road to the park and were pleased to find the gates open, although a large sign fixed to the railings wasn't exactly welcoming:

> **BEWARE. STAY ALERT. COVID RISK.**

Once inside the park we found the area containing the children's play equipment closed off, with another warning sign:

> **KEEP OUT. COVID RISK.**

I could understand why this area wasn't open as it would have been virtually impossible to maintain social distancing between young children. We'd been warned by government scientists that the virus could stay active on surfaces for many hours, even for more than a day. For the same reason the park benches had been cordoned off with yellow-and-black hazard tape, making the seats appear more like crime scenes rather than places to rest and enjoy the scenery.

Jamey looked longingly towards the children's play area and tugged Paula's arm as we passed.

'We can't go in there,' she told him. 'Not today.'

'Why?' Jamey asked. He was saying 'why' now as well as 'what' and 'when', as his young, questioning mind sought answers about the world around him.

'Because of the virus. Dirty,' Paula replied, pulling a face.

Jamey looked at his hands, associating dirty with having to wash them after he'd got them dirty playing in the garden.

'No, love,' I said. 'Your hands aren't dirty. It's the virus. Let's go and feed the ducks instead.'

He gazed at them for a few moments longer and then came with us to the duck pond, which is in another area of the park. There were others walking in the park, including some neighbours who said hello as we passed. People weren't stopping to talk much now, even from a distance, due to the fear of catching the virus. Diagram warnings had begun appearing on television showing just how far the airborne virus could travel when speaking or coughing.

The ducks didn't share our concerns or wariness, though, and were clearly hungry, presumably from the lack of visitors in the previous weeks when the park had been closed. As soon as we approached the pond they swam across and waddled in a group up the bank; a dozen or more, quacking loudly. Jamey took a few steps back. Paula showed him how to throw the duck food on the ground a little distance away, so they didn't come too close. He relaxed and began to have fun. But once the bag of food was empty, the ducks marched right up to him, quacking loudly, and tried to snatch the bag from his hand. Paula picked him up. They were still hungry, but fortunately an elderly man had arrived on the other side of the pond and began throwing in food. They turned and paddled over towards him.

'Ducks gone,' Jamey said, now looking disappointed.

'We'll come again another day,' I reassured him, as Paula put him down.

'Why?' he asked.

'Because we are out of food and someone else is feeding the ducks.'

'OK,' he said cutely.

Easter weekend was warm and sunny. Most businesses were closed Friday and Monday, but we were all warned to stay in our local areas and not take advantage of the fine weather and go to the coast or countryside. Jamey wanted to feed the ducks again so on Saturday, after we'd phoned Lacey and had lunch, we took some more duck food and set off. When we arrived at the park we found it was very busy, more so than I'd seen it in a long while. Families were sitting on the grass having picnics, groups of teenagers were playing football, other young people were just hanging out, and joggers were running along the paths. I didn't think it was just the good weather that had brought so many out, but also the need to socialize – to see others – when we'd been spending so long in our own homes. But of course it was exactly what we'd been told not to do and I had Jamey to think about, so as soon as we'd fed the ducks we returned home. Pictures on the news that night showed parks teeming with people, and another warning was issued instructing us to stay away.

On Sunday we had our Easter-egg hunt in the garden – just Paula, Jamey and me. Of course I knew where the eggs were, as I'd hidden them, but Jamey didn't know that. The race to find the eggs was real to him and Paula and I were as enthusiastic in our surprise and delight at discovering an egg as Jamey was. They were under bushes and plants, behind pots on the patio, and beside the children's play apparatus at the bottom of the garden. There was even one in the sand pit. Paula and I found a few, but naturally Jamey found the most and ended up with a basket full. I let him eat one and then suggested we put the rest indoors so they wouldn't melt in the sun.

Later Lucy posted a video clip on our family's WhatsApp group of their egg hunt in their flat. Emma was so cute carrying her little Easter basket over one arm and wearing furry bunny ears while hunting for the eggs.

The news that evening on the television was a mixture. While the number of new cases of coronavirus was falling in some areas, it was rising in others, and critical-care wards in some hospitals were near capacity. The Prime Minister had been discharged from hospital to continue his recovery at home, but there was still a shortage of

PPE equipment for healthcare workers, and the death toll continued to rise in countries badly affected by Covid. I thought of my dear parents and how they'd had to cope with far worse, having lived through the Second World War. I now felt I had a better appreciation of their generation's stoicism and bravery. My generation had had it relatively easy until now. On a positive note, Siobhan texted to say her father was recovering well. I was so pleased.

It was nearly 10 p.m. when the landline rang, which was late for a friend or family to be phoning for a chat. I picked up the handset in the living room where I'd been sitting reading a book, hoping the ringing hadn't woken Jamey. As soon as I heard Lucy's voice I knew there was something wrong.

'Mum, I'm sorry to call so late. You're not in bed, are you?'

'No, love. What's the matter?'

'Bonnie just phoned. She wants to see Emma tomorrow!'

'Oh, I see.'

Bonnie was Lucy's birth mother – Emma's grandmother. Lucy had come to me as a foster child many years ago and I'd adopted her. She couldn't be more loved and cherished if she'd been born to me and I knew that Paula and Adrian loved her as much as I did, and she them. I'd had to work with Bonnie in the past, as she and Lucy had maintained some contact. They saw each other once or twice a year at the most, when it suited Bonnie. I tell Lucy's story in my book *Will You Love Me?*

'I haven't heard a thing from her all year and now she wants to see Emma in the middle of a pandemic!' Lucy exclaimed, clearly agitated. I could understand her annoyance.

'What did you say?' I asked.

'That she wasn't allowed to come into the flat because of lockdown. She said we could meet outside. But I won't be able to stop her from touching or cuddling Emma. She could be carrying the virus, even though she says she isn't.'

'How does she know? Has she been tested?'

'No, she says she doesn't feel unwell.'

Lucy knew, as I did, that it was possible to carry the virus and pass it on without showing any symptoms at all.

'How have you left it with her?' I asked.

'I said I'd speak to Darren and phone her back. He agrees with me. We're not being unreasonable, are we? I mean, we're not seeing you or his parents.'

'No. Why does she want to come tomorrow?'

'She said she'll be in the area and hasn't got anything to do.'

Which was usually how Bonnie contacted Lucy – nothing for months and then a sudden text or phone call to say she was in the area and wanted to see her. One time she just turned up at their flat shortly after Emma had been born and then criticized Lucy for being in a mess. They'd argued and I'd had to telephone Bonnie and smooth things over.

'Do you want me to call her and explain?' I offered.

'No, it's OK, I'll phone her. Darren can talk to her if necessary. But what shall I say?'

'I think you've already said it, love. Remind her that grandparents can't see their grandchildren at present –

that I haven't seen Emma and neither have Darren's parents. Perhaps send her some recent photos of Emma.'

'Will do.'

'Let me know if you want me to speak to her.'

'Thanks.'

Lucy had grown to accept her birth mother's shortcomings, and while she was happy to see her every so often, she didn't want any more. Neither did Bonnie, who, although not a bad person, was unreliable, self-centred and continued to face many challenges in her own life.

Lucy must have phoned Bonnie straight away, for five minutes later she texted: *It's OK. Spoke to her. She's got other plans for tomorrow now anyway*.

Whether Bonnie had other plans I wasn't so sure; perhaps she was just trying to save face. I felt sorry for Bonnie, but Lucy was right not to see her during lockdown, even outside. She'd have to wait, like all the other grandparents who were separated from their grandchildren.

With my usually busy life now on hold and spending so much time at home, I was finding the days were starting to blur and merge. When I woke in the morning I had to think what day of the week it was. Paula was finding the same and would sometimes pause from what she was doing, look up and say, 'It's Tuesday today, isn't it?' (or whichever day it was).

'Yes, all day,' I replied.

We weren't the only ones. Jokes were still circulating on social media and many of those were now about time passing in lockdown. Others showed parents struggling to teach their children at home as teachers set work online. These witty gems were like breaths of fresh air when they arrived.

The only appointments I had in my diary now were for the three video calls each week – Kat on Tuesday and Thursday, and Lacey on Saturday. My life was looking after Jamey (with Paula's help), a weekly shop, a daily walk and – the highlight – the 'clap for carers' on a Thursday evening. I was writing my memoirs in the evening and early morning before Jamey was up. Paula and I continued to watch the news on television at some point each day to keep up with any changes.

It was inevitable that after spending so much time together, Paula and I would grow very close to Jamey. The three of us were in our own little bubble. As a foster carer you know that at some point the child you are looking after is likely to leave you – to return home, to a relative or a forever family – so you have to factor that into your feelings and expectations. It doesn't stop you loving and caring for the child, but it does give you some protection when the inevitable happens and you have to say goodbye. I knew that Jamey had grown very close to us too. He had arrived neglected, wary, developmentally delayed and with little emotional attachment to his mother so had bonded with us quickly. At some point, when the decision on where he would live permanently was made, he would – through a planned introductory programme of visits – gradually transfer his affection to his forever family.

But that was in the future; for now, our lives were governed by the pandemic and all that entailed – hand washing, social distancing and hoping for a vaccine.

With more Covid testing now taking place, the number of people testing positive was rising sharply. Our government announced that lockdown would be extended for another three weeks at least. Also announced, and very worrying, was that the figures emerging showed that some sections of the community were being affected more than others. Those with black and Asian heritage, for example, were more likely to die from coronavirus than others. Scientists were looking into why this was happening.

As well as the toll the pandemic was taking on our physical health, it was affecting the population in other ways too. Our mental health was suffering, domestic violence was on the increase and more children were being brought into care as households already struggling were tipped over the edge. Thankfully, by the third week in April the government had tentatively suggested the numbers had peaked in the UK but issued a stern warning that social-distancing measures would remain in place possibly for the rest of the year. They said it was unrealistic to expect our lives to suddenly return to normal, which of course is what we'd all been hoping for.

Then, amid all the doom, gloom and soothsaying, came a ray of light in the form of ninety-nine-year-old war veteran Tom Moore. He began appearing on our television screens having pledged to walk one hundred lengths of his garden by 30 April – his one hundredth birthday. His goal was to raise £1,000 for the NHS, but he quickly captured the hearts of millions, so his story went viral and donations began pouring in, not just from the UK, but from around the world. Captain Tom, as he became known, was shown pushing his walking frame around his rather nice garden. He was recovering his mobility after a fall when he'd fractured his hip. An unassuming, gentle, kind man with a smiling face and a positive outlook, who'd already lived through many challenges. He set a fine example to us all. The donations kept coming and it wasn't long before a million pounds had been raised – and it was still climbing. My eyes always filled when I saw him interviewed – a true hero from my parents' generation.

Although I was aware that more children than ever were coming into care, it wasn't until Joy phoned me that what that meant for a foster carer truly hit me. In the past I'd fostered more than one child at a time, but as I looked after my granddaughter some days, I wasn't getting any younger and Adrian worried that I sometimes took on too much, I'd told Joy I preferred to foster just one child at a time.

All that was about to change.

Joy began by asking how we all were, as she always did, and if any of us were displaying symptoms of the coronavirus, waiting for a test or had been in contact with someone who had tested positive.

'No,' I replied. 'We are all fine. How are you?'

'Snowed under with referrals,' Joy replied with crispness to her voice. 'I'm phoning to ask if you can take another child or even a sibling group.'

'Really?'

'You have the room and we're running out of options. The children's homes are either full or having to self-isolate due to someone testing positive.'

'Oh, I see. How long for?' I asked.

'I haven't got a specific child in mind at present. I'm just phoning all my carers to see how many beds we have.'

'Well, yes, I could take two in an emergency,' I said. 'But will they be tested for Covid before they arrive?' It occurred to me that if they weren't, they could bring the virus with them.

'Not as far as I know,' Joy replied. 'But the situation is changing daily, so that might happen. We will try to ascertain if they or any family member have symptoms, but it can't be guaranteed.'

'Won't that be placing us at risk then?'

'To some degree, yes. But it can't be helped, and as a foster carer you will be following your safer-caring practice, and you should have access to priority testing.'

'You mean if we show symptoms we can get tested?'

'Yes.'

Which didn't reassure me at all. It felt a bit like closing the stable door after the horse has bolted. All foster carers have a safer-caring policy, but it didn't include an out-of-control lethal virus, which Joy knew. What we were facing was unprecedented. Paula and I were following the lockdown rules and being very careful to minimize the risk of us or Jamey catching the virus, but that wouldn't necessarily be true of the family the child came from. I could have said no, but I didn't. I agreed to take another child or two if necessary.

CHAPTER TWENTY-ONE

CORA AND THEO

Paula said if we did foster another child or children she could help me as she'd been furloughed, which I appreciated. I didn't tell Lucy or Adrian at that point. If it went ahead I would, but as it wouldn't directly affect them there was no need to worry them at present.

I wanted to do my bit to help in this crisis, but thoughts of Siobhan's Ted, who kept leaving the house and putting others' lives at risk, plagued me. Worst-case scenarios flashed through my mind, including Paula, Jamey and me catching coronavirus, going to hospital and even dying. It was unlike me to have such negative and morbid thoughts, but being subjected day after day to figures showing the rising death toll was having an effect, and my usual optimism was under threat. I quietly hoped that fostering another child or children during the pandemic wouldn't be necessary.

The hope was short-lived. As soon as I saw Joy's number flash on my phone I guessed what it was about.

'How are you all?' she began, as usual.

'Well,' I said.

'I know I always ask you this but can you confirm none of you are displaying symptoms of coronavirus, waiting for a test result or have been in contact with someone who has tested positive or is showing symptoms?' I assumed all social workers had been told to ask this whenever they spoke to a carer.

'That's correct,' I confirmed.

'Good.'

I now braced myself for what Joy was about to say as more worst-case scenarios popped into my head.

'I've had a referral for a sibling pair,' Joy said. 'We need somewhere to take them straight away and I've put your name forward. Their mother is in hospital after her partner attacked her with a knife. He's in police custody, and the children are with a neighbour, but she can't keep them.'

'I see,' I said. And my next thought, I'm sorry to say, wasn't for the trauma that poor family had suffered, but that the children were now in the neighbour's home, increasing their chances of catching and then transmitting the virus to us.

'You'll take them?' Joy asked, an edge of impatience in her tone. 'We need to move them straight away.'

'How old are they?'

'The girl is three and the boy is just a year old.'

'I'll take them,' I said.

'Thank you.' I could hear her relief. 'I'll phone their social worker now and she'll call you.'

Although two young children, in addition to looking after Jamey, would be hard work, I had Paula to help, and once they were here I could protect us all from the virus. At their age they wouldn't be breaking lockdown rules and going out. My spirits lifted and I breathed a sigh of relief. Would I have still felt the same protectiveness, care and concern towards them had they been teenagers who were being moved because of challenging behaviour, as Ted was when he arrived at Siobhan's? Yes, I hoped so, and I would work on changing their unsafe behaviour and making them feel part of the family, as Siobhan was trying to do.

I went into our kitchen-diner where Paula was at the table painting with Jamey. I told her that I'd agreed to take a brother and sister who were just one and three years old. Her eyes lit up.

'They'll be good company for you,' she said to Jamey. Then to me, 'When are they coming?'

'Today, I think. Their social worker is going to phone. But there's always the possibility they might not come after all,' I reminded Paula.

It had happened in the past, as it has to many foster carers. We agree to take a child, we start preparing for their arrival, and then we receive another call to say they aren't coming after all. Usually because a suitable relative has come forward and offered them a home – which is generally considered a better option than going to a foster carer they don't know – or because the judge hasn't granted the care order so they stay with their parents.

While Paula was keeping Jamey amused, I went upstairs and checked the bedroom the children would be sleeping in. The cot was assembled from last time.

From what Joy had said, I was expecting the children's social worker to phone quite quickly, so when an hour passed and I hadn't heard I began to think the children weren't coming. Then at three o'clock the landline rang.

'It's Gabi Dance, social worker for Cora and Theo,' she said. I realized then I didn't even know the children's names; it had all been arranged so quickly. 'I believe Joy told you their situation?'

'Yes, a little.'

'We're on our way and should be with you in about fifteen minutes. I'll talk to you while my colleague drives. In line with current guidelines, we won't stay long in your house; we'll just place the children and leave.'

'All right.' I reached for the pen and paper I kept by the phone to take notes.

'Cora is three and her brother Theo is fourteen months old,' Gabi said. 'The family has never come to the attention of the social services before and the children appear to have been well cared for. They are used to being looked after by their mother and are understandably distraught by what has happened and being separated from her.'

'Yes, I can imagine,' I said. My heart went out to them. I assumed the children were in the car, but I couldn't hear them. 'How is their mother?'

'Lucky to be alive,' Gabi said. 'She was operated on last night. The knife just missed an artery. It seems she and her partner had both been drinking heavily and they argued in the kitchen, where he picked up the knife and stabbed her. There is no record of any previous instances of domestic violence.'

'So when did all this happen?' I asked.

'Around ten o'clock last night. The children were in bed and a neighbour heard a commotion. She and her husband went out to see what was happening and the children's father came out covered in blood. He said there'd been an accident and he had called an ambulance. The neighbour's husband went in and did what he could to help. When the police arrived they were asked to take the children in as they knew them. But they are an elderly couple and can't keep them. They are obviously very upset by what has happened.'

'Yes, it's dreadful.'

'We understand there are some grandparents who we're trying to contact but so far without success. We haven't been able to go into the family home yet as it's a crime scene, so the children just have what they are wearing – nightclothes. As soon as the police have finished and let us go in, we'll get some more of their belongings. You have spares they can use for the time being?' I could hear the tension in her voice.

'Yes, plenty. Do you know anything about the children's medical history? If they have any allergies or take medicine?' It was important I knew.

'We don't think so and they appear to be in good health.'

'No special needs?'

'Not that we are aware of, but we should know more over the coming days. I need to check you can keep them for as long as necessary?'

'Yes.'

'Once their mother is well enough we'll try to arrange a contact video call to her in hospital.'

'All right. They'll be sleeping in the same room here – I assume that is OK?' I checked. 'I have another child here, Jamey Durrant.'

'Yes, it'll have to be. There is no one else in the area who can take them. Everyone is full. You have a cot for the baby?'

'Yes. It's in the room ready.'

Suddenly I heard a child cry out, 'Mummy! Mummy!'

'She's in hospital, love,' Gabi said. Then to me, 'We'll see you in about five minutes. I'll answer any more questions you have then.'

I replaced the handset and returned to the living room where Paula was with Jamey.

'The children and their social workers will be here in five minutes,' I said, and any concerns for my own welfare vanished. Two small children had been taken from their home in the night in terrible circumstances and were now separated from their parents indefinitely.

'We're going to be looking after a little boy and a girl,' Paula told Jamey.

He looked at us, bewildered, as well he might, then, reaching up, he gave Paula a big hug.

I didn't have time to become nervous as I sometimes do when I have plenty of notice of a child arriving. I went straight upstairs to put linen on the cot and bed, and as I finished the front doorbell rang.

'Stay with Jamey in the living room, please!' I called to Paula as I ran downstairs. I thought if we all rushed to the front door it would be overwhelming for the little ones.

I opened the door to two social workers, with a child each – Cora, three, and Theo, one – dressed in pyjamas and dressing gowns. 'Come in,' I said, and stood aside to give them room.

'I'm Gabi and this is Kyle,' Gabi said, coming in first. She was holding Cora's hand and Kyle was carrying Theo.

Both children looked scared and miserable. Although they weren't crying now, they clearly had been, for their eyes and cheeks were red.

'We're in the living room,' I said, and led the way down the hall. 'This is my daughter Paula, who will be helping me, and this is Jamey, who is staying with us.'

'He's one of Shannon's?' Gabi asked, referring to their social worker.

'Yes. Do sit down. Can I get anyone a drink?'

'Not for us,' Gabi said, perching on the edge of a chair. 'We won't stay long.'

Cora sat on Gabi's lap and looked at me warily. Kyle had Theo on his lap while I sat on the sofa beside Paula and Jamey – on the other side of the room. Jamey was staring distrustfully at the sudden arrival of strangers. It did feel strange when there'd just been us for so long.

'The children have had lunch,' Gabi said. 'Their neighbour gave them something, but she said they didn't eat much.'

'I'll give them dinner before long,' I said. 'Has Theo been weaned?'

'I assume so,' Gabi said.

'Yes, he must have been,' Kyle added. 'The neighbour gave them pasta for lunch.'

'OK, good. Do either of them have any special dietary requirements?' I thought to ask.

'Not as far as we know,' Gabi replied. 'Here is the placement information so far. Can you sign the placement agreement form, please?' She took some printed forms from her bag and set them on the coffee table. 'I'll email the rest as soon as I have a chance. My contact details are on there.'

'Thank you.' I signed the relevant form and handed it back.

Both children were still staring at me guardedly and I

smiled. 'Would you like to play with some of these toys?' I suggested, picking out a couple from the toy box.

Cora clung tightly to her social worker and shook her head, while Theo looked at the toys but didn't move. I heard Kyle's phone bleep. He took it from his pocket and checked it, then showed the screen to Gabi.

She sighed. 'Tell her we're looking, but everywhere is full. I'll phone her tomorrow.'

I guessed this was about another child. Kyle texted a message and returned his phone to his pocket. It wasn't long before it bleeped again.

'Do you have everything you need here?' Gabi asked me.

'Yes.'

'We'll just have a quick look around before we go. Come on, Cora, let's see where you'll be sleeping for now.'

She eased Cora from her lap and stood. Cora grabbed her arm, clearly not wanting to be parted from her. Kyle also stood but was still carrying Theo.

'Does Theo walk?' I asked.

'Yes, he was at the neighbours', but he cries if I put him down,' Kyle said. Which was understandable. He felt more secure being held.

Paula stayed with Jamey in the living room as I showed the social workers, Cora and Theo around. The kitchen-diner first, then the front room and upstairs. It was the quickest tour I'd ever given. Normally we lingered in each room so the children got used to their new home and the social workers had a chance to ask questions. Today they were just poking their heads around the doors and moving on.

'This is the children's bedroom,' I said, pushing open the door. I waited outside.

'That's fine,' Gabi said, quickly going in and out.

There was no reaction from the children; they looked dazed.

'We'll leave you to it and I'll phone tomorrow,' Gabi said, heading downstairs. 'I'll just get my bag.'

Cora clung to Gabi as she went into the living room. I heard Gabi say goodbye to Paula and Jamey as I waited in the hall with Kyle and Theo.

'Are you going to come to me?' I said, offering my arms to Theo.

Theo drew back and buried his face in his social worker's shoulder. At some point he was going to have to come to me, upsetting though that would be for him. Gabi returned with Cora still clinging to her, then as she said goodbye Cora screamed.

'I want to come with you!' She burst into tears.

Gabi bent so she was at Cora's height. 'Don't upset yourself, pet. Remember what I said in the car. You're going to stay here with Cathy and her family until Mummy is better.'

'I want to go home!' Cora wailed. Which set Theo off crying too.

Kyle's phone started ringing. It was chaos in the hall. He glanced at the screen and showed it to Gabi. 'They'll just have to wait,' she said, stressed.

Both children were crying loudly and it was obvious that neither of them were happily going to stay with me, not yet at least.

'I think we'll just have to go,' Gabi said, passing Cora's hand to me. 'I'll phone you tomorrow.'

'I want my mummy! Daddy!' Cora wailed.

'I know, love,' I said, and drew her close.

Kyle handed Theo to me and they let themselves out. I'm sure they felt as bad as I did, leaving to the sounds of the children crying, but there was nothing else they could do. It would take time before the children settled, and the longer they were in the house, the greater the risk of transmitting the virus. While we'd been in the hall handing over the children all social distancing had gone.

Theo was struggling to be put down, so now the front door was closed I gently lowered him to the floor where he collapsed in a heap, sobbing loudly. Cora continued crying, 'I want my mummy! Daddy! I want to go home.' She was becoming hysterical.

As I soothed her, the living-room door opened and Paula and Jamey appeared looking very worried.

'If you could bring Theo, I'll bring Cora,' I said to Paula. 'They'll soon be all right,' I told Jamey with a reassuring smile.

I knew from experience that the first twenty-four hours would be the most traumatic for the children, then, with lots of care, concern and reassurance they would begin to adapt and settle into their new home. I had no idea how long Cora and Theo would be with me; I assumed Gabi would include their care plan in her email.

Paula and I gradually encouraged the children into the living room and then distracted them with toys. Ten minutes later, tears spent, Cora and Theo had stopped crying. Theo was exploring a toy box with Jamey, while Cora was talking to us, asking questions, answering ours, and saying how much she loved and missed her mummy and daddy. Their resilience, fortitude, and courage was admirable, as it is in so many children who come into care. They are truly little heroes.

But what struck me was the developmental gap between Cora and Jamey. Cora was probably only six months older than Jamey but could have been years ahead of him. Even little Theo at fourteen months was confidently exploring items and naming some of them, his vocabulary similar to Jamey's when he'd first arrived, aged two and a half. It highlighted more than ever how important those early years are, and while Jamey was doing well, the effects of neglect were still obvious. I felt a surge of love and protectiveness towards him and gave him a big hug.

CHAPTER TWENTY-TWO

COVID CHANGED OUR LIVES

Dinner that evening was very different from usual with three little ones at the table. I would like to say it was lively, but Cora and Theo were subdued, although they did eat. Cora fed herself confidently using children's cutlery, while I helped Theo spoon-feed himself, loading the spoon and guiding it to his mouth. Jamey was still overawed by their sudden arrival and I was trying to make sure he had his fair share of attention, although in practical terms it was less than it had been, as Paula and I were now split between three and Theo needed a lot of attention.

But all three children ate a fair amount, including the yoghurt and diced fresh fruit I gave them for pudding. Cora said the yoghurt was like the one her mummy gave her, so I felt I had done something right.

Cora and Theo looked very tired. They'd had a traumatic and exhausting twenty-four hours and I knew they'd feel better after a good night's sleep. Paula offered to clear away the dishes and look after Jamey while I took them to bed.

'Call us when they're ready and we'll say goodnight,' Paula said.

I'd already taken fresh towels and face flannels from the linen cupboard and new toothbrushes from my spares and put them in the bathroom ready for bedtime. Cora and Theo were still dressed in the nightwear they'd arrived in and as I ran the water for their wash I suggested they might like to change into some clean pyjamas. Cora said a forceful 'No, I like these.' I didn't press it. They could have fresh clothes in the morning, and what they were wearing would be comfortingly familiar. It was all they had from home at present.

Although Cora and Theo had settled during the evening, now it was time for bed their tears and upset returned.

'I want to go home. I want my mummy!' Cora cried, then she grew angry and threw her toothbrush into the sink. I took it out and handed it back to her. 'I don't like you! I'm going to tell my daddy about you! Take me home now!' she demanded.

Theo, seeing his sister upset and angry, began to grizzle and then, dropping to the floor, started a full-scale tantrum, screaming, his arms and legs flailing. Hearing the commotion, Paula called up.

'Do you need any help, Mum?'

'I'll manage up here if you can stay with Jamey, please,' I said over the noise.

'Lucy just texted – shall I tell her Cora and Theo are with us?' Paula asked.

'Maybe wait until things are a bit calmer,' I replied. For I felt sure she'd phone when she found out.

I comforted and reassured both children enough to finish doing their teeth and have a wash, then I put Theo in a clean nappy. I fetched the bag of spare soft toys I kept in my bedroom and said they could choose one each to take to bed with them. Theo took the first one he came across – a cuddly elephant – but Cora spent some time rummaging in the bag and then tipped out the contents. Reluctantly, she settled on a velvet-smooth teddy bear.

'It's not the same as my bear at home,' she grumbled, clearly tired.

'No, but it's a nice bear with lovely soft fur,' I said encouragingly. 'I'm sure he will like you as much as you like him.'

'I don't like him at all,' she said, her face clouding.

'Would you like to choose another one then?'

'No. I want this one.'

'OK, love.' I would ask Gabi to bring some of the children's toys from home when she collected their clothes.

As I took the children to their bedroom Paula called up again. 'Shall I get Jamey ready for bed now?'

'Yes, please, love.'

'Where's his bedroom?' Cora asked as Paula brought Jamey upstairs.

'In there,' I said, pointing to his room. 'And that's Paula's room. You've already seen mine.'

'Where does his daddy sleep?' Cora asked. I guessed she thought I was married and that Jamey was my child.

'He doesn't live here,' I said. 'There's just us in this house. I am looking after Jamey like I am looking after you and Theo.'

Cora looked puzzled. This was probably the first time she'd come across fostering. 'Are you his mummy?' she asked.

'No, foster carer, like a mummy.'

'You're not my mummy.'

'No, foster carer,' I confirmed. Cora certainly knew her own mind!

Jamey seemed confused and worried by all the talk about mummies and foster carers, so I hugged and kissed him goodnight, then left him with Paula to get ready for bed, while I took Cora and Theo into their bedroom. I would have struggled to manage bedtime for three children without Paula's help.

The cot in the children's bedroom was on the opposite wall to the bed so Theo and Cora could see each other.

'Do we have to sleep here?' Cora asked mournfully.

'Yes, love. This is your bedroom for now, while you are with me.'

'It's too small,' she said. 'I have a big bedroom at my house and Theo doesn't sleep with me.'

'It's a bit different here, and I thought it would be nice for you and Theo to sleep in the same room. Let's see how it goes tonight.' I lifted Theo into his cot. If it didn't work out I could put the cot in my bedroom.

'I want to go to my home,' Cora said.

'I know, love, but that's not possible right now. There is no one there to look after you.' I encouraged Theo to lie down and tucked the cuddly elephant in beside him, then turned to Cora.

'Come on, love, into bed. You must be tired.'

She rubbed her eyes. 'Why isn't there anyone at my house?' she asked.

'Do you remember what your social worker told you? That Mummy was in hospital?'

She nodded. 'Where's Daddy?'

'I'm not sure, love. Now, into bed.'

'Why's Mummy in hospital?' she asked, then reluctantly climbed into bed.

'She was hurt and the doctors are making her better.'

Theo was now standing up in his cot, looking at us.

'Did Daddy hurt Mummy?' Cora asked. I had no idea how much she knew, and it wasn't for me to tell her that her father had stabbed her mother. Her social worker would tell her what she needed to know.

'Mummy and Daddy are safe,' I reassured her. 'Now, lie down and try to get some sleep. If Theo sees you going to sleep, he will too.'

Cora laid her head on the pillow, but instead of closing her eyes ready for sleep she began to weep. 'I want my mummy and daddy!' she cried.

'I understand, love.' I soothed her forehead.

I heard Paula leave the bathroom with Jamey and go into his bedroom.

As I comforted Cora, Theo began to grizzle so I went to pacify him. I laid him down again, tucked the cuddly in beside him and returned to Cora. I spent the next half an hour going between the cot and the bed, reassuring them and trying to get them off to sleep. The more tired they grew, the unhappier they became.

Then Cora said, 'Theo has a bottle at night.'

'Of milk?' I asked her.

'Yes.'

It's details like this that are really useful for the foster carer as they are part of a familiar routine for the child and can make them feel at home. I assumed that Gabi and Kyle had either forgotten to tell me or didn't know.

'Thank you for telling me,' I said to Cora. 'You stay in your bed and I'll get Theo some milk. Do you have a drink at bedtime?'

'No.'

Leaving their bedroom door open, I hurried downstairs and into the kitchen where I took a new feeding bottle from the cupboard and warmed some milk. I assumed Theo had cow's milk – most infants his age do. I tested its heat before returning upstairs. Having seen Jamey to bed, Paula was now waiting with Theo and Cora.

'Thanks, love,' I said.

'I'll be in my room if you need me.'

I went to lift Theo out of the cot to give him the bottle, but Cora said, 'He does it.'

'Thank you, you're a big help.'

I handed Theo the bottle and he lay on his side and began sucking on it while I sat on Cora's bed, watching him. I'd already dimmed the lights ready for sleep and we could just see him in the half-light. Gradually, as he sucked, his eyes began to close and before he'd finished he was asleep. I quietly removed the bottle from the cot.

'Now, I want you to go to sleep too,' I whispered to Cora. 'I'll leave the light on low and the door open, so call out if you want me in the night.'

'Can I see Mummy and Daddy tomorrow?' she asked, quietly.

'I don't know yet, love,' I replied truthfully.

'When can I see them?' Her bottom lip trembled.

'As soon as possible. Your social worker will tell us.' I put my arm around her.

'Can I see Nana and Grandpa?' she asked.

I really didn't know, and I couldn't give her false hope. Gabi had mentioned they were trying to locate some grandparents, but that was all I knew.

'I'm not sure yet. Do you see them often?'

She looked thoughtful and then said, 'Yes.'

'Do they live close?'

'We go in the car,' she said. Which of course could mean anywhere.

'Don't you worry. Your social worker will know. Now, off to sleep. We can go to the park tomorrow.'

'I like the park,' she said, and snuggled down.

'Good girl.'

I stayed with her until she was asleep, then tiptoed from the room.

It was nearly 9 p.m. and I was exhausted, but I knew I should start my log notes for Cora and Theo as well as writing up Jamey's. Downstairs in the front room I logged onto my computer. After I'd finished their daily records, I made a written note of all the questions I needed to ask Gabi when she next telephoned. I then looked at the placement information form Gabi had left. It showed the children's full names, dates of birth and that they were the subject of an Emergency Protection Order. Their parents' names and occupations were given; their father was a financial advisor and their mother was a beautician with her own business. The address of the family home surprised me. It was in an affluent area – a road of large, privately owned detached houses. They seemed to be an educated couple who had been doing well – on the outside at least. So what had gone so badly wrong that it had led to them drinking heavily, then him stabbing her? I wondered. It was a tragedy. The family had been torn apart, the father would face prosecution, so it was unlikely they'd ever be the same again. And the children would carry the memory of that fateful night with them for a very long time.

In the box on the form for other significant adults, the names of the maternal grandparents were given. There wasn't much else I didn't already know and I tucked the form into a new folder, which I would keep in a locked drawer. It was now after 10 p.m. and, aware that the children were likely to wake in the night, I locked up and went upstairs to bed. I checked on Cora and Theo, and they were both asleep. I tapped on Paula's bedroom door and went in. She was watching a film on her laptop. I told her I was going to bed and thanked her for all her help.

'Night, Mum. There's no need to thank me, I'm happy to help. But what will happen when I return to work? How will you manage then?' she asked.

'Don't worry. The children will be more settled by then,' I replied positively.

I kissed her goodnight and left her to finish watching her film. It was important she had some 'me time', as it is for all members of a family that fosters.

I checked on Cora and Theo at 2 a.m. and they were both sound asleep. Then around 5.30 I was woken with a start.

'Mummy! Mummy!' Cora cried, panic-stricken.

I grabbed my dressing gown and ran round the landing, hoping her cries hadn't woken Jamey or Paula.

'It's OK,' I reassured her, going in. 'There's nothing to be frightened of. I expect you wondered where you are.'

She was sitting upright in bed, staring around. Theo

was standing up in his cot and looked as though he was about to cry. I lifted him out and sat with him on my lap on Cora's bed as I comforted them both.

'Can we go home today, please?' she asked, her face crumpling. My heart went out to her.

'Not today, love,' I said gently, brushing a strand of hair from her face. 'But I'll find lots of nice things for you to do, like painting and model making. We can go to the park later, but it's a bit early yet. Do you think you can go back to sleep?'

'No,' she said, rubbing her eyes. 'I want my mummy.'

Although it was very early, I thought she'd feel happier if she was occupied. I could gradually ease them into a better routine over the coming days when they were more settled.

'If you really can't go back to sleep, we'll go downstairs and find something for you to play with. But we need to be quiet so we don't wake Jamey and Paula. We also need to change Theo's nappy first. So quietly.'

I helped them into their dressing gowns and changed Theo's nappy, making a mental note that I would need to buy more nappies when I went shopping.

Downstairs I made them both a drink, following Cora's instructions on what they liked. Then I took them into the living room where I kept them amused with toys, puzzles and games. After an hour Theo fell asleep on the sofa, while I sat with Cora and read her some stories. She was interested in the books and said her mummy read to her, but I was tired and could easily have nodded off. Then I heard Jamey get up to use the toilet. Theo was awake now and I took him and Cora upstairs, where Jamey was waiting for me on the landing.

'Good boy,' I said.

He was in trainer pants at night but now used the toilet on waking. I waited until he'd finished washing his hands. Paula was still asleep so rather than bath and dress the children now and risk waking her I took them downstairs for breakfast. We were all still in our dressing gowns, but it didn't matter as we were in lockdown and weren't going anywhere.

I asked Cora what she would like for breakfast and showed her the cereal we had. 'That one,' she said, pointing to the packet of hot oat cereal.

'Does Theo have the same?'

'Yes.'

Jamey wanted the porridge too and I seated all three children at the table – Theo in a baby booster seat with a tray – while I made the porridge with warm milk.

'We have honey with it,' Cora said as I set the bowls on the table. So I fetched the honey. I sat at the table eating my toast and coffee and helping Theo.

As we ate Paula came downstairs in her dressing gown and, saying hello to all three children, made herself tea and toast. Once I'd finished my breakfast, I left her in charge while I went upstairs to shower and dress. Then it was her turn to shower and dress, after which we bathed and dressed all three children – Cora and Theo in clothes from my spares, which Cora didn't like at all. Although she and Theo were less tearful than yesterday, she was a bit grumpy and, when not fully occupied, asked for her mummy and daddy, which was only natural. I reassured her as best I could and said I hoped to hear from her social worker today. Theo just wanted to be held or sit on one of our laps.

I thought we'd leave going to the park until the after-noon so Cora and Theo had a chance to familiarize themselves with their new home. Once we were all dressed, Cora said she wanted to go in the garden, which I understood she'd been doing at home. The weather had turned cool for the end of April, but I was pleased she was taking an interest and wanted to do something. I found them both jackets in my spares and we all went into the garden where we got out toys from the shed.

My neighbour and friend Sue must have heard us, for she called over the fence: 'Are you OK, Cathy? Sounds like you've opened a nursery there.'

'It feels like it!' I called back. 'We're all well. How are you?'

'So far so good. Stay safe and see you when we are allowed to.'

'Yes, indeed.'

This was similar to the conversations we were all having with our friends and family – stay safe and see you as soon as we are allowed. How changed our lives were as a result of the pandemic.

CHAPTER TWENTY-THREE

SAMANTHA

Joy phoned my mobile while we were in the garden and I went inside to take the call, leaving Paula with the children. Joy knew Cora and Theo had arrived yesterday and asked how their first night had gone. I told her they'd slept reasonably well and I was waiting to hear from their social worker about contact with their mother and getting their belongings from home. She asked if I had all the equipment I needed for fostering them, and I said I'd have to buy another car seat when we began going out again in the car. I had a booster seat for Cora but only one child seat, and both Jamey and Theo would need to use one. She said she'd ask around to see if another carer had a spare. I'd shared my equipment before when it wasn't in use. She said she'd video call me later in the week in place of the home visit she would have normally made when a new child arrived.

After lunch, at 1 p.m., I made the contact video call to Kat using my mobile but she didn't answer. I texted her to say I'd tried and that Jamey was well and we were going to the park. As we walked there, Theo in the stroller, Cora walking by my side and Jamey holding

Paula's hand, Kat replied by text: *Thanks. Give him my love.* But she didn't return the call. I quietly told Jamey his mother had texted and sent her love.

The children's play area in the park was still taped off, as were the benches, so we played on the grass with a ball I'd brought from home. Then we fed the ducks. Theo and Cora weren't frightened of them as Jamey had been, and Cora said they saw ducks with their mummy and daddy. I noticed Jamey was quieter than usual and I made sure he was included in all conversations and activities. Not an assertive child who would push himself forward, he kept giving way to Cora – standing aside and holding back. Cora was very confident and clearly used to being heard and having her own way, so quiet, unassuming Jamey could easily fall into second place if Paula and I hadn't kept encouraging him. I didn't want the progress he'd made coming to a halt, with the possibility of him regressing.

When the children had had enough of the ducks and the park we took a slow walk home. I made us a drink and a snack and Theo had a little nap in his cot. It was 4 p.m. before Gabi phoned. She began by asking how the children were and I told her what I'd told Joy, adding that we'd been in the garden and to the park. I said Cora and Theo weren't as upset as they had been yesterday.

'Good. Their mother, Samantha, wants to speak to them. Can you video call her, please? She's still in hospital but has her phone with her. She's likely to be in there the rest of the week.'

'Yes, what time?'

'As soon as you can. She's expecting your call. Her number is ...' Gabi read it out and I made a note. 'I haven't had a chance to get the children's belongings from home. Samantha's parents have keys and will get some of their things. Are you managing for now?'

'Yes. Cora is asking about her nana and grandpa.'

'They see the children regularly and Samantha is planning on going to stay with them when she is discharged from hospital. She wants the children to go there too. I've spoken to her parents, Mr and Mrs Sutton, and I'll be doing a virtual visit on Thursday. They are naturally distraught at what has happened, even more so as they can't visit their daughter in hospital because of the Covid restrictions.'

'So is it likely the children will go to their grandparents?' I asked. Clearly a lot had changed in the last twenty-four hours since the children had arrived.

'It's a strong possibility, but don't tell the children until it's certain. I need to see Mr and Mrs Sutton and complete some checks first.'

'I won't.' I'd been fostering long enough to know that arrangements can change, so I would only tell Cora and Theo they were going to their grandparents once Gabi confirmed it and a date had been set.

She wound up by saying she'd be in touch and asked me to phone Samantha now. I stayed in the hall where I'd gone to take the call, out of earshot of Cora and Theo, and keyed in Samantha's mobile number. Samantha answered straight away and I was immediately reminded how intrusive video calls can be. The poor woman was in bed, propped up on a mound of pillows and wearing a hospital gown. She looked pale and very tired.

'Samantha, I'm Cathy, your children's foster carer,' I said.

'Oh,' she gasped, and struggled to sit up but winced with pain.

'Are you all right?'

'Just a bit sore. Where are they? I've been worried sick. Can I see them now?'

'Yes, of course.'

'Thank you.'

I took the phone into the living room where Paula was looking after the children. 'Mummy is on the phone,' I said.

'Mummy!' Cora screeched at the top of her voice.

I took Theo on my lap and positioned my phone so they could both see the screen.

'Mummy! Mummy!' Cora cried, and burst into tears. 'Where are you? I want you. Where's Daddy? I want to go home!'

'I'm all right. Don't upset yourself. You're making me cry,' Samantha said, her eyes filling.

I tried to reassure Cora. 'Mummy is safe in hospital.'

'Mummy! Mummy!' Cora screamed again, becoming hysterical.

Jamey was in the room looking worried, so I asked Paula to take him to another room to play. 'Calm down, love,' I said to Cora, and wiped her eyes. 'Mummy is all right. She's in hospital being looked after by the doctors and nurses.' Samantha was wiping her eyes.

'I'm going to be all right,' she said, her voice shaking. 'Let's be happy. It's so good to see you both. I've missed you so much.'

'I've missed you. I want to go home,' Cora said, fresh tears falling.

'We can't go home yet,' Samantha said. 'But you'll

be going to stay with Nana and Grandpa soon.' I hoped she was right. 'I'll join you there as soon as I can leave hospital.'

'I want to be with you,' Cora cried.

'I know, love. We'll all be together soon.' Samantha was struggling to maintain her composure.

Theo was on my lap staring wide-eyed at his mother's image. 'Wave to Mummy,' I encouraged him.

'Theo, it's Mummy. Are you OK, love?' Samantha asked.

He smiled.

'I love you,' Samantha said, waving.

'Wave to Mummy,' I encouraged him again, and he did.

'Can I wave?' Cora asked.

'Yes, of course, love,' Samantha said.

'They are both fine,' I reassured her. 'They're obviously missing you but I'm keeping them occupied with games and stories. We went to the park this afternoon.'

Her eyes filled. 'Thank you so much. Are they eating all right?'

'Yes. Gabi said they didn't have any food allergies – is that correct?'

'Yes.'

'They both had porridge for breakfast and then the meals I'm cooking. Is there anything in particular they like or dislike?'

'Not really. I make sure they have fruit and veg each day. But they like most things. I can't believe this has happened to me.' Samantha was clearly still struggling to come to terms with what had happened. 'The surgeon said I could easily have died. My poor children. I am grateful to you, but they will be better off with my parents. They know them well.'

'Yes, Gabi said, and Cora has mentioned her nana and grandpa a lot.'

'Has the social worker told you when my parents can collect them?' Samantha asked, again trying to sit more upright.

'No, she's going to let me know.'

'Mum and Dad offered to collect them today, but the social worker said she needed to do some checks first and see their house. Dad wasn't happy.'

'It's normal practice,' I said. 'It sounds to me as though it's going through very quickly. Sometimes these checks can take months.'

'Mummy, I want to go home,' Cora said. 'I don't like it here.'

Samantha looked embarrassed.

'Don't worry,' I said with a smile. 'I understand. Of course they'd rather be with you.'

'Are you hurt?' Cora asked her mother.

'I was, but the doctors are making me better. I'm going to be all right, love.'

'Where's Daddy?' Cora persisted.

'At home,' Samantha replied. So I assumed he'd been released from police custody.

'Can I go home?' Cora asked.

'No, love, not yet. We're going to stay with Nana and Grandpa.'

'Why?'

'It's better that way.'

Clearly Samantha wouldn't want to go into the details with Cora, so I changed the subject.

'Tell Mummy what you've been doing,' I encouraged. 'We saw some ducks in the park and played ball.' But she shook her head.

'Theo looks content,' Samantha said, brightening slightly.

'Yes, he's fine. Try not to worry. My adult daughter and I are taking good care of them both.'

'Gabi said you'd been fostering a long time. I expect you're used to things like this happening, but I can't believe it. Neither can my parents. He just lost it.' I assumed she meant her partner. Her eyes glistened with tears again, then a nurse appeared and said something to her. 'Cathy, can I call you back a bit later?'

'Yes, of course.'

'Bye, Cora. Bye, Theo. Love you, speak soon.'

As Samantha ended the call Cora began to cry. I comforted her and then we went to find Paula and Jamey. They were in the front room playing on his tablet. I thanked Paula for looking after him and then organized an activity for us all to do.

Samantha video called half an hour later and Cora wasn't so upset this time. They talked for about fifteen minutes. Theo was playing and I positioned the phone so Samantha could watch him. She asked me if she could phone again later when they were in bed to say goodnight and what time would be good.

'Seven o'clock,' I suggested.

'Thank you, Cathy.'

There was no reason why Samantha shouldn't phone her children. Indeed, as it seemed they would be shortly returning to her care there was every reason why they should – to maintain their bond. Being separated would have some effect, but it was important to minimize it as much as possible and the video calls would help.

That evening Paula took care of Jamey's bedtime while I bathed Cora and Theo and got them ready for bed. Once they were in bed I made the video call to their mother, but it was bittersweet. While it was a lovely idea for her to say goodnight, they couldn't cuddle or kiss each other as they usually did and it reminded Cora of what she was missing. She soon became tearful again, which unsettled Theo.

'It's awful seeing them upset when I can't do anything,' Samantha said, also close to tears.

'Maybe just say goodnight. I'll stay with them until they are asleep,' I reassured her.

'Thank you, Cathy. I'll say goodnight and phone again in the morning.'

'OK.'

She blew them both a big kiss and said, 'Night, night, I love you both so much. You go to sleep now and I'll phone tomorrow.'

I encouraged the children to say goodnight and wave and then we ended the call. I dimmed the light, then sat on the floor space between the cot and the bed, from where I comforted both children until they were fast asleep. It took nearly an hour. Had they been staying for longer I would have gradually eased them into a better routine where I kissed them goodnight and came out, leaving them to go to sleep, and repeating as often as necessary. But they'd had a lot of upset and changes in the last few days and would very likely be facing another move soon.

Once they were both soundly asleep I came out, leaving the door slightly open, and went downstairs, where I wrote up my log notes. Then I spent some time talking to Paula before having a soak in the bath and going to bed.

Cora and Theo only woke once in the night and slept in a little longer than the night before – until 6 a.m.!

Their mother phoned at 8 a.m. while they were having breakfast. They stopped eating so she said she'd phone back when they'd finished. She did, at 8.30, and then again at 9.15. While it was nice for them all to be in regular contact, and reassuring for Samantha, it was unsettling for Theo and Cora, as contact often is for children in care. Cora was constantly asking when she could see Mummy again, and I even found her with my phone trying to call her. Theo, not really understanding where his mother was, just looked bewildered and unhappy after each call. I distracted them both with toys and games until they settled again.

Wednesday presented another challenge. I needed to do a big food shop at the supermarket but I couldn't take all three children with me in my car. Also, it would be impossible to socially distance them from other shoppers as we were being asked to do. I didn't feel comfortable leaving them all with Paula as it was a huge responsibility, so I suggested to her that I took Jamey with me if she could look after Cora and Theo. This would also give him a break from them and allow us some one-to-one time, which had been sadly lacking since their arrival. Paula agreed although she asked me to change Theo's nappy first, which I did.

We explained what was happening to the children.

'I want to come,' Cora said, pulling a face.

'I'd like you to stay here with Paula and Theo,' I said. 'I'll only be a couple of hours and then we can go to the park later.'

'I go shopping with Mummy,' Cora persisted.

'Yes, but it's a bit different now. I'd like you to stay and help Paula with Theo. She won't be able to manage alone without your help.'

Paula joined in my amateur psychology and agreed that she couldn't possibly manage without Cora's help. It did the trick. Saying goodbye, I left with Jamey while the going was good.

As I drove I talked to Jamey and asked him how he was feeling.

He met my gaze in the rear-view mirror but didn't reply.

'Happy, sad or not sure?' I asked him.

'Not sure,' he replied quietly.

'I understand, love, it's a lot for you to take in. I think you're doing very well. It shouldn't be for much longer.'

I'd think carefully in future about taking extra children while Jamey was with me, especially when Paula returned to work as I would be spread too thinly to help the children as much as I would like. Fostering isn't just about feeding and clothing the children, but also nurturing them to their full potential.

Jamey and I joined a socially distanced queue outside the supermarket, which gradually moved forward as customers left. I explained to Jamey what was happening, and it became a bit of a game with him taking two giant steps when we were allowed to as the queue inched forward. A member of staff positioned at the entrance smiled at Jamey as she sanitized the handlebar of the trolley. Once inside, as well as socially distancing we had to follow the one-way system marked out by arrows on the floor. Jamey liked those too and we were progressing well until I realized I'd forgotten the honey, and we had to do an entire lap of the store to return to the aisle where the honey was. Jamey chuckled.

Some of the shelves were low on stock, especially essential items, but thankfully there were nappies.

'Nappies,' Jamey said, looking puzzled as I put them into the trolley.

'For Theo,' I clarified. 'You don't wear nappies any more, you're a big boy.'

He smiled and glowed with pride. I kissed his cheek. He was adorable and I'm not ashamed to say I loved him dearly. Since leaving the house and there had just been the two of us he'd relaxed, started to come out of his shell again and was now enjoying himself.

'Apples,' he said, as I parked the trolley beside the fruit display.

'That's right. How many shall we buy? One, two, three …' I began counting out the apples and putting them into the bag Jamey was holding.

Jamey repeated the numbers, although I knew he couldn't count yet, unlike Cora who could confidently count to twelve all by herself. But children develop at different rates and Jamey hadn't had a good start in life. It would take time for him to catch up.

As we steered the trolley through the clothes section I paused to select a new outfit each for Theo and Cora, and pyjamas. I didn't know if or when their clothes would come from home, and while I had plenty of spares, these would be theirs to keep. I also bought Jamey another tracksuit. As we approached the checkout my phone went off and I saw it was a video call from Samantha.

'I'm in the supermarket,' I said. 'I'll call you once I'm home.'

'Is it safe there for Cora and Theo with all those germs?' she asked, immediately anxious.

'They're at home with my daughter Paula. Don't worry. I'll video call you once we're back.'

I think we were all worrying more about our family's health during the pandemic. However, I didn't have a chance to return Samantha's call, for as I was unpacking the shopping she phoned again. I left Paula and Jamey to continue the unpacking in the kitchen while I went into the living room with Cora and Theo.

'Sorry if I'm making a nuisance of myself,' Samantha said. 'But all I've got to do is lie here and worry about my children.'

'I completely understand,' I said. 'I'm sure I'd be the same. Here they are.'

CHAPTER TWENTY-FOUR

NANA AND GRANDPA

Samantha phoned about every hour on Thursday morning. During at least one conversation she told Cora and Theo their nana and grandpa would be collecting them on Saturday. I sounded a note of caution and said I hadn't heard from Gabi yet.

'I'll call her now and tell her to phone you,' Samantha said.

Samantha seemed brighter and stronger and was hoping to be discharged from hospital at the weekend. She would go to her parents to continue her convalescence. If Cora asked about Daddy, Samantha just said he was all right and at home, then changed the subject.

On Thursday afternoon I managed to get through to Kat for Jamey's video call. Paula was looking after Cora and Theo in another room, and Kat had a reasonable conversation with Jamey, although it was short. She showed him where she was living by panning her phone around the room. It was a small bedsit and very untidy, but she seemed not to mind. More importantly, she made an effort to talk to Jamey and asked him what he'd been doing.

'Playing and park,' he said.

'That's nice. Are you being a good boy?'

'Yes,' Jamey dutifully replied.

Their conversation lasted about ten minutes, during which time she didn't stay in the same place for more than a couple of seconds. She paced the room, sat on the bed, stood up again and paced some more. She seemed on edge and nervy, as she had at other times. It wasn't long before she said she had to go and after telling Jamey to be good she said goodbye. Jamey, of course, just accepted it and said a quiet 'bye'. He didn't really expect any more from his mother and I thought how very different Kat's interaction with Jamey was compared to Samantha's with her children. Indeed, how different their lives had been. We're not born with parenting skills; we learn them as we go along and also from the example our parents set us. And of course it's very difficult to raise a child if you are battling your own demons, as Kat was.

That evening at 8 p.m., when all three children were asleep, Paula and I went outside to 'clap for carers'. After we returned indoors we video called Lucy and Adrian for a chat. Emma was in bed, but Lucy called us at other times when she was awake so we could speak to her. While these video calls were enjoyable, I was starting to feel that much of my life was becoming virtual – online meetings with family and friends, and for fostering. Like many, I craved a time when we would all be able to meet again as normal, in person, with family hugs and kisses.

Joy scheduled a virtual supervisory meeting for 10 a.m. on Friday. She was more adept with the software now, as indeed I was. I was using my tablet in the front room, while Paula kept the children amused with activities at the table in the kitchen-diner. Joy started by asking if we were all well and I told her we were. Then I said that Samantha seemed to think her parents would be collecting Cora and Theo on Saturday and taking them to live with them, but I hadn't heard anything from Gabi. Joy said she'd phone her as soon as we'd finished to find out what was going on. Communication and updates were proving more difficult with so many not being in the office.

The rest of her 'visit' took the usual format, only of course it was online rather than in person. Joy asked how I was managing with three children and I said that the practical aspects worked with Paula at home, but that I didn't think having two more children in the house was doing Jamey any good. Joy felt that part of this could be due to him being an only child who wasn't used to mixing with other children – he'd only just started play-group when we went into lockdown. I felt he lacked confidence because of his early life experience. She asked what I was doing by way of activities, and I gave examples and described an average day. As I talked I could hear Paula playing with the children in the kitchen-diner.

Joy asked if any of the children had had any accidents or illnesses – as she was required to do at each visit. I confirmed they hadn't. She said she'd read and signed my log notes online and asked if I could do the same with her supervisory report from her last visit. She said training for foster carers had resumed and was now online and I should log in to the local authority's portal and sign up for the training I needed. She said she wanted to see the children, so I took the tablet into the kitchen-diner and propped it on the table. Cora and Theo were crayoning. Theo was on Paula's lap.

'This is Joy, my supervising social worker,' I said, more for Cora's and Theo's benefit than Jamey's, as he'd met her before.

'Hi, Jamey, Cora and Theo,' Joy said, with a smile. 'Hi, Paula. You're doing a good job.'

'Thank you,' Paula said, and stopped Theo from trying to eat a crayon.

'How are you all?' Joy asked.

'Good,' Paula replied.

Cora paused from colouring to look at Joy and then continued, a grumpy look on her face.

'Can I see your pictures?' Joy asked.

Cora ignored her but Jamey held up his picture.

'That's wonderful. I think I can see lots of blue sky and the sun.'

Jamey smiled, pleased. It looked like the sky and sun, and I guessed he'd had some help from Paula.

'Can I see your picture?' Joy asked Cora.

She shook her head.

'What have you been doing?' Joy asked. 'Cathy tells me you've been going to the park.'

'Ducks,' Jamey said.

'You saw the ducks?'

He nodded.

'What about you, Cora, did you see the ducks?' Joy tried, but Cora ignored her. 'Have you got everything you need?'

Jamey nodded, bless him. Cora continued crayoning, while Theo tried to eat another crayon.

'Not to worry,' Joy said to me. 'I've seen them. I'll do a virtual tour now and then leave you to it.'

I picked up the tablet. 'I'll be back soon,' I said. 'I'm just going to show Joy around the house.'

'Why?' Cora asked.

'Because she has to see it as part of her visit,' I replied.

Jamey slipped from his chair and came with me. I took my tablet in and out of the rooms, giving Joy the tour she would normally have done in person – downstairs and then upstairs and a quick look in the garden. Once we'd finished, she said she'd phone Gabi to find out about Saturday, and we said goodbye. Rather than seeing her to the front door, I closed the app and then the tablet.

'Gone!' Jamey said.

'Yes, gone,' I agreed.

Joy's 'visit' had lasted about an hour and when I checked my phone I saw I had two missed calls from Samantha. I phoned her back.

'Has Gabi called you?' she asked.

'No, but I've just been talking to my supervising social worker and she's going to phone her now to find out what's going on.'

'Gabi told me she'd call you to tell you my parents will be collecting Cora and Theo on Saturday morning,' Samantha said, clearly irritated.

'OK, but I will need to hear it from Gabi. I'll give her a ring too.'

'I've got to stay in hospital until Monday as I have a temperature.' She sighed, exasperated.

'I am sorry. I hope you feel better soon.'

'Yes, thanks. Phone Gabi now, please.'

I called Gabi but her line was busy, so I left a message. Samantha phoned again half an hour later and I told her I still hadn't spoken to Gabi.

'I have,' she said. 'Just now. She said she'd call you straight away.'

'All right.'

But Gabi didn't phone and when Samantha called again I still hadn't had confirmation from her that the children would be leaving on Saturday. 'I expect she is very busy,' I told Samantha. 'With so many working from home during the pandemic everything is taking longer.'

'It really isn't good enough,' Samantha said, exasperated.

I empathized with her, although there wasn't much else I could do.

It was 4 p.m. when Gabi finally phoned to say that Cora and Theo would be collected by their grandparents – Mr and Mrs Sutton – the following morning. They were expecting to arrive around midday, and she'd given them my address and mobile phone number. She told me to have the children ready as the grandparents wouldn't be coming into the house due to Covid restrictions.

'Have they managed to get the children's belongings from home?' I asked. 'If not, I'll pack clothes from my spares.'

'You'll have to ask Mr and Mrs Sutton when they arrive,' Gabi said a little tersely. I guessed she was feeling the strain too.

I was now finally able to tell Cora and Theo they would be going to their Nana and Grandpa's.

'Good,' Cora said. 'I love Nana and Grandpa.'

'I know you do.'

Five minutes later my phone rang and it was another video call from their mother.

'Has Gabi phoned you now?' she asked.

'Yes, and I've just told Cora and Theo.'

'Put them on, please. I need to see them.' Her cheeks were flushed, and I thought all this stress wasn't helping her recovery.

I positioned my phone so Cora and Theo could see their mother.

'Nana and Grandpa are coming tomorrow to take you to their house,' she told them. 'They are going to collect some of your belongings from home first. I've texted them a list of what you need. I've got to stay in hospital for a few more days and then we'll all be together.' So that answered my question about the children's belongings. But it was all too much for Cora and she burst into tears.

'I want to go home!' she cried.

'You are going to Nana and Grandpa's. You like it there and I'll join you as soon as I can. Don't cry, you'll upset Theo,' Samantha said.

I dried Cora's tears and sat beside her as Samantha reassured her. I encouraged Theo to interact with his mother and wave, but he wanted to play with some toys on the floor, so I put him down. Paula was with Jamey in another room. At one point Cora asked Samantha if Daddy was going to Nana's too. Samantha replied 'no' and changed the subject. After about fifteen minutes she wound up and said she'd phone again later, which she did. She also phoned at bedtime to say goodnight, as she had the evening before.

'Tomorrow night when I phone you'll be at Nana and Grandpa's,' she told them. 'Love you both, my darlings. Goodnight.'

'Night, Mummy,' Cora replied, close to tears again.

Once Samantha had gone, I settled Theo in his cot and stayed with them until they were asleep.

The following morning they woke early. Cora was excited to be leaving and asked how long it was until Nana and Grandpa came.

'Six hours,' I said.

Jamey, having heard Cora and Theo, was up early too but was very clingy. He wouldn't let me out of his sight, and I explained that he wasn't leaving but Cora and Theo were. All the changes were unsettling for him. Cora and Theo had arrived under a week ago, been part of our family, and now they were suddenly going. It was difficult for him to grasp, as it had been for my children when they'd been young and a child had arrived and then left.

Cora was so excited she couldn't eat breakfast, then she grew tearful when her nana and grandpa didn't immediately appear. I showed her how long it was on the clock until midday, and Samantha supplemented this by phoning about every twenty minutes with updates on her parents' progress: Nana and Grandpa were up and dressed and having their breakfast. They were getting ready to leave soon. (I gathered they lived about an hour's drive away.) They were on the motorway, then eventually they were on their way to collect the children's belonging from home – as well as some clothes for Samantha. It went quiet for about three-quarters of an hour and I

wondered if something had gone wrong, but then
Samantha phoned to say her parents would be about
fifteen minutes, and would I please make sure the children were ready as her parents were eager to get home.

I changed Theo's nappy, then brought down the bag
containing his and Cora's belongings and set it in the hall.
I had packed the nightclothes they'd arrived in, the
clothes I'd bought for them and the soft toys they'd been
using. As we waited I told Cora and Theo that we'd liked
looking after them but understood they would rather be
with their nana and grandpa. This was more for Cora's
benefit, as Theo was too young to understand and was
content if he was sitting on someone's lap and being kept
amused.

A few minutes later the front doorbell rang and Cora
ran down the hall.

'Nana! Grandpa!' she cried as I opened the door. She
threw herself into her nana's arms.

Mr and Mrs Sutton were a smartly dressed couple in
their late sixties. They stood well back from the door as
we spoke.

'Here's their bag,' I said, passing it to Mr Sutton. 'I'll
get Theo. I know you don't want to come in, but do you
want a drink?'

'No, thank you,' Mr Sutton replied a little stiffly.

Paula came into the hall carrying Theo, with Jamey at
her side. She passed Theo to me; I kissed him goodbye
and handed him to Mr Sutton.

'Would you like a kiss goodbye?' I asked Cora, who
was still clinging to her nana.

'I don't think that's wise with this virus,' Mrs Sutton
said, which was hardly relevant given the children had

been living with us for nearly a week. I didn't comment, and Cora didn't want a kiss from me anyway.

'Thank you for having them,' Mr Sutton said.

'Yes, thank you,' his wife added.

'It was a pleasure,' I replied. 'I hope Samantha recovers quickly. If she or the children would like to phone us, we'd be pleased to hear from them.'

'I'll tell her,' Mr Sutton said.

Paula, Jamey and I stood at the door and saw them off, then returned inside.

'Gone,' Jamey said as I closed the door.

'Yes, gone,' I replied. 'What would you like to do?'

'Park,' he said. 'Feed ducks.'

'Well done, good boy.' It was almost a three-word sentence.

'Let's go now and we'll have lunch when we get back,' I suggested. I felt in need of fresh air and a walk. I put a snack and a drink for Jamey in my bag.

It felt strange, just the three of us again, out walking, but also something of a relief. If I'm honest, even with Paula's help we'd been stretched to the limit, and now we could relax and concentrate on Jamey again.

We spent about an hour in the park and on the way back I suddenly realized I was supposed to have phoned Lacey at 1 p.m. In all the upheaval of Cora and Theo leaving, then going straight to the park, I'd forgotten. The video conferencing app we used – that the social services had recommended – was on my computer at home. It was 1.20 when we arrived and I went straight into the front room to call Lacey, while Paula took Jamey to the toilet, as he needed to use it. Lacey was waiting for the call and I began by apologizing.

'I am sorry we're a bit late. I had to say goodbye to the brother and sister we've been fostering, then we went to the park. I forgot all about it,' I admitted, not for one moment thinking there would be a problem.

'Brother and sister?' Lacey queried. 'Who?'

'We fostered them for a week, and they've gone now.'

'Where?'

'To their grandparents.' There was no issue in telling her this. She didn't know the family.

'How did they manage that in a week?' Lacey asked suspiciously. 'I've been waiting months to have Jamey live with me.'

'All cases are different,' I replied.

'You're telling me! This is totally unacceptable. Also, I thought we were supposed to be in lockdown. How do you know those children weren't carrying the virus?' Which of course had crossed my mind. 'I'll be speaking to Shannon first thing on Monday. I'll talk to Jamey now.'

'He's coming.'

Pity I'd mentioned Cora and Theo, I thought as I went into the hall. Paula and Jamey were coming downstairs and I took him into the front room. He smiled when he saw Lacey, which helped lighten her mood, and they had a good conversation. It lasted nearly half an hour, during which time she read to him, turning the book so he could see the pictures, and showed him a new puzzle she'd bought for him. He was enthralled. Lacey was used to working with children who had additional needs in her role as a teaching assistant and knew how to engage their attention. I sat out of view during the contact. When they'd finished Lacey didn't want to speak to me as she usually did. Saying goodbye to Jamey, she blew him a kiss and ended the call.

I could appreciate why Lacey was annoyed. Apart from the issue of the coronavirus, without knowing all the facts it could appear that different standards were operating in respect of Cora and Theo going to their grandparents so quickly. But as I'd told Lacey, each case was different. Sometimes when a child goes to live with a relative or other 'connected person', as they are known, the social services' assessment is done largely after the child moves, which could be the case with Mr and Mrs Sutton. Although another factor was that the children would be living with their mother too. Their situation was very different to Jamey's, who would either live permanently with his aunt or stay in foster care. However, in both cases the social services would continue to monitor the children after they moved until they were satisfied they were being well looked after and not in any danger.

CHAPTER TWENTY-FIVE

LIFTING LOCKDOWN

Saturday evening was the first time in a week that Paula and I were able to sit down together, relax and watch some television. While Cora and Theo had been with us the evenings had disappeared with dinner, story time, bath and bed – when Paula had taken care of Jamey and I'd seen to Cora and Theo, staying with them until they were asleep.

We caught up with the news and what was going on in the world, which was still dominated by the coronavirus. The number of new cases, hospital admissions and deaths were rising in the UK, as they were in many countries, but there was more testing available so this could account for some of the data. We learnt that, despite these figures, lockdown in England was having a positive effect and we were past the peak. Plans to ease the restrictions were to be announced soon, although we could expect some to remain in place to avoid a second wave of infections later in the year. Dear Captain Tom Moore had celebrated his one hundredth birthday, finished his walk and raised £30 million for the NHS! The Queen made him an honorary colonel in recognition of his wonderful achievement.

On Sunday I stripped the bed and cot in what had been Cora and Theo's bedroom and gave the room a good clean, while Paula played with Jamey downstairs. We went for a walk and then returned home where Jamey was content to just sit and play. I think he enjoyed having his own space again. Once, he asked where 'they' had gone. I explained that Cora and Theo had gone to live with their nana and grandpa – the man and woman who had come here to collect them. He nodded thoughtfully, although I'm not sure he fully understood. As well as playing with Jamey, Paula and I also did some activities with him that would help him learn and gradually add to his numeracy and literacy skills.

That evening I was planning to see Jamey to bed as I hadn't done it all week, but he wanted Paula, so while she took him upstairs to get ready I went online and began a foster-carer training module. I broke off to say goodnight to Jamey and then returned to finish it. The great advantage of online training was that I could fit it in when I had the chance, rather than having to attend in person on a set day, but of course it lacked the personal touch that having a lecturer present added. Also, the lunch breaks were nice, as carers could meet and catch up. I completed the module – Encouraging Positive Identity and Self-esteem (in looked-after children) – and then watched some television with Paula.

Joy telephoned on Monday morning to ask if Cora and Theo's move had gone to plan. I said it had and they'd been collected by their grandparents at twelve o'clock on Saturday. I said that Cora, especially, had been overjoyed to see them again. Joy asked if I'd heard any more from Samantha, which I hadn't. I told Joy I'd video called

Lacey slightly later than usual and she hadn't been pleased when I'd mentioned the two other children I'd been fostering, and she was going to phone Shannon.

'Don't worry,' Joy said. 'Shannon can answer any questions she might have.'

Joy thanked me for looking after Theo and Cora and we then spent some time discussing Jamey. I explained I was concerned about fostering additional children while he was with me because of the impact it had on him.

'But you would in an emergency?' Joy asked.

'Yes.'

Shannon emailed later, advising me that she was arranging a virtual visit on Wednesday at 10 a.m. The child's social worker is expected to visit a child in care at least every six weeks. I made a note in my diary. Apart from that and the video calls to Kat and Lacey, my diary remained unsurprisingly empty as lockdown continued.

On Tuesday Kat didn't answer the video call, so I texted her saying I'd tried and that Jamey was doing well and I'd phone her again on Thursday. She texted back: *Thanks*. Jamey was none the wiser, as I always made the call in another room and only took the phone to him if she was there. At his age it was the right thing to do. He didn't need any more disappointment in his short life. It would have been more difficult to protect an older child, as they would know exactly when they were going to speak to their mother; indeed, their lives often revolved around contact with their family.

On Wednesday I used my tablet again for Shannon's virtual visit as I guessed she'd want to have a look around the house, as she would have done in person. She began by asking how we all were and in particular how Jamey was. She was aware that Cora and Theo had been with us last week; her permission would have been needed before they were placed. I told her that Jamey was fine now but had been overwhelmed at times, especially around Cora as she was very confident, and he just shrank back in her presence. I said he had preferred to play alone but sometimes with Theo, apart from when Paula and I organized activities they were all involved in. I noticed as we spoke that Shannon was working from home with a backdrop of bookcases. Bookcases and shelving seemed to feature a lot in the backgrounds of video-conferencing calls. I sometimes found myself trying to read the titles on the spines of the books.

Shannon asked about Jamey's health, including his weight, so I read out his weight gains from the record book I was keeping as the clinic was still closed. She wanted to know about his routine in lockdown and the activities we were doing. I told her and described an average day. I said at present he was playing in the living room with Paula. She then asked about contact: 'With his mother first.'

I checked back in my log and told her of the times Jamey had spoken to her, roughly for how long, what they'd talked about and how positive the experience had been. I had to be honest, uncomfortable though that was for me, as Shannon had asked me to monitor contact so was expecting truthful feedback. This was the only feedback on contact now, as there was no face-to-face interaction due to the Family Centre remaining closed. I had to include the many times Kat hadn't answered her phone but had texted a reply.

'And his aunt?' Shannon asked, making a note.

'Good.' I described their virtual contact, again using my log.

'Has her partner Andy been joining in?' Shannon asked.

'No.'

'Lacey wants him included. Does Jamey ask for him?'

'No, but he doesn't really ask for anyone,' I replied. 'Although he enjoys the online contact with Lacey. She makes it fun and knows how to involve him.'

'Thanks. We can think about including Andy at a later date. So overall contact with Lacey is positive?'

'Yes. Has she phoned you? She wasn't happy about Cora and Theo.'

'She has been in touch; so has one of her legal team. I'm afraid they are going to have to be patient – everything is taking longer due to Covid. I've agreed for her to have an additional video call on Wednesdays at one o'clock in the afternoon.'

'Starting from today?' I asked.

'Yes, please.'

Her front doorbell chimed loudly. 'Can someone get that?' Shannon called, and was about to continue when it rang again, longer and more insistent. 'Just a minute,' she sighed, clearly not pleased, and left.

I heard her shout, 'Couldn't someone else have got this?' Then the front door opened and she said, 'Thank you,' before it closed again. She returned.

'Sorry about that. It was a parcel. Same thing happened yesterday when I was talking to a judge in child-care proceedings. My teenagers can order stuff online, but they can't get off their beds to collect it from the door!'

I smiled.

'Let's continue. Is there anything else you want to say about Jamey? I've read your reports.'

'Only that he's a lovely child and a pleasure to look after.'

'Good. I'll see Jamey now then.'

'I'm using my tablet, so I'll take you to him.'

Picking up the tablet, I went down the hall and into the living room where Jamey and Paula were doing a large-piece jigsaw puzzle on the floor.

'Jamey, your social worker would like to speak to you,' I said, propping my tablet on the coffee table. I pulled up the child's stool for Jamey to sit on, but he continued playing.

'Can you talk to me for a few minutes?' Shannon asked. 'Then you can play.'

Reluctantly Jamey stood and sat on the stool. He was usually very compliant. Perhaps he'd had enough of social workers online.

I stood to one side so I wouldn't distract Jamey, and Paula left the room.

'How are you?' Shannon asked him.

Jamey smiled and nodded, as many children his age would.

'Are you doing a jigsaw?'

'Yes.'

'What's the picture of?'

'Animals,' Jamey replied correctly. 'Farmyard.'

'Very good. I used to do jigsaws with my children when they were young. Does Cathy help you?'

Jamey nodded.

'What else do you like doing?' Shannon asked.

'Playing,' Jamey replied.

'With what? What do you like playing?'

Jamey fell silent and looked thoughtful. It wasn't for me to prompt him or speak on his behalf on this occasion. This conversation was between him and his social worker, as it would have been had she been here in person. It was different when he spoke to his mother or aunt; then I prompted him when necessary so it was a positive experience.

'What do you like doing?' Shannon asked again.

'Ball and painting, and Paula,' Jamey said.

'Wonderful. Paula is Cathy's grown-up daughter.'

Jamey nodded enthusiastically.

'You like playing with her?'

'Yes.'

'What do you like to eat?' Shannon asked.

'Chips,' Jamey replied. I hoped Shannon didn't think that was all I gave him.

'And what else?'

'Beans.'

'Good boy. Is there anything you want to tell me?' Shannon asked.

Jamey shook his head.

'If you need anything, who do you ask?'

'Cathy,' he replied, pointing at me. 'And Paula.'

I was pleased by his response. He'd understood the question and had replied appropriately.

'Thank you for talking to me,' Shannon said. 'You can play now.'

Before she had a chance to say goodbye Jamey left the stool. 'Paula?' he asked me.

'She's in the kitchen, love.'

He ran from the living room to find her. I picked up the tablet.

'Do you have any worries about him?' Shannon asked.

'He's happy enough and putting on weight, but his learning is still behind where he should be.'

'Yes, I can see that. Once all the services are up and running again I'll request that assessment he missed. Then we can see what help he needs and make the necessary referrals.'

'Thank you.'

She made a note and then asked, 'Can you show me around your home now, please?'

'Yes, of course. The living room.' I panned the tablet around the room so she saw all of it, and through the patio windows, then I went into the kitchen. Paula was making Jamey a drink and a snack and looked a bit self-conscious, but she said hello. Once Shannon had seen the kitchen-diner, I continued her virtual tour down the hall, into the front room where I'd previously been, then in and out of the rooms upstairs. I lingered in Jamey's bedroom so she could see it all, then returned downstairs. Shannon thanked me, said she'd be in touch and we said goodbye. I closed the app and then my tablet.

'Gone,' I found myself saying, just as Jamey did.

That afternoon I made the video call to Lacey using the computer in the front room, which had the bigger screen. I made sure she was there first before I got Jamey. Lacey seemed in a better mood and asked me how I was.

'Good, thank you, and you?'

'All right. I'm just grateful I haven't caught the virus,' she said.

I agreed it was all very worrying and then went to fetch Jamey. His face lit up when he saw his aunt.

'Hello, my precious,' she said. 'How are you?'

'I'm fine,' he said. He must have heard me use that phrase.

'Great. I'm fine too,' she said. She asked him what he'd been doing and then began reading from a new book, designed to help children learn their numbers. It said the number as the button was pressed. Jamey was enthralled. It was a pity he couldn't play with the book in person, but nevertheless he enjoyed it and the other books she read. The call lasted over half an hour, and it was a good contact for both of them.

'See you again on Saturday,' Lacey said, winding up. 'We can call twice a week now. I love you.' She blew him lots of kisses, then added, 'I've spoken to Mummy and she sends her love.' Jamey just accepted the mention of his mother without any comment or reaction.

The week continued and the weather grew warmer by the day. In fact, May turned into the sunniest on record. Lockdown continued but didn't seem so bad in the sunshine. Paula, Jamey and I spent most of our days in the garden, playing, gardening and having picnic lunches. It was a shame that Emma and the rest of my family couldn't join us, but there was light at the end of the tunnel. We were told the lockdown was having the desired effect and that the government was preparing to gradually ease the restrictions and recharge the economy. Millions of pounds were being poured into businesses and our society would reopen. Those who couldn't work from home were allowed to return to the workplace but were advised to avoid using public transport if possible. Employers had to put in place safety measures for their employees. We were allowed to go outside to exercise more than once a day but were told to maintain social distancing. The government changed its message from 'stay at home' to 'stay alert'. At the end of May, we held our last 'clap for carers', which seemed to be a landmark in our recovery.

By 1 June shops, garden centres, estate agents and sports courts had reopened, and schools were about to start a phased reopening. Television soap dramas could be filmed again and competitive sport was allowed, though without a live audience. We were told to wear face coverings in enclosed spaces such as shops, and those arriving from abroad had to quarantine for fourteen days, as was happening in some other countries. The furlough scheme was extended until October, which was costing the government £14 billion a month. Paula heard from her manager that she would continue to be furloughed, but the nursery where Darren worked said he would probably be needed soon as people returned to work and they had more children attending. Although Covid-19 hadn't been eradicated by lockdown, we were beating it. Deaths from the virus were down and optimism abounded. Cautionary warnings about a possible second wave were easy to ignore.

But Lacey wasn't in a happy mood, as she told me at the start of the next video call.

'I've spent weeks trying to get through to that bloody social worker and the Guardian! Nothing has happened in the last month. I don't even know if she's finished our assessment. I've had enough of waiting. I've put in a complaint, telling them I'll sue them.'

'I'm sorry, I don't know any more than you do,' I said.

CHAPTER TWENTY-SIX

HINDSIGHT IS A
WONDERFUL THING ...

As June began so did the rain. It poured down day after day, flooding some areas as rivers burst their banks. The weather was behaving strangely all around the world, and most people now accepted it was due to global warming and urgent action needed to be taken to reduce carbon emissions.

Lacey told me she had received a letter from the social services acknowledging her complaint, apologizing and reassuring her it would be fully investigated. This appeased her a little, although I'm not sure it actually changed anything. As far as I knew the final court hearing was still scheduled for the end of July. I assumed that before long the assessments and reports – including the Guardian's recommendations – would be submitted to the court if they hadn't been already. Lacey's solicitor would be sent a copy of these.

Now the lockdown restrictions had been substantially lifted and we were allowed to meet another household outside, Lacey felt she should be seeing Jamey in person. If it was decided that Jamey was going to live with her then contact would be increased, presumably to include face-to-face meetings rather than just virtual ones, in the lead-up to the move. But if it wasn't then it would be reduced – probably to nothing. I didn't know what the decision would be or even if the hearing would go ahead as scheduled. Sometimes they are postponed even in normal circumstances, and there was so much uncertainty at present that a delay was possible. I assumed Lacey's lawyer had told her that, and while it was important for Jamey to be settled with his forever family as soon as possible, I was in no rush to see him go. Neither was Paula.

'He's like my little brother,' she said.

Now households were allowed to meet outside, we saw Lucy and family, and then Adrian and Kirsty. It was wonderful to see them in person, and of course my granddaughter, Emma, wanted a hug, which I gave her. I'm sure I wasn't the only grandparent to break the social-distancing rules for a few seconds. The rest of us did the elbow bump.

'I don't think Nana would have thought much of that!' Lucy exclaimed, and I agreed. We were a family who hugged a lot in normal circumstances.

Although news of the pandemic was cautiously optimistic, there were other matters of concern. Brexit talks were continuing on a roller coaster of deal or no deal, and election campaigning resumed in the US. But what dominated the news and appalled us all was the death of George Floyd. His murder by a white police officer in Minneapolis had given rise to mass protests in support of the Black Lives Matter movement, which was gathering momentum around the world and raising public awareness of institutional racism. Like many, I was shocked and saddened that in this day and age such prejudice still existed. I'd naively assumed that was all in the past, but the more I listened to the news reports, discussions and documentaries, the more I realized this wasn't so and we still had a long way to go. Martin Luther King's famous 'I have a dream …' speech in 1963 about equality was still just that for many – a dream. I sincerely hoped this was the turning point and that we were now heading for a more enlightened and equal future.

Just as May had been the sunniest on record in the UK, so June was turning into one of the wettest, and we dodged the showers to go out. But life was returning to normal. If we all behaved ourselves and followed the remaining restrictions then hairdressers, pubs, restaurants, tourist attractions, art galleries, museums, theme parks, libraries, places of worship and community centres would all be allowed to reopen in July. We would also be allowed to holiday in the UK. But if we didn't follow the rules and the infection rate began to rise again then we faced more restrictions – even another lockdown. The R number was the indicator of the number of people being infected. If the R value was higher than one then the number of cases snowballed. By the beginning of July it was between 0.3 and 0.8 depending on the area, so generally we were all doing well.

Jamey, of course, didn't know or care about the R number or the rain. He was as happy playing in the puddles with his wellington boots on as he was in the garden in his shorts when the sun shone. I often watched him and thought back to the child who had arrived just before Christmas and my heart swelled with love and pride. Bless him, I loved him so much and I would be devastated when he left. Naturally, as a foster carer I knew that was likely to happen, but tell me how you stop yourself from loving a child? I'd been fostering for over twenty-five years and still hadn't learnt. In order to do our job properly you have to love, but then, of course, fostering is not so much a job as a vocation.

By the end of the first week in July, when tourist attractions, playgrounds and many businesses were reopening, I'd completed another three online training modules so I was on course to meet my training requirements for the year. Then one morning I answered the doorbell to be presented with a beautiful bouquet of flowers. Puzzled as to who they could be from, I thanked the delivery driver, closed the door and unpinned the envelope containing the gift card. Paula and Jamey, intrigued by who was at the door, had joined me in the hall.

'It's not my birthday,' I said, taking out the card.

Dear Cathy
I hope you and your family are well. Thank you for
looking after Cora and Theo.
Best wishes,
Samantha and family

'What a lovely surprise,' I said. 'How very thoughtful.'

'That was nice of her,' Paula said, looking at the message.

'Yes, it was.'

'Flowers,' Jamey said, pointing.

'That's right, love. Aren't they beautiful?'

I hadn't heard from Samantha since the day her parents had collected Cora and Theo two months before, so this was completely unexpected. A really touching gesture. I put the flowers in a vase of water and then found Samantha's mobile number and texted her.

Thank you so much for the beautiful flowers. Very kind of you. We are all well, I hope you and your family are too. Cathy x

She texted back: *Glad you like them. We are all well. Thanks again. Sam*

I didn't know if she and the children were still living with her parents or had returned to the family home, and it wasn't appropriate to ask. Once a child leaves a foster carer, we are not usually updated unless the family keeps in touch.

The second week in July, Shannon emailed to say that Andy could be included in virtual contact now. I knew then that there was a very good chance the social services were recommending that Jamey went to live with his aunt and her partner. Laccy confirmed this at the start of our next video call. 'The Guardian agrees with the social services' recommendation that Jamey should live with us,' she said. 'But we still have to go to court – virtually. I have to phone in.'

'I expect you're pleased.' She looked relieved.

'Very. It's been an uphill battle, but we got there in the end. There are still some details to sort out, which the court will address. Kat wants contact, which is fine with me, but the social services want it supervised at the Family Centre for a set number of times a year. I suggested it was left up to me. I mean, she's my sister and Jamey's mother.

I'm sure we can be trusted. Jamey will still be monitored by the social services for at least a year after he moves in with us, but our lawyer says that's normal.'

'Yes, it is,' I confirmed.

'At the end of that time we can apply for special guardianship, and then goodbye social services!'

I smiled.

'Has Shannon told you about future contact being in person?' she asked.

'Not yet.'

'Why does everything take so flipping long?' she exclaimed. 'She's supposed to be arranging it.'

'I'll email her when you've finished talking to Jamey and find out what's happening. I'll need to know the arrangements too.'

I fetched Jamey and as usual he was pleased to see his aunt. He'd brought his tablet with him and showed her the game he'd been playing. She admired and praised his work and they talked for a while, then she said, 'Andy is here and he'd like to talk to you. He's looking forward to seeing you again.'

Jamey looked slightly puzzled when he first appeared, but once he spoke Jamey seemed to recognize his voice and smiled.

'Hi, mate, do you like my beard?' Andy asked, rubbing his chin. So I guessed it was new.

'Yes,' Jamey said, rubbing his own chin.

'You haven't got a beard yet, mate,' Andy laughed. 'But you will when you're older if you eat all your meals and grow big and strong.'

Andy was built like a house, and I guessed he did weight training, but he had a gentle manner with Jamey.

I hardly knew anything about him, but as he talked I warmed to him. He told Jamey about the trucks he drove for a living and showed him some photographs of him beside huge lorries. Jamey was enthralled.

'Big lorries,' Jamey kept saying, pointing.

'Yes, I can sleep in it at night when I have to go a long way,' Andy said. 'Sometimes I have to go abroad across the Channel. I'll show you one of my lorries for real one day. Would you like that?'

Jamey nodded enthusiastically.

Lacey re-joined the call after a few minutes, sitting beside Andy. They talked to Jamey about all the things they were going to do when he lived with them, including swimming, trips to a zoo, theme park and castle, going on holiday, and so forth. I hoped they remembered and kept all their promises, as Jamey certainly would remember. I'd seen parents of children in care promise them the world (and shower them with gifts) in the build-up to them returning home, only for their relationship to falter once home as they'd struggled to meet their child's inflated expectations. I find the best policy with children is to under-promise and then over-deliver to avoid disappointment and give the child a nice surprise.

Andy went to watch some sport on television and Lacey continued talking to Jamey. She mentioned the nursery he would go to three days a week while she worked.

'Like the playgroup,' I explained to Jamey. Although I'm not sure how much of that he remembered now.

After another fifteen minutes or so Jamey grew restless and wanted to leave. Lacey understood and called to Andy to come and say goodbye.

'You've done well, mate,' he said, 'sitting there all that time. I'm sure I couldn't. I used to get told off for fidgeting in class at school.'

'Best not put that idea in his head,' Lacey said, which was exactly what I'd been thinking.

We all said goodbye, I closed the app and Jamey went to find Paula. I emailed Shannon, saying the virtual contact with Lacey and Andy had gone well and that Lacey seemed to think they were having face-to-face contact soon in preparation for him moving in with them. Half an hour later Shannon phoned.

'I'm sorry I haven't been in touch. My mother had suspected Covid and was quarantined in the care home, but it was a chest infection.' Shannon had previously told me her mother was in a care home and she hadn't been able to see her due to Covid restrictions.

'What a worry for you,' I sympathized. 'Have you been able to see her?'

'Yes, through a window. Not ideal but better than nothing. At least she's feeling better. Is everyone there well?'

'Yes.'

'No one is having to self-isolate or waiting for a test result?'

'No.'

'Good. Lacey has told you of our recommendations then?'

'Yes, so Jamey is definitely going to live with her?'

'Assuming the judge agrees. I've set up an hour's contact at the Family Centre on Monday at eleven o'clock.'

'Is it open again then?'

'They are offering a limited service and you will need to wear a mask. Jamey is exempt at his age. The contact will be held mainly outdoors, so if it's raining please bring rainproof coats. I shall be there to observe.'

'Will Andy be there?' I asked. 'So I can tell Jamey.'

'Not on this occasion. It's just for him and Lacey. I'd like you to stay and tell Lacey what she needs to know about Jamey's routine and so forth.'

'Yes, of course.'

'Assuming there aren't any problems, there will be another contact on Thursday and then three more the following week, leading to a virtual home visit and then the move the day after the court case.' This was different to how we usually moved a child to permanency – I assumed because of Covid restrictions and the need to minimize contact between households. 'I'll put all this in an email to you and Lacey once I've confirmed the times with the centre.'

'You know we usually video call Kat on Tuesday and Thursday afternoons at one o'clock?' I reminded her.

'Does she answer?'

'Sometimes.'

'OK, call as usual. I'll be speaking to her soon.'

'And the video call to Lacey on Saturday? Is that still going ahead?' Normally details like this would have been addressed in a planning meeting where Shannon, Lacey, Andy and I would have sat around a table with our diaries and worked out a timetable leading to the move.

'Yes, phone Lacey as usual,' Shannon confirmed. 'It will keep the contact going over the weekend. I'll speak to Jamey now, please.'

I could tell Shannon was in a hurry so I quickly took the phone into the living room where Jamey was playing with a toy lorry on the floor. Paula had popped into the kitchen.

'Jamey, your social worker wants to talk to you,' I told him, and held the phone to his ear.

He carried on pushing the toy lorry across the floor so I had to keep up with him in order for him to hear. I could hear Shannon trying to explain that he would be seeing Aunty Lacey soon in preparation for going to live with her and wouldn't that be nice. Jamey was more interested in his toy lorry.

'I'll explain step by step as we go,' I told Shannon, and we said goodbye to the sound of lorry noises.

Paula appeared and I told her that Jamey would be going to live with Lacey and her partner in two weeks' time.

'Oh,' was all she said, but her face said much more.

We sat in silence on the sofa for a while watching him play, then Paula suddenly asked, 'Is Lacey nice?'

'Yes, from what I've seen of her. But clearly the social services know a lot more than we do, and they must be satisfied it's in Jamey's best interest to live with her and Andy.'

'And what about his mum?' Paula asked.

'There will be some contact.'

Like me, Paula often worried about the parents of the child if they couldn't return home. Sometimes we knew them or had at least met them at contact. In an ideal world no parent would suffer the pain of losing their child, but then no child should suffer as Jamey had. Now he was gaining weight and generally making progress, it was easy to forget the frail, neglected, frightened child who had arrived.

I wondered what Kat was thinking. She would know now that the social services and the Guardian were recommending that Jamey went to live with her sister permanently. How was she feeling? Was she angry, as she had been when I'd first met her? Or remorseful? Or were her thoughts still so clouded by substance misuse that she had lost touch with reality and had few feelings for Jamey at all? Since publishing my fostering memoirs, I've heard from parents who have lost their children into care and, looking back, bitterly regret what they did or didn't do to stop it from happening. Substance misuse often features in the social services' decision to remove a child, as does domestic violence – when a woman opts to stay with a violent partner rather than leave and keep her child. Looking back, these parents didn't know how they could ever have made such disastrous choices, but then hindsight is a wonderful thing. That expression is attributed to William Blake, a famous English poet, although the rest of the quote is even more profound: 'Hindsight is a wonderful thing but foresight is better, especially when it comes to saving life, or some pain.'

I had no idea how painful all this was for Kat – she hadn't answered the video calls for weeks. But that was about to change.

CHAPTER TWENTY-SEVEN

SAYING GOODBYE TO MUMMY

The next day, I left the living room where Jamey was playing to video call his mother so he wouldn't be disappointed when she didn't answer. To my amazement she did answer and her live image appeared on my phone screen.

'Oh, you're there,' I said. 'I'll put Jamey on.'

'Can I talk to you first?' Kat asked, her voice flat. She looked very down.

'Yes. Just a minute.'

I stuck my head around the living-room door and asked Paula to look after Jamey while I was on the phone. I then went into the front room and closed the door, wondering what Kat could possibly want with me. She'd hardly said a word to me all these months.

'Are you all right?' I asked her. The skin on her face had broken out in red sores and she had dark rings under her eyes. She was sitting on a chair in her bedsitting room.

She shrugged. 'I want to talk to you about Jamey.'

'Yes, of course.' I also sat down.

'Did you know he's going to live with my sister and her bloke, Andy?'

'Yes, Shannon told me.'

'I didn't want him to go there to begin with, but I've accepted it now. They won't let him come back to me any time soon, so better her than someone I don't know.'

I nodded.

'The thing is,' she said, nervously biting her lip, 'I don't want Jamey to think badly of me. Does he ever mention me now?'

Difficult, I thought. 'Not so much recently,' I replied diplomatically, for in truth he never mentioned her at all.

'I guess that's for the best then. I don't want him pining and fretting for me. He deserves to be happy after all the crap I gave him.' She paused and took a breath. 'You know Jamey better than anyone now – even Lacey – and he's doing well with you; Shannon told me. He trusts you, so can you tell him that I'm not a wicked person? I just got it wrong and made a lot of mistakes. I want him to be happy, and hopefully in time he'll forgive me.'

'I see.' I swallowed the lump rising in my throat. Kat looked so despondent and alone. 'Jamey doesn't think badly of you.'

'Good. But if he asks you about me or says something bad, can you tell him I'm sorry? I won't be seeing him again for a very long time.'

'Shannon told me we should video call you next week as usual,' I said.

'I don't want you to. I'll tell Shannon.'

'All right, but haven't you been offered a goodbye contact at the Family Centre so you can see Jamey?' This was usual when a child couldn't return to their parents.

'Shannon said something about that, but I'm not taking it up. What's the point? I haven't seen Jamey in ages, and he's got a new life now. Why bugger it all up for him? And it would be painful for me too.' Which I could understand.

I'd taken children to the Family Centre for a final goodbye contact before and it's heart-breaking for everyone. It's supervised and the parent(s) and child spend an hour or so together and then part knowing they won't see each other again or will have very limited contact. Some children in long-term care see their families for an hour or two a few times a year, while others just have 'letterbox' contact at Christmas and on their birthdays. I knew the contact arrangements for Kat and Jamey had yet to be finalized at court, but it seemed that Kat wasn't expecting to have regular contact with him.

'Jamey trusts you,' Kat said again, in the same sad, fragile voice. 'Please make sure he knows I'm not a bad person and I never meant to harm him.'

'I will. Are you receiving support?' I asked.

'I've been offered counselling if I want it,' Kat replied.

'What about rehab?'

'What about it? I'm not in the right frame of mind for that now.'

So it appeared that, even after all that had happened, Kat couldn't give up the drugs and alcohol that were ruining her life.

I nodded solemnly. 'Hopefully you will feel able to go into rehab one day,' I said, and left it at that. It wasn't for me to lecture her on the damage she was doing to her health.

'Can you put Jamey on now so I can say goodbye before I lose my nerve?' she said.

I could see she was anxious, but I hesitated.

When Shannon had told me to continue the video calls to Kat I was sure she hadn't envisaged a virtual goodbye contact, which was what this was going to be. It could be very upsetting for Jamey, and in normal circumstances Shannon and a contact supervisor would have been present at their last contact. It crossed my mind that perhaps I should refuse and say we needed to discuss this with Shannon first. But then I thought the chances of Kat attending a formal goodbye contact – either in person or virtually – were very slim. This could be her only chance to say goodbye to Jamey and try to right the wrong she'd done to him.

'You know I'll be present?' I checked with Kat.

'Yes.'

I returned to the living room and signalled to Paula she could go.

'Your mummy would like to talk to you,' I told Jamey, and I sat on the sofa beside him.

'Mummy?' he asked questioningly.

I held my phone so they could see each other.

'Hello, Jamey,' Kat said, raising a small smile. 'It's Mummy. How are you?'

He looked at her, puzzled, and then said, 'I'm playing.'

'Can you stop playing for a little while so I can talk to you?'

He nodded obediently.

'Good boy. You're doing very well. Your social worker told me how well you're doing, which is good. In fact, you've changed so much you don't look like my son any more.' She gave a small, nervous laugh.

'This is difficult for me, Jamey,' Kat continued. 'I've had time to think and I know I wasn't a good mother when you were living with me. Do you remember the time you lived with me?'

He gave a small nod and his face grew serious.

'What do you remember?' Kat asked.

Jamey shrugged, then pointed and said, 'You.'

I would stop the contact if it became distressing for Jamey.

'What do you remember about me?' Kat asked.

Jamey shook his head.

It was impossible to know how much Jamey remembered of the time before he came into care, and he really didn't need reminding of it now. He was looking worried, as if he'd done something wrong. I waited to see what Kat would say next.

'Do you remember me leaving you alone in your cot while I went out?' Kat asked him. 'I bet you don't remember me cuddling you and reading you stories like Cathy does, because I didn't. I didn't do any of the things a good mother does.' Her eyes filled, but if she needed to confess and purge herself of her guilt then she needed to do it with a counsellor, not Jamey.

'Kat,' I said, interrupting. 'At Jamey's age he's unlikely to remember much from that time, and what he can remember will be hazy. I think it's best if you say what you felt you needed to about being sorry and wish him well,' I prompted.

'Typical me! Getting it wrong again,' Kat said.

'I didn't mean it like that, but I have to think of Jamey's feelings.'

'Like I didn't.' She rubbed her hand agitatedly across her forehead and took another deep breath. 'Jamey, what Mummy is trying to say is that she is sorry. I should have been a better mother and done it all differently. You're going to live with Aunty Lacey and she'll look after you. But I want you to remember that it wasn't my fault. All my problems were caused by drugs. So don't ever take drugs, Jamey. Do you understand?'

'Yes,' he replied, appreciating that this was serious but not understanding why.

'Good boy. I know you'll do better than me. Is there anything you want to say to me?'

He shook his head.

'Not like your dad then. He always had plenty to say to me.'

Jamey had no relationship with his father, and Andy was about to fulfil that role, so I felt there was no point in going on a trip down memory lane now. I sensed Kat was about to continue in the same vein, so I thought it was time to wind up.

'I'm sure Jamey will be fine and continue to make good progress,' I reassured her. Then to Jamey, 'Say goodbye to Mummy, love.'

'Bye,' he said in the same small voice.

'Can you blow me a kiss?' Kat asked.

Jamey dutifully blew her a kiss.

'I should have kissed you while I had the chance,' Kat said, her face crumpling. 'But then I should have done lots of things I didn't. Forgive me, son. Whatever happens to me, remember I love you. Do you love me?'

Jamey nodded.

Kat gazed at him for a moment longer and then ended the call. Jamey stayed where he was, staring at the blank screen. I closed the app and put my arm around him.

'Mummy upset,' he said.

'Yes, but Shannon will look after her.'

I cuddled Jamey until he'd recovered and wanted to get down off the sofa and play. Once he was settled, I phoned Shannon. It went through to voicemail, so I left a message: 'It's Cathy. We've just video called Kat and I'm concerned. She seems very low and doesn't want us to phone any more. She said goodbye to Jamey and was talking of not seeing him again.'

I knew that Kat had overdosed at least once and seemed so low I thought she could do it again. Shannon would be able to offer some support, although most counselling and therapy was still taking place online.

That evening, when I wrote up my log notes, I made sure I included Jamey and Kat's call, as I was supposed to. The following day I received an email from Shannon acknowledging my message and saying she'd spoken to Kat and she was all right. We weren't to phone her any more, and Shannon finished by saying she'd see Jamey and me on Monday at 11 a.m. at the Family Centre with Lacey.

CHAPTER TWENTY-EIGHT

LOVE YOU TOO

Jamey took the impending momentous changes to his life as he did most things: quietly and in his stride. Not so for Lacey. When we video called her on Saturday she was very excited to put it mildly, as was Andy, although he wouldn't be seeing Jamey on Monday.

'We'll be outside so we can play ball, and they have tricycles and other toys at the centre,' Lacey enthused.

Jamey smiled and nodded as Lacey continued telling him about all the fun they were going to have. Once she'd exhausted Monday, she ran through her plans for the rest of the week and then read him a story. When he'd had enough he said, 'Bye, Lacey,' and took himself off to play. He was starting to develop a character – stoical, which would seem him through a lot.

'Oh, he's gone,' Lacey said, a little put out. 'He doesn't seem overjoyed to be seeing me again.'

'I'm sure he is,' I replied. 'It's going to take him time to process all the changes – remember, it's seven months since he last saw you.'

'That's why I should have had contact sooner!' she declared, forgetting that she hadn't been approved to foster Jamey until now.

'Don't worry. I've moved lots of children to permanency,' I reassured her. 'Once they start seeing their forever family regularly like you will be doing over the next two weeks they soon bond.'

'Do they?'

'Yes. Trust me. You'll be in a different place in two weeks' time.'

'He's very reserved for a child his age, don't you think?' Lacey said. 'He was when I used to look after him. He never asked for anything or made a fuss. One of the reports said he was withdrawn as a result of severe neglect.'

'I haven't seen the reports, but if an infant's needs aren't met, they stop asking. He's got better since he's been here. And once he's settled with you, I am sure his progress will continue. Andy's lorries will help,' I added with a smile. 'He hasn't stopped talking about them.'

Lacey smiled too. 'Good.'

One of my roles as a foster carer is to prepare the child for leaving – moving to permanency, as it's known. I talked to Jamey about what was going to happen, explaining that he would see a lot of Lacey over the next two weeks, first at the Family Centre with Shannon on Monday, when I would stay, and then just with Lacey and Andy until he went to live with them. I said we'd pack up all his toys and clothes – of which there were many now – so he'd take all of his belongings with him. He didn't say much, but I could see he was taking it all in. He hugged Paula and me that little bit more, as we did him.

Shannon had emailed the timetable for the introductory period and I would explain to Jamey what he was doing each day. Although we were out of lockdown, restrictions still applied. To minimize the risk of coronavirus spreading between households, Jamey wouldn't spend time inside Lacey and Andy's flat until he moved there. Usually a child visits for a few hours and then spends some nights sleeping there before the move, after which they return to the carers for a night before saying goodbye. In place of this Lacey and Andy were going to show Jamey a short video of their home, and he was likely to have some recollection of staying there before. We couldn't give Jamey a leaving party as I normally did when a child left, because of Covid, but I had bought him a giant magnetic construction kit as a leaving present and a card. I'd also bought him a remote-controlled lorry for his birthday, which was a week after he left.

On Sunday, Paula and I took Jamey to an outdoor activity centre, which had just reopened after lockdown. Social distancing and restrictions on numbers applied, but Jamey loved it. We took lots of photographs, some of which would go with him in his Life Story Book and some we'd keep. Paula and I were making the most of our time with Jamey as his departure date loomed.

On Monday morning I reminded Jamey where we were going that day – 'To see Aunty Lacey at the Family Centre.'

The weather was fine, but I took our waterproofs just in case as we'd be outside. Going there in the car, Jamey seemed more interested in the lorries we saw than where we were going. 'Lorry!' he cried at the top of his voice every time he spotted one, even from a distance. 'Another lorry! Another!'

'Yes, well done.'

As I pulled up outside the Family Centre he fell silent. Then, as I opened his car door to let him out, he asked, 'Mummy?' The last time he'd been here was to see Kat.

'No, love. You are going to see Aunty Lacey and Shannon today. You've said goodbye to Mummy.' Harsh though that sounded, it would help Jamey come to terms with his past and the new life that awaited him.

I put on my mask and Jamey tucked his hand into mine as we went up the path to the security-locked main door. I pressed the buzzer and waited, then a voice came through the grid. 'Hello?'

'It's Cathy with Jamey. He has contact here today.'

'Just a second. I'll let you in the side gate.'

This was different; usually we went in through the main door.

A few moments later a member of staff unlocked the side gate. 'They are in the playground at the back,' she said. 'Shannon and Lacey are already there.' So I guessed they'd come early.

'Do I need the mask outside?' I asked. She wasn't wearing a mask.

'No, just if you come into the building to use the bathroom. There is hand sanitizer by the entrance at the back.'

'Thank you.'

I tucked my mask into my pocket, and Jamey and I went through the gate and then round to the rear of the building. Lacey and Shannon were standing by the children's play apparatus talking, with the contact supervisor a short distance away. They stopped when they saw us.

'Jamey!' Lacey cried, delighted, and spread her arms to greet him.

He hesitated for one second – I think he was struggling to believe she was actually there in person rather than online – then he shouted, 'Lacey!' and ran full pelt towards her.

She picked him up and cuddled him for all she was worth. Her arms wrapped tightly around him and she showered him with kisses. As I drew near I could see her eyes glistening with tears. She couldn't speak for a moment and then said, 'Finally, I get to hold you again.'

I felt my own eyes fill.

To begin with Jamey wanted me to stay close as he played with Lacey, but as his confidence grew and he felt safer, he was happy for it to be just her, while I stood to one side. Shannon stayed to observe contact for about half an hour, and I got the chance to ask her how her mother was. She said she was reasonably well, although there had been many cases of Covid in the care home and some residents had died, which was very sad and worrying. When she left she said goodbye to us all and that she'd be in touch for updates on how the introductory period was going.

As Jamey pedalled up and down on a tricycle, Lacey and I talked about Jamey – his routine, likes and dislikes, and how Shannon wanted him weighed every two weeks. Lacey was open and willing to learn as much as possible, recognizing how much Jamey had changed since she'd last cared for him. I said I'd give her his record book from the clinic together with his Life Story Book. I told her he was supposed to have had another medical on 23 March but that it had been cancelled due to lockdown and Shannon was following it up. I also said speech therapy had been suggested and I felt Jamey would benefit from it, although much of the service was online at present. Lacey was aware that Jamey had started playgroup before lockdown, and she planned for him to go to nursery three days a week while she worked when the schools reopened for the new term in September, assuming they did reopen then. Some government advisers were worried that reopening too soon would rekindle the transmission of the virus. I told Lacey I'd let her have Jamey's savings in cash, as due to lockdown I hadn't been able to open an account for him. All carers are expected to save for the child they are fostering.

'Thank you so much. And if I have any problems I can phone you?' Lacey asked.

'Yes, of course.'

'It sounds silly – I've known Jamey all his life,' she said. 'But now I'm about to be his parent I'm feeling nervous.'

I smiled knowingly. 'I'm like that before a new foster child arrives,' I admitted. 'Once the child is with me I'm too busy to worry and I just enjoy having them. I'm sure you'll be the same with Jamey.'

She looked at me carefully. 'Are you all right about him coming to live with me?'

'Yes, of course. We'll miss him dreadfully, but it's right he's going to family as he can't live with his mother.'

'Good.'

The hour flew by and when it was time to go Jamey wanted to stay and play.

'We'll come here again on Thursday,' Lacey told him. 'I'll see you then and Andy will be with me too.'

'Lorry?' Jamey asked.

'He can't really bring his lorry here, love,' she replied with a smile. 'But I promise you'll see it before long.'

We said goodbye to the contact supervisor and left by the side gate. Lacey came with us to my car, kissed Jamey goodbye and then returned to her own car.

'Lacey gone,' Jamey said sadly.

'Only for a little while,' I said, fastening his seatbelt. 'You'll see her again very soon.'

'Love Lacey,' he said, bless him.

'Good. She loves you too.' I kissed his cheek.

He reached up and wrapped his arms around my neck. 'Love Cathy,' he said.

'I love you too, very much.'

CHAPTER TWENTY-NINE

SAYING GOODBYE

The introductory period went as planned and the Family Centre became a drop-off and collection point only, where I met Lacey and Andy at the start and end of contact. The first week they stayed in the grounds of the Family Centre with a contact supervisor. The second was 'community contact' where they spent time in the community, as shops, parks and cafés were now open. As their time together increased I saw Jamey slowly transferring his affection from me to them. Sad though this was, it meant we had done our job and Jamey would soon be ready to leave to start his new life.

The last weekend Jamey was with us we met Adrian and Kirsty, and Lucy and family, in a park so they could say goodbye to Jamey. They'd bought him leaving gifts and cards, which was kind of them. Emma was sweet – now nearly two years old, she understood that Jamey was going and wanted to hold his hand the whole time and kept giving him kisses. Because of lockdown we hadn't been together as a family as much as usual, so the bond between the rest of my family and Jamey probably wasn't as strong as it might have been. All the same, goodbyes aren't easy, but they are important, as they allow everyone to move on.

On the afternoon of the court case Shannon phoned to confirm the judge had ruled that Jamey should live with Lacey and Andy so the move would go ahead as planned. Then Audrey Bashir, the Guardian ad Litem, phoned to say goodbye.

She asked me how we all were and then spoke to Jamey. 'So, you're going to live with Aunty Lacey and Andy,' she said. 'How do you feel about that?'

'Love Lacey,' Jamey said, smiling.

'That's wonderful. And what about Andy?'

'Love Andy,' Jamey replied. In fact, at present Jamey loved everyone, including our cat – 'Jamey love Sammy,' he often said.

Audrey thanked me for all I'd done for Jamey, adding, 'I think it's the right decision, don't you?'

'Yes.'

'Time will tell. Let's hope for the best.'

The Guardian's role usually ended with the court proceedings.

By the morning of his move I had everything packed, including Jamey's leaving presents and cards, which he would open in his new home. He was quiet as Paula and I stacked all the bags and boxes containing his belongings in the hall. Then we sat in the living room playing games one last time as we waited for Lacey and Andy to arrive. Normally when a child leaves the new parents come into the foster carer's home for a short while, but that wasn't going to happen today due to the current advice around coronavirus. Evidence was showing that the virus was less transmissible in the fresh air, so Lacey and Andy would collect Jamey from the doorstep, then we'd say goodbye outside.

Jamey had been quiet all morning and wanted lots of hugs from Paula and me, which was understandable. We were putting on brave faces as it wouldn't help Jamey if he saw us unhappy. This was a big step for him too. A few minutes before Andy and Lacey were due to arrive, while we were still in the living room, I heard a loud rumble outside but didn't think much of it. The doorbell rang.

'That'll be Lacey and Andy,' I said, standing.

The three of us went down the hall and I opened the front door. Sure enough, there stood Andy and Lacey, looking very happy. And behind them, parked in the road outside, was a very large lorry. Jamey saw it too. You couldn't miss it!

'Lorry!' he cried, pointing.

'Yes I wonder who that belongs to,' I said, puzzled.

'Well, you did say he had a lot of things to move,' Andy said, grinning.

'You're joking! It's yours?' I exclaimed. 'However did you manage that?' The company's logo was emblazoned all along the side.

'My boss knows what a big day this is for us all and how much Jamey likes lorries, so he's letting me use it for the move.'

'Amazing. That was nice of him. Well done, Andy.'

Jamey was jumping up and down, unable to contain his excitement. 'Lorry! Lorry!' he cried.

'You can sit in the cabin with Lacey while I load up all your things,' Andy told Jamey.

He lifted Jamey onto his shoulders – he was very high up – and carried him to the cabin where he sat him in the front. You could hear Jamey's squeals of delight up and down the street. Lacey climbed in beside him, and Andy, Paula and I began loading Jamey's belongings into the back of the lorry. It was huge inside.

'You did well, thinking of this,' I told Andy, as we worked.

'Thanks. I'm glad he likes it. I've fixed his car seat in, so he'll be riding safely.'

I checked the hall was clear of Jamey's belongings, then it was time to say goodbye. Paula and I stood on the pavement by the cab. Lacey helped Jamey out so he could say goodbye, then climbed out herself.

'Goodbye, my precious,' I said, giving Jamey a big hug and a kiss. 'It's been wonderful looking after you. I'll phone you on your birthday.' Lacey and I had already agreed this, and how we would keep in touch.

'Bye, Jamey,' Paula said, bending down to hug him.

'Bye, Paula,' Jamey said, and he began to look very sad.

'I think it's time to go,' I said to Andy and Lacey, and they agreed.

'Thanks for everything,' Lacey said. 'I'll be in touch.'

We couldn't hug so the adults elbow bumped. Paula and I stayed on the pavement as Lacey and Jamey returned to the cab and Andy climbed into the driver's seat. They looked so high from where we stood. Lacey closed the passenger door and lowered her window.

'Wave goodbye,' she told Jamey.

He was completely engrossed in what Andy was doing but he managed a small wave. Andy started the engine and Jamey gave a cry of delight.

'Bye, take care!' Andy called.

Then, slowly and majestically, the lorry rumbled away as neighbours looked out of their windows to see what the noise was all about.

'How to stage an exit!' Paula said with a smile.

'Absolutely.' In all the years we'd been fostering we'd seen many children off at the door but never so grandly. Bringing the lorry had been a lovely idea.

Goodbye, Jamey. Good luck x

A couple of thoughts to leave you with:

- When the social worker and police went to Kat's home there was no heating and Jamey was in his cot. The bedding was sopping wet and stank of urine, and there were teeth marks on the bars of the cot where Jamey had spent so long going hungry. Shannon said that, on reflection, it was felt that he should have been removed sooner.

- In the first wave of the pandemic referrals to children's services rose by 44 per cent.

For an update on Jamey and the other children in my books, please visit https://cathyglass.co.uk/updates/

SUGGESTED TOPICS FOR
READING-GROUP DISCUSSION

———————

Neglect is a form of abuse. Discuss. How was Jamey's physical and psychological development affected by neglect?

With the arrival of coronavirus and lockdown the internet played an even more vital role in everyday life and work than before. What are the pros and cons of conducting meetings, assessments and training virtually?

Kat and Lacey are very different. Describe their personalities and lifestyles.

Cathy is asked to supervise phone contact. Why might this be difficult for a foster carer while trying to build a relationship with the child's family?

Cathy and Paula become very attached to Jamey but know at some point he is likely to leave. How do you think foster carers prepare themselves for a child leaving?

Cathy says: 'Fostering isn't just about feeding and clothing the children, but also nurturing them to their full potential.' What does this mean in real terms?

What effect does the arrival of Cora and Theo have on the Glass household?

Jamey's aunt, Lacey, says she should have done more for Jamey. What more could she have done and what do you think stopped her?

At the end we are told that Shannon felt Jamey should have been removed from home sooner. Discuss. What other options were there?

Cathy Glass

———

One remarkable woman, more
than **150** foster children cared for.

Cathy Glass has been a foster carer for
twenty-five years, during which time she has
looked after more than 150 children, as well
as raising three children of her own. She was
awarded a degree in education and psychology
as a mature student, and writes under a
pseudonym. To find out more about Cathy
and her story visit **www.cathyglass.co.uk**.

An Innocent Baby

Abandoned at birth, Darcy-May is brought to Cathy with a police escort

Her teenage mother wants nothing to do with her, but why? She is an adorable baby.

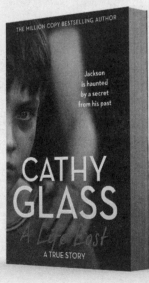

A Life Lost

Jackson is aggressive, confrontational and often volatile

Then, in a dramatic turn of events, the true reason for Jackson's behaviour comes to light ...

A Terrible Secret

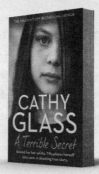

Tilly is so frightened of her stepfather, Dave, that she asks to go into foster care

The more Cathy learns about Dave's behaviour, the more worried she becomes ...

Too Scared to Tell

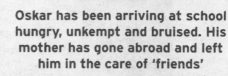

Oskar has been arriving at school hungry, unkempt and bruised. His mother has gone abroad and left him in the care of 'friends'

As the weeks pass, Cathy's concerns deepen. Oskar is clearly frightened of someone – but who? And why?

Innocent

Siblings Molly and Kit arrive at Cathy's frightened, injured and ill

The parents say they are not to blame. Could the social services have got it wrong?

Finding Stevie

Fourteen-year-old Stevie is exploring his gender identity

Like many young people, he spends time online, but Cathy is shocked when she learns his terrible secret.

Where Has Mummy Gone?

When Melody is taken into care, she fears her mother won't cope alone

It is only when Melody's mother vanishes that what has really been going on at home comes to light.

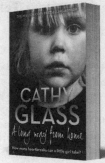

A Long Way from Home

Abandoned in an orphanage, Anna's future looks bleak until she is adopted

Anna's new parents love her, so why does she end up in foster care?

Cruel to be Kind

Max is shockingly overweight and struggles to make friends

Cathy faces a challenge to help this unhappy boy.

Nobody's Son

Born in prison and brought up in care, Alex has only ever known rejection

He is longing for a family of his own, but again the system fails him.

Can I Let You Go?

Faye is 24, pregnant and has learning difficulties as a result of her mother's alcoholism

Can Cathy help Faye learn enough to parent her child?

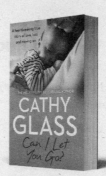

The Silent Cry

A mother battling depression. A family in denial

Cathy is desperate to help before something terrible happens.

Girl Alone

An angry, traumatized young girl on a path to self-destruction

Can Cathy discover the truth behind Joss's dangerous behaviour before it's too late?

Saving Danny

Danny's parents can no longer cope with his challenging behaviour

Calling on all her expertise, Cathy discovers a frightened little boy who just wants to be loved.

The Child Bride

A girl blamed and abused for dishonouring her community

Cathy discovers the devastating truth.

Daddy's Little Princess

A sweet-natured girl with a complicated past

Cathy picks up the pieces after events take a dramatic turn.

Will You Love Me?

A broken child desperate for a loving home

The true story of Cathy's adopted daughter Lucy.

Please Don't Take My Baby

Seventeen-year-old Jade is pregnant, homeless and alone

Cathy has room in her heart for two.

Another Forgotten Child

Eight-year-old Aimee was on the child-protection register at birth

Cathy is determined to give her the happy home she deserves.

A Baby's Cry

A newborn, only hours old, taken into care

Cathy protects tiny Harrison from the potentially fatal secrets that surround his existence.

The Night the Angels Came

A little boy on the brink of bereavement

Cathy and her family make sure Michael is never alone.

Mummy Told Me Not to Tell

A troubled boy sworn to secrecy

After his dark past has been revealed, Cathy helps Reece to rebuild his life.

I Miss Mummy

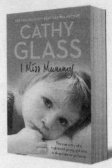

Four-year-old Alice doesn't understand why she's in care

Cathy fights for her to have the happy home she deserves.

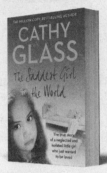

The Saddest Girl in the World

A haunted child who refuses to speak

Do Donna's scars run too deep for Cathy to help?

Cut

Dawn is desperate to be loved

Abused and abandoned, this vulnerable child pushes Cathy and her family to their limits.

Hidden

The boy with no past

Can Cathy help Tayo to feel like he belongs again?

Damaged

A forgotten child

Cathy is Jodie's last hope. For the first time, this abused young girl has found someone she can trust.

Run, Mummy, Run

The gripping story of a woman caught in a horrific cycle of abuse, and the desperate measures she must take to escape.

My Dad's a Policeman

The dramatic short story about a young boy's desperate bid to keep his family together.

The Girl in the Mirror

Trying to piece together her past, Mandy uncovers a dreadful family secret that has been blanked from her memory for years.

About Writing and How to Publish

A clear, concise practical guide on writing and the best ways to get published.

Happy Mealtimes for Kids

A guide to healthy eating with simple recipes that children love.

Happy Adults

A practical guide to achieving lasting happiness, contentment and success. The essential manual for getting the best out of life.

Happy Kids

A clear and concise guide to raising confident, well-behaved and happy children.

CATHY GLASS WRITING AS
LISA STONE

www.lisastonebooks.co.uk

The new crime thrillers that will chill you to the bone . . .

THE COTTAGE

Is someone out there?

TAKEN

Have you seen Leila?

THE DOCTOR

How much do you know about
the couple next door?

STALKER

Security cameras are there to
keep us safe. Aren't they?

THE DARKNESS
WITHIN

You know your son better than
anyone. Don't you?

Be amazed
Be moved
Be inspired

Follow Cathy:

/cathy.glass.180

@CathyGlassUK

www.cathyglass.co.uk

Cathy loves to hear from readers and reads
and replies to posts, but she asks that no plot
spoilers are posted, please. We're sure
you appreciate why.